ROBERT WHITING, a graduate of Japan's Sophia University, has spent most of his adult years living and working in Asia. He has been a contributor to *Sports Illustrated* and numerous Japanese sports publications, but his efforts have been devoted mainly to creating multimedia educational materials for children. His work has been published by Encyclopaedia Britannica, Grolier International, and Time-Life Books. Mr. Whiting is at present a resident of Tokyo.

THE CHRYSANTHEMUM AND THE BAT
BASEBALL SAMURAI STYLE

ROBERT WHITING

 A DISCUS BOOK/PUBLISHED BY AVON BOOKS

To my mother and father, Margo and Ned

Picture Credits

Baseball Magazine, Tokyo—Pages 21, 34, 39, 42, 45 bottom, 47,
51, 55, 58, 63, 67, 97, 101, 103, 111, 134, 168, 171, 175, 185, 219,
234 right, 244, 245, 247
Kyodo News Service—4, 29, 75, 80, 89, 93, 113, 131, 133, 137, 153,
155, 156, 160, 162, 163, 165, 183, 189, 196, 200, 205, 218, 243
Chunichi Newspapers—Opposite 1, 9, 14, 37, 84, 127, 146, 214,
230, 237
The Nikkan Sports Press—23, 45 top, 70, 73, 123, 140, 178, 212
Pacific League Office—224, 234 left

AVON BOOKS
A division of
The Hearst Corporation
959 Eighth Avenue
New York, New York 10019

Copyright © 1977 by Robert Whiting
Published by arrangement with Dodd, Mead &
Company, Inc.
Library of Congress Catalog Card Number: 76-27708
ISBN: 0-380-63115-6

The Dodd, Mead & Company, Inc. edition contains the
following Library of Congress Cataloging in
Publication Data:

Whiting, Robert.
   The chrysanthemum and the bat.

   1. Baseball—Japan—History. I. Title.
GV863.77.A1W46   796.357'0952   76-27708

First Discus Printing, May, 1983

FOREWORD

This book, the result of more than ten years of baseball watching in the Land of the Rising Sun, was written to show a very different culture through a familiar window.

At first glance, baseball in Japan appears to be the same game played in the U.S.—but it isn't. The Japanese view of life stressing group identity, cooperation, hard work, respect for age, seniority and "face" has permeated almost every aspect of the sport. Americans who come to play in Japan quickly realize that Baseball Samurai Style is different. For some it is fascinating and exciting; for others, exasperating, and occasionally devastating.

Baseball seems an ideal framework from which to approach Japan. It is not only a familiar sport but also a cross-cultural one that people can relate to emotionally as well as intellectually. A study of how the game has been modified to accommodate Japanese social values illustrates many differences between our two countries.

Western businessmen are able, should they choose, to isolate themselves from Japanese society. Yet the American ballplayer is in a unique position. He is constantly with the team and continually exposed to pressures from club management, the press, and his teammates. Such pressures, a direct reflection of contemporary Japanese attitudes, are examined in detail.

I have attempted to present a true picture of Japan through its baseball world. If at times I seem critical, this in no way reflects on my affection and abiding respect for the Japanese people among whom I have been most fortunate to spend a good part of my adult life.

My experience in Japan has given me a chance to broaden my outlook on life. And it's this I should like to share with you.

Robert Whiting
Tokyo, 1976

acknowledgments

I would like to thank the following for their help in putting this book together: Hiroshi Akimoto, correspondent, *Tokyo Chunichi Sports;* George Altman, former infielder, Hanshin Tigers; Toshiro Ashiki, Public Relations Director, Chunichi Dragons; Kaoru Betto; Clete Boyer, Coach, Taiyo Whales; Shinichi Eto, outfielder, Lotte Orions; Hiroshi Gondo, Coach, Chunichi Dragons; Norio Hattori, *Baseball Magazine,* Ikuo Ikeda, Director, *Baseball Magazine;* Hideyuki Inubushii; Shigeo Ishida, Writer, *Nikkan Sports;* Kazuo "Pancho" Ito, Public Relations Director, Pacific League Office; Dave Johnson, infielder, Yomiuri Giants; Takeaki Kaneda, Asian Director, *Sports Illustrated,* Noboru Kawai, Publishing Department, *Hochi Shinbun;* Koichi and Machiko Kawamura; Tadasu Kimura, M.D.; Sadao Kondo, Head Coach, Chunichi Dragons; Jim LeFebvre, infielder, Lotte Orions; Joe Lutz, former Manager, Hiroshima Carp; Tsuyoshi Miyakawa, AIPS Acting Vice-President, *Kyodo News Service;* Nariyashu Morishita, Rikio Murano, and Toshio Naka, Coaches, Chunichi Dragons; Hiroo Nakao, President, Grolier International (Japan); Leslie Nakashima, Sports Editor, UPI Asia; Masanori Ochi, Sports Director Nippon TV; Dave Roberts, former infielder, Yakult Atoms; Toshiyaki Sakai; *Tokyo Chunichi Sports;* John Sipin, infielder, Taiyo Whales; Daryl Spencer, former infielder, Hankyu Braves and presently Manager, Coors baseball team; Takejuh Suzaki, writer and Professor, Meiji University; Toshiro Suzaki; Naokazu Tsukada, Trainer, Chunichi Dragons; Tadahiro Ushigome, Public Relations Department, Taiyo Whales; Wally Yonamine, Manager, Chunichi Dragons, and his wife, Jane.

I would also like to give special thanks to Machiko Kondo for her help in translations from Japanese and in the typing of the manuscript; to Dale Miller for his help in the revisions of the original draft; and finally, to Dwight Spenser, who, more than anyone else, is responsible for the existence of this book. To him, I owe a special debt of gratitude.

contents

Tokyo's Korakuen Stadium

1 outdoor kabuki

The big Seiko clock above the electronic scoreboard in center field read 6:20—thirty minutes before game time. The two-tiered 50,000 seat Korakuen Stadium was already filled to overflowing. In the special "jumbo stands" down the left and right field foul lines, policemen were urging standing-room ticketholders to move a little closer together so that even more people could be packed in to see the game.

The *sushi, sake,* and *hotto dogu* vendors had sold out their first loads and were hurrying back for refills before the aisles became completely clogged with fans.

Behind both dugouts, camera crews from two major networks were setting up their equipment to televise the game. In the pressbox, sportswriters from Japan's five major sports dailies were getting ready to report the evening's contest.

As a soft female voice announced the starting pitchers, the ticket windows outside the massive stadium closed, causing hundreds of irate fans to storm the gate. One old man was trampled in the rush and carted off to the hospital.

The event was a game between the two teams tied for first place in the Central League—the Yomiuri Giants of Tokyo and their traditional rivals from Osaka, the Hanshin Tigers. It was the first day of June and the season was only seven weeks old.

Each spring when the cherry blossoms come into bloom, the Land of the Rising Sun starts its annual love affair with the game of baseball. Almost overnight, Japan is transformed into a nation of starry-eyed pitchers, catchers, and home-run hitters; a nation of *bēsubōru* nuts.

White-collar workers grab the company ball and bat at lunchtime

1

and head to the nearest park for a quick game of work-ups under the noonday sun. Delivery boys park their motorcycles between noodle deliveries and pull fielder's gloves from back pockets for a leisurely game of "catch-ball" in the nearest alley.

Platform conductors in train stations practice shadow swings with their red signal flags or work on their pitching deliveries with discarded candy wrappers, while those with enough time throng to the nearest "batting range" for 100 yen worth of swings against a mechanical curve-ball pitcher. And all across the five main islands of the tiny nation thousands of diamonds are filled with aspiring sluggers, ready to fight it out for the prestige of wearing that school uniform.

Each season, millions of fans pour through the turnstiles to see their favorite teams in action—from the little leagues all the way up to the professionals. The sport is so popular that even high school and college games draw capacity crowds.

The annual ten-day national high school championship tournament at Koshien Stadium in Osaka draws over 400,000 and is, in Japan, an event equal in significance to the Stanley Cup playoffs in hockey or the World Cup finals in soccer. There is hardly a TV set in any house, coffee shop, or tearoom around the nation that is not turned on NHK (Japan's government owned national TV network) to see the continuous nine-to-six live daily coverage of the tournament.

College teams, such as those in Tokyo's glamorous Big Six University League, are followed with the fervor that Americans usually reserve for Saturday afternoon collegiate football. The semiannual three-game series between Tokyo's traditional crosstown rivals, Keio and Waseda, for example, draws well over 60,000 spectators per match and commands a nationwide TV audience. For sheer spectacle, this event outdoes a Michigan–Ohio State football game. Karate-chopping cheerleaders and raven-haired pom-pom girls lead a stadium full of frenzied students wildly screaming *"ganbare"* (Let's go) in unison. A series win for Waseda touches off a wild night of merrymaking in the narrow twisting sidestreets of Shinjuku (Tokyo's version of Greenwich Village) that is reminiscent of Times Square on New Year's Eve. A Keio win brings a similar fate to the downtown area of the Ginza.

The national obsession with *yakyu* (field ball), as it is commonly known, hits its peak when the glamor boys of Nippon—the professionals—take the field. Each year, nearly twelve million *bēsubōru* fanatics turn out to watch the twelve teams of Japan's two professional leagues, the Central and the Pacific. While two and a half million—or one out of every four spectators—flock to Korakuen Stadium to see the darlings of Japan, the Yomiuri Giants—the oldest, winningest, and most popular team in the country.

For those who stay home, there is a pro game on national TV nearly every night during the season. On weekends, a fan can plop down on his straw mat floor with his bottle of *Kirin* or *Asahi* beer and, with a flick of the dial, choose from two and sometimes even three games being broadcast simultaneously.

Baseball has become a fixture in Japanese life since it was first introduced in 1873, some twenty years after Commodore Perry and his "Black Ships" visited the island nation and thus ended more than two centuries of isolation. An American named Horace Wilson, a professor at a Tokyo university, is recognized as having first taught the game to the Japanese. Initially played by Kimono-clad youths in sandals, the game has flourished on a high school and collegiate level from the turn of the century. There were detractors, however, like critic Inazo Nitobe, an educator who later became an official of the League of Nations. He called baseball "a pickpocket's sport . . . in which the players are tensely on the lookout to swindle their opponents, to lay an ambush, to steal a base. It is, therefore, suited to Americans, but it does not please Englishmen or Germans."

The first professional league in Japan was not officially established until 1936, two years following a tour of American major-league all-stars led by Babe Ruth, Lou Gehrig, and Lefty O'Doul.

Before that visit, few Japanese believed professional baseball could succeed in their country. The sport was undeniably popular—Big Six college games drew enormous crowds. But tradition-bound Japanese were expected to remain loyal to favorite college teams, leaving the pros with no one to cheer them on. Furthermore, monetary considerations would, it was argued, so dilute the purity of the sport that right-thinking people would turn away in disgust.

A Taiheiyo Club Lions' cheerleader in action

These dark prophecies proved false, however. So overwhelmingly popular were the American stars, particularly the 39-year-old Ruth (who walloped 13 home runs in the 18 games he played in Japan), that in 1935, Matsutaro Shoriki, owner of the prestigious *Yomiuri Shinbun* (Japan's largest daily newspaper and the sponsor of the tour) decided to form a pro-baseball team of his own, the Tokyo Giants. A year later, several other firms followed suit and Japan's first professional league was born. By 1940, there were nine teams.

With the coming of Pearl Harbor, baseball took a back seat to Japan's all out drive for victory. By 1944 the season had dwindled to a mere 35 games, with only six teams contending for the pennant. It hardly mattered, for by this time baseball, like every other aspect of Japanese national life, had become a tool in the fanatical war effort. The Tokyo Giants were renamed "*Kyojin Gun,*" or "Giant Troop." (It was as if the New York Yankees had been dubbed the "Yankee Battalion.") Such English baseball terms as 'strike' and 'ball' imported from enemy America were scrapped for the Japanese '*yoshi*' and '*dame*' (good and bad). A shortstop became a '*yūgeki*' (freelancer) and when a runner slid into home plate the umpire would pronounce him 'alive' or 'dead' (*ikita* or *shinda*) instead of 'safe' or 'out.'

In 1945, the year of Tokyo fire bombings and the Japanese surrender, play was suspended altogether. But when occupation forces under Douglas MacArthur moved into Japan, baseball quickly recovered. In 1948 eight teams played a total of 105 games. MacArthur himself, recognizing the Japanese love for this alien game, personally issued the order to clean up Korakuen Stadium, home of the Tokyo Giants. The ball park had been used as an ordnance dump during the war.

Baseball thrived so well in the early postwar years that by 1950 two leagues were formed. That year, there were 15 teams but the number eventually dropped to 12, six teams in each league. Meanwhile the game's popularity soared, surpassing even traditional Japanese sports like *sumo* wrestling.

Today baseball is unquestionably Japan's favorite sport. The teams in the Pacific and Central Leagues each play a 130-game schedule and the two pennant winners meet in October in the Japan Series, the Oriental version of the American World Series.

Three of Japan's 12 pro ball clubs make their home in Tokyo, four in Osaka, and one each in Nagoya, Fukuoka, Kawasaki, Hiroshima, and Sendai. Most teams are owned by business firms and exist primarily for public relations purposes. This results in some rather unlikely names. The *Taiyo Whales* of Kawasaki are owned by the Taiyo Fishery Co. and the *Yakult Swallows* of Tokyo are the property of a major health food company. The *Hankyu Braves*, the *Nankai Hawks*, the *Kintetsu Buffaloes*, and the *Hanshin Tigers* (all of Osaka) are owned by private railways. Others include the *Lotte Orions* of Sendai (chewing gum), the *Chunichi Dragons* of Nagoya (newspapers), the *Yomiuri Giants* of Tokyo (newspaper/TV), the *Hiroshima Toyo Carp* (owned jointly by the citizens of Hiroshima and Toyo Kogyo—a major automobile manufacturer), and the *Nippon Ham Fighters* of Tokyo. The *Taiheiyo Club Lions* of Fukuoka are privately owned, but have a primary advertising contract with the Taiheiyo Club Corporation, a major land developer.

The professionals stock their teams with college and high school standouts in an annual draft. And the players, often stars in their own right, sometimes command large bonuses.

Baseball owes much of its status as the premier sport in Japan to an enlightened media that not only knows the game, but also understands how to make it interesting. Japanese TV and radio announcers working in teams can elevate the most routine encounter between a pitcher and a batter into a moment of high drama. Between pitches— and throughout the game—sportscasters discuss the comparative strengths and weaknesses of the man at the plate and the man on the mound: "This pitcher usually tires after seventy pitches and he has already thrown seventy-four. . . . Notice how the batter has widened his stance? (*Camera shot of stance*) He wasn't doing that a month ago. I think that's why his batting average has fallen. He is not putting his hips into his swing and he is also taking his eyes off the ball. . . . Let's take a look at that last pitch in slow motion. See how the pitcher's leg came down too soon? That is why the pitch was high . . ."

Announcers discuss previous encounters between the pitcher and the batter. With the help of computer records, they predict, sometimes with amazing accuracy, what pitch will be thrown and what the batter is likely to do in a given situation: "Watanabe has a .220 lifetime average batting against this pitcher Suzuki; however, he is .314 against him this season. What do you think accounts for the difference?/Well, let's see. Suzuki used to retire him on a high outside slider. However, this season Watanabe has learned to punch that particular delivery to the opposite field./What do you think Suzuki will use this time?/It is difficult to say, but, with two out and a runner on second, I don't think he will use the slider. In my opinion he will throw an inside fastball at the chest. Look how Watanabe is crowding the plate. It would be easy to get him with that pitch./If Suzuki throws an inside fast ball, I think Watanabe will try to foul it off and wait for a better pitch./Maybe so, but, since Watanabe is batting second tonight, it might be a good idea for him to reach first and let Kobayashi try to drive the runs in./I don't think so. Kobayashi has the power, but his lifetime batting average against Suzuki is less than .100. He is lefthanded and Suzuki is lefthanded./Yes, but . . ."

And so it goes, sometimes seemingly forever. There is never enough time between pitches for Japanese announcers to say all they have to say. They are often accused of talking too much, and their frequent mistaken predictions are a standing joke. But the interest and excitement they can generate in a slow moving game is truly amazing.

On televised games in the States, if a pitcher shakes off a sign three or four times and steps off the mound, boredom ensues. The announcer will talk about the wonderful dinner he had the night before, discuss his latest fishing expedition, or welcome a group of visiting firemen—anything except what is going on down on the field.

In Japan, when a pitcher keeps shaking off a sign, the tension mounts. The announcer pays attention. He becomes more excited: "He shook the sign off again! What do you think he wants to throw? Ah! He just shook it off a third time!/I think the pitcher wants to throw his fast ball and the catcher wants him to come in with a curve? /Why?/Because in a similar situation last month . . . etc."

When a batter keeps fouling off a 3–2 pitch with a runner in scoring position on second base, the typical U.S. announcer will run down the league standings, report on the top ten batters, or tell the viewer about the Goodyear blimp. In Japan, the announcer tells the viewer *why* the batter keeps fouling off so many pitches. The fan learns that the rightfielder has a weak arm and that the batter is waiting for an outside pitch he can poke to right.

When a player slides into base, the Japanese TV baseball viewer (or listener) gets lessons on how to slide. He learns whether the slide was a good one or not. When an infielder makes a play, the fan gets advice on playing the infield in various situations. He gets lessons on how to bat, how to pitch, how to throw, how to steal signs, and how to manage a team.

Thanks to excellent TV coverage the Japanese fan cannot help becoming involved in the details of the game as he is drawn into the intricacy of each play. Games in Japan last nearly three hours on the average, much longer than games in the U.S. Yet, in Japan, the broadcasts somehow never seem as dull or as long as they do in the States.

Japan is a baseball fan's paradise. And the baseball addict who must have his regular dose of baseball news, capped off by a night game, is indeed fortunate to be born there. Consider the day of an average baseball nut—a Tokyo *salariman* who is, no doubt, a Giants fan.

On his way to work he stops at the newsstand in front of his train station. Here he has a choice of five major daily sports newspapers: *Chunichi Sports, Hōchi Shinbun, Nikkan Sports, Sports Nippon, Sankei Sports*, as well as *Daily Sports*. (There are none in the United States.) Each paper sells for 50 yen (15 cents a copy) and it tells him every conceivable thing he might want to know about the previous night's baseball activities.

As the "platform pusher" wedges him into the already packed morning express, he eagerly scans the headlines: GIANTS SLASH TIGERS! "Ah! My team won." Crammed against the door of the train and unable to turn around, he struggles to unfold his paper and prepares to enter the separate reality of baseball.

Sub-headlines quickly summarize the story. *Giants Open Up Two-Game Lead Over Tigers in Tight C.L. Pennant Race. Win on 'Sayonara' Hit in 12th Inning. Oh Blasts 40th Home Run. Horiuchi Struggles to Victory. Notches 13th Win of Year on "Guts" Alone. Hurls 179 Gritty Pitches.* And next to the large photo showing the Yomiuri Giants leftfielder scoring the winning run in the 8–7 victory, he finds the details of the game.

31 August, Showa 48. Korakuen Stadium. Yomiuri Giants vs. Hanshin Tigers. Season record: Giants 10 wins; Tigers 10 wins; 1 tie. Starting time: 6:50. Attendance: 50,000. Final Score: Giants 8, Tigers 7. Extra-inning game, 12 innings. Winning pitcher: Horiuchi; 13 wins, 14 losses, 36 games. Losing pitcher: Wako; 2 wins, 4 losses, 16 games. Home runs: Oh (3 runs 1st inning) 40 (Enatsu); Horiuchi (3 runs–7th inning) 2 (Wako); Kirkland (3 runs–5th inning) 17 (Horiuchi); Toi (2 runs–8th inning) 6 (Horiuchi); Tabuchi (2 runs–8th inning) 33 (Horiuchi).

The August moon hung forlornly in the sweltering summer mist over Korakuen Stadium as ace Giant pitcher Horiuchi trudged wearily off the mound. He stopped once and turned to glance at the clock over the huge electronic scoreboard out in centerfield. The hands had just passed ten o'clock.

Horiuchi was thinking the same thought that was running through the mind of everyone else in the park: Would the game reach the 13th inning before the 10:10 curfew? Could the Giants score the winning run in the bottom of the 12th? Would the game end in a tie? As Horiuchi confessed later: "I wanted the time to run out. Their clean-up trio would be leading off the

Front page of Chunichi Sports, one of Japan's five major dailies devoted to sports

top of the 13th. I could see that the ball had heavy eyes. It wouldn't do what I wanted it to. . . . Anyway, all I was thinking of was a tie."

At 10:10, the game would be three hours and twenty minutes old and would not enter a new inning. Pitching with two days rest, Horiuchi had gone the full 12 innings and had thrown 179 grueling pitches. He was tired and wanted the game to end. Everyone was in agreement. Coach Makino instructed: "I don't want to go into the 13th inning." Everyone knew what he meant. The Giants would play for time.

Horiuchi, batting eighth in the Giant lineup, led off the bottom of the 12th inning. The Giant bench continuously called him back for advice. To stall for time, he kept changing bats, stepping out of the box, knocking the dirt from his shoes, putting resin on his hands, conferring with the third-base coach and stroking his bat. After Horiuchi struck out, centerfielder Shibata came to bat. Shibata alone used up five minutes at the plate. The clock then passed 10:10. The Giant bench breathed a sigh of relief. The Giants could not lose this game now.

Shibata drove the next pitch into left field for a single. The Giants were beginning to hear the sounds of a 'sayonara' hit. With two out and Shibata on second as a result of Doi's grounder to third, Takada came up and blasted Wako's first pitch into shallow center. Shibata rounded third and rushed into home plate with the winning run.

The Giants, who had been content to tie, saw a victory come tumbling their way, magically appearing out of the humid summer night. Takada's comrades in the dugout on the first-base side emptied onto the field to welcome home their hero, who had blasted the 'sayonara' hit.

Said the happy Takada: "When I hit the first pitch thrown by Wako in the 10th inning and grounded out to third, it was a *shūto bōru* (screwball). I had an idea he might be throwing the same pitch again, so I was ready. I was just trying to meet the ball." And so, with this determined spirit, Takada settled the question that had been on everyone's mind for three hours and twenty-four minutes, this hot summer night of August 31.

Horiuchi, in his typical manner, frequently exasperated the Giant fans during the game. He was given a 3–0 lead in the first inning, when Oh lined a 1–2 low-outside fastball into the leftfield stands for a three-run home run, and in the third inning was presented with another run. But, in the fifth inning, with two men on, the erratic young hurler gave up a home run to the black foreigner Kirkland and allowed the Tigers to tie the score.

Whenever it looked as though the Giants would win, Horiuchi would do something to throw the game in doubt. He indeed lived up to his nickname of "Bad-Boy Taro." To his credit, however, he did pitch out of several tight spots from the eighth inning on. So perhaps this grueling 12 inning, 179 pitch win is evidence that Horiuchi is regaining some of the fighting spirit he had last year when he won 26 games.

As the train makes another stop and the platform pusher shoves a few more passengers in, our baseball fan, barely able to move, delves deeper into his 16-page paper. *Spiritless Dragons Lose Fire—Face Major Shake-Up.* "They'll need it." *Carp Sink Into C.L. Cellar.* "What's new?" *Braves Slice Nippon Ham. Hawks Fly Low—Drop Third In A Row. The Foreigner Comes Through—Repoz Blasts 'Sayonara' Home Run.* "Hmmm."

"This looks like a good story. *The Cowardly Pitcher: Down After Only 46 Pitches.*"

The performance of Hanshin's ace pitcher, Enatsu, last night was shameful. It was even more shameful because the Tigers started him to satisfy the fans' expectations. The spiritless pitching of this twenty-game winner has seriously damaged Tiger chances in the pennant race. True, it may be said that he had only two days rest and was tired. But, the same was true for his pitching rival Horiuchi. Furthermore, this season, the Tiger star had a record of 8–2 when starting with two days rest, while Horiuchi was an abysmal 0–3 before last night's game. It would seem that Enatsu would be far superior.

But, he wasn't. Consider the first inning. Enatsu gave up a walk, a sacrifice, and another walk. There were runners on first and second, and one out. Then C.L. home-run leader Oh blasted Enatsu's first pitch into the left-field stands. The Giants led, 3–0. Enatsu's listless pitching continued into the third inning. Giant batters hit his half-hearted balls for another run and Enatsu was taken out of the game.

And that is not all. Enatsu's remarks in the locker room were not those of a man aware of the crucial importance of this encounter. For example, he said casually, "You say that I was beaten by Oh. Well, Oh has 40 home-runs. The one he hit off me tonight was just one of the forty home-runs that man has hit this season. When he came up in the third inning, I put him out on a fly to right, didn't I? I am just an ordinary human being. I'll try to do better in my next start against the Whales."

Well, of all the nerve! I must say that Enatsu may be ordinary, but the four runs he surrendered may be the catalyst that will turn his Tigers into ordinary cats. The Tiger batters came through quite splendidly. But, unfortunately, their ace let them down.

With two days rest, Horiuchi pitched erratically, desperately and frantically. But, he showed his true fighting spirit by throwing 179 agonizing pitches. Enatsu threw only 46 pitches and returned quickly to relax in the baths of the Midori Inn. In my opinion, that is the difference between the fighting spirit of Enatsu and Horiuchi.

The train pulls into Tokyo Station and our friend hurries to his office in Marunouchi, Tokyo's business center.

Comfortably seated at his desk, with a cup of green tea before him, he opens his paper again. After glancing to see who won the best player and fighting spirit awards for last night's games, he turns to the statistics with a tinge of anticipation. And, what statistics!

Ten-column box scores on each game. (Those in U.S. papers are usually six columns or less.) Times at bat, runs scored, hits, RBIs, strikeouts, walks, sacrifices, stolen bases, errors, and adjusted seasonal batting averages. Down below are nine-column boxes for the pitchers: Innings pitched, number of batters faced, number of pitches thrown, number of hits allowed, strikeouts, walks, runs surrendered, earned runs surrendered, and adjusted season ERAs. And if this is not enough, our fan can turn to the inning-by-inning batter-by-batter account of what happened in each game.

If he still has time before his boss catches him loafing, he can pore over the standings that show how each team is doing against every other team in the league. This data includes the total number of games each team has played, total wins, losses, ties, percentages, home runs, runs scored, runs allowed, and team batting and pitching averages.

During his mid-morning break, he can study the upcoming schedule detailing who is playing whom, when, and where for the next ten games. Or he can read a summary of how each team has performed for the last ten games.

At lunch over fish, rice, and *misomiso* soup, he can discuss the previous night's game with his colleagues and pick up any details of the encounter his newspaper might have missed (improbable as it may be).

During his afternoon break, he returns to his paper to review individual batting and pitching performances. There he finds the following statistics for the top thirty batters in each league: Batting average, games played, unofficial times-at-bat, official times-at-bat, runs scored, hits, home runs, total bases, RBIs, strikeouts, walks, sacrifices, and stolen bases. And for the pitchers: ERA, games pitched, hits allowed, home runs surrendered, strikeouts, walks, runs allowed, and earned runs allowed.

If there is a lull in the late afternoon, he can sneak a look at what the managers had to say about the games the night before, in the *Kantoku No Hanashi* (The Manager Speaks) section of the paper. The following are samples of what he might find.

(On winning three in a row):

I can't believe it. I think they were in worse condition than we were. I don't know what happened. I tried a number of new strategies in this series, and I think I learned something. But, I also think they learned something. So I don't know what will happen next time.

(On losing seven in a row):

I apologize to the fans for this disgrace. I just hope we will get better. I don't know what has come over my pitching staff. They have lost their fighting spirit.

(On an upcoming series with the Giants):

I have formulated a plan to overcome the Giants. We will defeat the Tigers three in a row in our upcoming series, and then we will win three of our four games with the Giants. I cannot reveal the details of my plan at this moment.

(On being in last place):

This cannot continue. Our baseball is a product that we are selling to our fans. No matter how low we sink in the standings we must strengthen our resolve and play to the utmost of our ability for the rest of the season. It is a professional responsibility we have. My men must try harder tomorrow. I will hold a meeting to discuss the matter with them. My humble apologies.

After this, our fan may well take a quick look at what the players had to say.

(A pitcher on his disappointing defeat):

I'm sorry. I wanted to throw my curve ball, but they were aiming for it, so I had to go with my *shūto bōru* (screwball). Unluckily, my *shūto* was too sweet and so they hit me. I will do my best to redeem myself in the future

Box scores in Chunichi Sports

(A pitcher on pitching while sick and winning):

I tried to pitch at *mai-pēsu* (my pace) all throughout the game. It was very painful, but fortunately my slider was razor sharp. I was lucky to win. From now on I am not going to think about my health anymore. I vow to think solely about pitching to help the team win the championship for our fans.

(A pitcher on his six-hit shutout):

I do not want to be rude to the Lions, but I have the fullest self-confidence when I am pitching against them. I have no inclination to lose against them. It was very easy.

(A pitcher on getting his 20th win):

My condition was not good tonight, but I had to win at all costs, so I struggled desperately. I gained these 20 wins because of the manager and my teammates. I was filled with dread that I would not be equal to the task at hand. I pitched with all my might. It was very painful, but I am deeply satisfied with this game and with this season. I will now aim for the best pitching percentage in the league.

(A pitcher upon winning his third game in a row):

I have pitched over 200 balls in the past three days. But I am not tired. I have only been pitching in this league for three years, and I am not thinking of the long run. I want to play for a long time, but the important thing at the moment is a man's spirit. I have not been pitching long in the professionals, so there is no depth to my pitching. I am young and my mind has not developed yet. However, I will pitch as the team wants me to pitch and vow to do my best.

(A batter on his prolonged batting slump):

I don't know what is wrong. I am seeing the ball well. I feel I am in good condition. I am eating well and my bowel movements are regular. I must ask the batting coach for guidance.

(An outfielder on dropping a fly ball to lose the game):

Damn it! I had the ball right in my hands. And it just popped out again. I am really ashamed of myself. I truly apologize to my teammates and to the fans.

After this, there is still the baseball gossip in the gossip column (*Eto Files For Bankruptcy. Harimoto Arrested In Drunken Brawl—Out For Two Weeks*) as well as all the latest college, high school, and industrial league baseball news.

After work, our fan stops to buy a copy of *Bēsubōru*, a popular weekly magazine. A typical table of contents might include the following:

1. I Owe My Career To My Mother—She Did My Homework For Me While I Practiced Baseball.
2. The Change In Bad-Boy Taro. Could It Mean Another Pennant For The Giants?
3. How I Keep My Batting Eye—I Only Read Comic Books.
4. Oh Sets His Sights On Aaron: What Breaking Hank Aaron's Home-Run Record Will Mean To Sadaharu Oh.
5. America's Unforgettable Baseball Games.
6. *Heartbreak Column:* Yoshida Tries To Forget The Pain.
7. Why Nagashima Hides In The Dugout.
8. The Garlic *Shochu* Craze (drink made from distilled sweet potatoes): How It Gives The Players Vim And Vigor And Keeps The Fans Away.
9. What It Means To Be A Yomiuri Giant.
10. *Tears And Laughter In Baseball:* When A Backache Becomes Too Much Too Bear.
11. *Foreign Topics:* Streaking In Major-League Parks.
12. *The Daimyō* (Lords) Of Professional Baseball.
13. The Dilemma Of The Lions And Monster Frank Howard: Is He Worth The Money?
14. Dr. Baseball: Clete Boyer Of The Whales.
15. Fiction: The Seven Samurai Of Baseball.
16. *Baseball Diet Corner:* Snakes, Frogs And Other Energy Foods.
17. The World Series And Japan.
18. Rookie: Fresh Ham Of Nippon Ham.
19. The Burning Ace Of The Burning Dragons.
20. The Pen-Pal Corner (where one finds such letters as the following):

If you are a girl and you consider yourself the number-one fan of the Nankai Hawks, why don't you write to me and we can exchange opinions. For I am the number one fan of Nankai in Sakai City.

Kenji Wakisaka (16) (male)

I have been a very faithful fan of Lotte for seven years. I am waiting for letters from girls all over Japan who are especially interested in the Pacific League.

Toshio Tarui (19) (male)

I am a fan of Chunichi, Lotte, Hanshin, high school baseball, university baseball, Elton John and Morio Kita (a contemporary writer). Please, someone, write to me.

Mitsue Uchiumi (15) (female)

Returning home, our fan nods to his wife as he walks through the door, takes a quick bath, and changes to his *yukata* (a casual summer robe). He hastily downs his dinner of fish and rice and is ready for more baseball.

From 6:30 to 7:30, he listens to the game on radio and then switches to watch all the action live on his Sony color TV. Then, at precisely 8:56, he hears the announcer say: "We deeply regret this, but unfortunately our broadcast time has once again expired. It is deeply disappointing to us, but thank you for tuning in. The results will be reported on the sports news at 11:10. We will be back on the air tomorrow night at the same time.

In Japan, for some inexplicable "aesthetic" reason, games are invariably telecast for one hour and 26 minutes, no matter who is playing. This can be infuriating, especially when in the 9th inning, with the score tied and bases loaded, the game goes off the air.

With a groan, our fan returns to his radio and listens to the last few innings. After the game he watches the sports news so he can see that home run he missed when the TV broadcast was cut off.

Tired, and perhaps even sated, he then crawls between the *futon* (Japanese bedding) laid on the floor by his patient but baseball-weary wife and goes to sleep.

2 when a manager
is not a manager

Reporters packing the tiny conference room at Osaka Stadium glanced at their watches in anticipation. They had been alerted by General Manager Tachibana of the Nankai Hawks that there would be an important announcement at 6:40 that evening.

The press sensed something dramatic about to take place. The Hawks, defending Pacific League champions and a perennial power-house in Japanese pro ball, were occupying an unfamiliar position—last place. In the first two months of the season they had managed to lose two out of every three games. It was one of the worst starts in club history.

At exactly 6:40—the appointed hour—General Manager Tachibana strode through the press room door. By his side walked Kazuto Tsuruoka, the Hawks' field manager. A hush fell over the room as the newsmen recognized Tsuruoka. Nicknamed "The Boss" by his players, the venerable manager had piloted the Hawks for nearly twenty years, winning seven pennants and one Japan Series. What, the reporters wondered, might his presence at this press conference mean?

The general manager bowed to the assembled reporters and began to speak in measured tones: "As of today, Manager Tsuruoka has relinquished command of the Hawks as a means of taking responsibility for the team's poor showing in recent games. Hopefully the manager's action will stimulate the Hawk players to reflect on their performance on the field."

Tachibana added that he deeply regretted Tsuruoka's decision but that, as General Manager, he had no choice except to accede to the field manager's request. Head Coach Kageyama had been instructed to act as manager in Tsuruoka's absence. Tachibana went on to express his own hope that Tsuruoka's action would breathe new life into the team. Tsuruoka, he added, would retain the title of manager for the time being.

Reporters sat in stunned silence as Tachibana announced that Tsuruoka would now answer questions.

The tall, courtly 46-year-old manager lit a cigarette and began to field questions from the press. He spoke deliberately, without emotion: "Team performance has been poor . . . as manager I must assume responsibility . . . if the commander cannot lead his troops, they will die . . . I hope that my departure will inspire the Hawk players to reflect on their performance . . . For the moment I don't want to see any baseball, I just want to rest."

A shock wave passed through the Japanese baseball world. The Hawk head coach Kageyama, who had just been appointed acting manager, hoped that "Manager Tsuruoka's brave action will move the Hawks to fight harder."

"What the hell made the boss quit? Who's responsible for this?" grumbled the Hawks' leading home-run hitter. And the veteran shortstop lamented, "It's all my fault. The Boss was like a father to me. If I hadn't been injured he might not have left the team. We will all have to do our best so he can return."

By mid-July the Hawks were back in the pennant race, riding the crest of an 11-game winning streak. Acting Manager Kageyama told the press: "Everyone knows the Boss is a more skillful manager than I am. Perhaps it is time for him to return to the team." Requests from the Hawk players and a petition signed by the fans added to the pressure for Tsuruoka's return, and, on August 9, he was reinstated as field manager. The Hawks went on to finish second in the Pacific League that year.

When an American major-league team is mired in last place, it is usually time for the manager's head to roll. "A change has to be made," and that is that. A new manager steps in, the players adjust, and the old manager goes job hunting, taking the whole thing philosophically. After all, his job is to produce a winner.

In Japan nothing is ever quite so simple. The owner of a baseball team must consider more than just his responsibilities to the fans; he must also bow to the dictates of Japanese group dynamics, which take into account the personal relationships between manager and players. In addition, he must think of his own obligations toward the manager and, finally, the feelings of the manager himself. A club owner will try his best to smooth things over while keeping the manager, even though this may result in a losing season and a drop in attendance.

Confusing as this may sound to Americans, it makes sense in the context of baseball samurai style. American pro-baseball teams are run like corporations, with their members united by a common ability to play and their desire to make money. Not so in Japan, where a baseball team is more like a cohesive extended family unit held together by a complex web of interlocking personal obligations. The kind of intersquad bickering that characterizes some U.S. teams is virtually unknown.

There is an off-the-field camaraderie seldom seen in America, where players are used to "doing their own thing" and rarely see teammates outside the stadium. Most bachelors on a Japanese club, for example, live in the team dormitory. They are together nearly 24 hours a day. Married players will drink beer or play mahjong with teammates in their free time, and during the off-season it is not uncommon for an entire first team to get together for golf outings.

The club ownership sponsors social functions and group rituals to help foster feelings of solidarity and belonging. At the start of each season, a team will visit a Shinto shrine to pray for good luck, and when spring training ends, the players form a circle around the pitcher's mound for the traditional hand-clapping farewell ceremony. In December, everyone connected with the squad, from owner down to bat boy, gathers for the annual *nōkai* (year-end party). These are all demonstrations of group unity and harmony.

In spite of the high level of industrialization, Japan remains a paternalistic society with values deeply rooted in Confucianism and agrarian tradition. The older, established members of a group have clearly defined responsibilities toward the younger and vice versa. In the business world this is reflected in a lifetime employment system that gives workers maximum job security in return for allegiance to

Players perform ritualistic farewell ceremony as the Yomiuri Giants prepare to break camp

the company. Job-hopping, layoffs, and lengthy labor–management disputes are relatively rare.

The same mentality is reflected in baseball. Trades do occur and players are released outright, but far more than his American counterpart the Japanese ballplayer can look forward to a lasting association with the parent team—even after his playing days are over. A retired Nippon Ham Fighter, for example, may find himself selling ham for a living. A Chunichi Dragon taking off his uniform for the last time may move to shuffling copy for *Chunichi Sports.* At the very least, every retired player can look forward to the annual "Old Boys" party sponsored by the team. (For one such event, team alumni gather at a hot spring resort for a geisha party, followed by a golf tourney the next day.) Despite the westernization of baseball, the front office still feels strongly obligated to the player who has served his team well.

Japanese paternalism is most evident in the relationship between the manager and his players. Ideally each team should function as one happy family with the manager presiding in the role of surrogate father—a stern disciplinarian, somewhat aloof, yet never failing to show concern for the players' welfare.

Consider the case of Kazuto Tsuruoka, who resigned as manager of the Nankai Hawks to accept responsibility for a disappointing loss to the Tokyo Giants in the 1965 Japan Series. (This was four years after his earlier sabbatical.) One of the best-loved managers in the history of the sport, Tsuruoka refused an offer to manager a rival club in the Pacific League because he could not bear to fight against his former team. Head Coach Kazuo Kageyama, who initially had offered to resign along with Tsuruoka, was subsequently persuaded to take over as manager. But when Kageyama died suddenly of an acute malfunction of the cerebral cortex (reportedly a result of fatigue caused by his managerial duties), Tsuruoka turned down a lucrative contract with a team in the Central loop and returned to his old post as Hawk manager. The interests of his former team took precedence over any other considerations.

The manager sometimes gets involved in the players' private lives. For example, he may act as a "go-between" to arrange brides for single players. One manager, Kaoru Betto of the Taiyo Whales, traveled the breadth of Honshu—from Tokyo to the Japan Alps—just to persuade an unrelenting father that a Whales' reserve outfielder was worthy of his daughter's hand.

The manager makes laudatory speeches at players' weddings. He consoles bereaved players at the funerals of deceased relatives. He presents gifts and good wishes to players with newborn children along with prudent advice on the responsibilities of fatherhood. In addition, he is often ready with words of admonition for players who stray too far from the flock.

"Toshiro, I'd like to have a minute with you. You will be 29 years old next month and I think it is time you settled down and got married like everyone else. A man cannot play at his best without a sense of responsibility. You need a wife, children and a home."

"Hideyuki, you have been married for a year and a half, now. Don't you think it is about time you had a child—a son? A man has to carry on the family name you know. No arguments, now. You are a Japanese, aren't you? Well, act like one."

"Koichi, the batting coach tells me that you lost 150,000 yen ($500) at the race track last night. And he told me before that you lost another 100,000 yen playing *hana-fuda* (a Japanese card game). Two weeks ago, it was 75,000 yen at the bicycle races. And I, myself, remember you losing over 200,000 at roulette last January when you

The marriage of Koichi Tabuchi, Hanshin Tiger slugging star

took that trip to Seoul. I hate to see you throw away your money so foolishly. But, more importantly, we have an image to protect. We are providing an example for the youth of Japan to follow and what you do in your private life reflects on the good name of this team. If the press ever finds out how much money you are losing, it will seriously damage our image. So I am ordering you from now on to give up gambling and concentrate solely on baseball."

"Katsu, congratulations on your new child. I hear you are taking him to the shrine tomorrow. Here is a little something from me. Please take it and let me give you some advice on how to raise him: Always try to make him proud of his family name. Understand?"

"Tatsuo, I have been hearing too many stories about you. First it is a Ginza night club hostess. Then it is a bar girl in Shinjuku. Now, you are spending all your time at the Turkish Baths in Asakusa. You smoke one and a half packs of cigarettes a day and I think you are hitting the Suntory whiskey a little too much. I don't have any complaints about your play on the field, but I do about your 'loose' behavior. And I think it's time you began to mend your ways."

"Tadasu, your mother wrote and told me you haven't written her in two months. Write! Today! Also get a haircut and shave off that mustache. This is a team of baseball players, not movie stars."

Such fatherly concern is bound to result in a strong emotional bond between players and managers. And this sense of collective responsibility translates—hopefully—into success on the playing field.

When a team goes into a slide, the owner is likely to view the problem in emotional terms. He may go so far as to talk to the players, reminding them of their obligations toward the manager and the organization, or he may appeal to their sense of pride in being Hawks or Ham Fighters.

If nothing else works, he can resort to *kyūyō*, a drastic but highly effective strategem introduced into the world of professional baseball by the face-conscious Japanese. A *kyūyō* literally means a rest or recuperation. In baseball, it consists of the owner of a sagging team "allowing" his manager to take a rest. The head coach is usually appointed acting manager while the manager goes off by himself to meditate on the situation. The stated purpose of a *kyūyō* is to "refresh the mood of the team."

Incredible as this sounds, the wise owner knows that a *kyūyō* can be a very useful device. First of all, he realizes that if the players really respect their manager, they will feel they have let him down. His departure may be just the spark needed to ignite their flagging spirits—to shame them into playing better baseball. Their shame—and the trauma of separation from their surrogate father—will be ended when play improves.

Illness, real or imagined, is often given as the reason for a *kyūyō*. (Mental fatigue is the diagnosis most commonly associated with losing streaks.) Whatever the excuse, it is seldom clear how the *kyūyō* is initiated. The announcement to the press almost always reads the same: "So-and-so-*san* requested a leave of absence and permission was granted." But, often as not, the request originates in the front office. Inevitably, the *kyūyō* is accompanied by a flurry of statements from the owner, the front office, the coaches, and the top players to the effect that the responsibility for the slump lies with everyone—the owner, the front office, the coaches, and players—not just the manager!

Sometimes the *kyūyō* works miracles. In 1967, Osamu Mihara, one of Japan' all-time great managers, was having trouble with his Taiyo Whales. Mihara "requested" and received permission to take a

12-day leave of absence. Stories appearing in the Japanese press hinted that the manager's leave might be prolonged—depending on how the team performed.

Head Coach Kaoru Betto stepped in as "acting manager" and the Whales promptly responded by winning ten games in a row. Following the tenth win, Betto paid a visit to the club owner, Kenkichi Nakabe. Betto argued that he was only a coach, not a manager, and that the job should go back to the true manager. Nakabe agreed, and Mihara was reinstated, ending one of the shortest *kyūyōs* in baseball history.

Another *kyūyō* that worked out well involved Michio Nishizawa, manager of the Chunichi Dragons from Nagoya. In May 1967, Nishizawa left the team on account of "illness." His departure was all the more dramatic because, the season before, Nishizawa had vowed to bring the team a league championship.

At the start of the season, Nishizawa had been bothered by stomach pains. And when the Dragons went into a tailspin around the first of May, the pains grew more intense. Unable to conceal his condition, Nishizawa began bringing his medicine along to games.

A week later, with his team floundering in last place, Nishizawa underwent a physical examination. His doctors advised him to rest for a month. But Nishizawa, recalling his promise of the previous year, resolved to stick it out. Since his health appeared to wax and wane according to the Dragons' fortunes on the diamond, Nishizawa may have hoped that a few timely wins would restore his vigor.

Continued losses, however, soon quashed such hopes. Nishizawa's pain was excruciating and growing worse with each defeat. It reached a peak of intensity, apparently, after a meeting between Nishizawa and the Dragons general manager. Nishizawa paid another visit to the hospital and, soon after, the Dragons' owner ordered the ailing manager to take a *kyūyō*. Pitching Coach Sadao Kondo was asked to take over the team in Nishizawa's absence.

"It's detrimental to morale to have the manager leading the team while he's rubbing his stomach," explained the Dragons' general manager. Nishizawa protested to the press that he would return in a few days, but the general manager was not so sure. He cautioned that

Nishizawa's recovery might take "quite some time."

Predictably, Acting Manager Kondo warmed up to his new role with a declaration of collective responsibility: "I think it's a regrettable thing we have done to our manager. The present problems of the team are the responsibility of the coaches and the players. The trouble is mental more than anything else. I'm going to put forth my best effort to pull the team out of its slump and get it on the right track for the manager's return."

True to his word, Kondo proceeded to lead the Dragons to eight wins in ten games. And there can be little doubt that the team's comeback helped speed the recovery of the ailing manager, who convalesced at home in front of his TV set.

Returning to the Dragons in Hiroshima, after a mere two weeks' absence, Nishizawa was greeted like Odysseus back from his years at sea. The Dragons' star leftfielder blasted a three-run homer to highlight an 8–0 shutout, and then summed up the mood of the team when he told the press: "I am delighted that I could celebrate the manager's return with a home run."

In the visitors' clubhouse after the game, a beaming Nishizawa could not believe the change that had come over his team. "The batters are swinging better than before I left . . . even the mood on the bench is improved . . . I have never been so happy." Adding that his stomach felt "unbelievably well," he rushed back to the inn where the players were staying and, in a rare display of gratitude, personally thanked each one of them.

Nishizawa's *kyūyō* worked out remarkably well. This usually happens, however, only when the manager is an established name— when his age, seniority, and past achievements have solidified his image as *pater familias*. The departure of such a beloved figure inevitably triggers guilt in the players. They try harder and usually play better as a result.

Kazuto Tsuruoka of the Nankai Hawks was far and away the most established manager in baseball. He had already led the team through some 20 seasons when he took his *kyūyō*. Even though he declared that he would not return, no one dared take him seriously.

Sure enough, the prospect of a shameful rupture in team (family) relations had the desired effect. Playing his role to the hilt, Tsuruoka held out stubbornly until an 11-game winning streak, a climb into contention, a plea from his players and coaches, a petition signed by the fans—and a two-month rest—had mellowed him enough to change his mind.

Sometimes it becomes obvious that a managerial rest won't accomplish a thing. By mid-season there is no longer any doubt that the manager must go if his team is to move out of last place. At this point, the manager himself usually makes the first move. In the grand Japanese tradition of accepting responsibility, he will step forward and offer to depart.

The operative word is still *kyūyō*. The same as before. It still means "rest and recuperation" and is written with the same Chinese characters. But this time everyone knows the manager will not be coming back. Although it is usually not publicly announced as such, his *kyūyō* is permanent. It is in fact a resignation.

Such verbal camouflage is used for several reasons. First of all, for a manager to resign or be fired precipitously would involve a loss of face all around. It almost never happens; instead, official announcements are postponed until after the season.

Another reason is that no Japanese likes to admit failure, which is precisely what a manager would be doing if he quit a losing team in mid-season. Furthermore, Japanese thinking holds that the owner who has to fire his manager is also a failure. He has not chosen carefully and, therefore, has failed in his responsibility to the fans.

This is where a *kyūyō* saves the day by letting team owners and managers part company while allowing each to retain a certain measure of personal dignity. The manager who takes a leave and doesn't come back hasn't really been fired and he hasn't really resigned. He just isn't there anymore. In Japan, form takes precedence over content, especially in such serious matters as changing managers.

The resignation *kyūyō* unfolds like an elaborately choreographed kabuki drama. A favorite opening act has the manager approach the team owner:

MANAGER (*bowing deeply*): I admit my responsibility for the team's poor performance. I wish to resign. I'm sorry to have caused you so much trouble.

OWNER (*shocked, indignant*): Nonsense. Don't be stupid. I refuse to consider it. I have asked you to lead my team to victory. I am depending on you. Besides, it isn't all your fault. The players, the coaches, and we in the front office are all to blame. Don't quit now, just when I need you most. Where is your courage? Go back down on that field and get to work.

In the second act, the manager returns to his team and tries to revive his flagging enthusiasm in the hope that some of it will rub off on his dispirited players. After a few more weeks of losing baseball, he again decides that he has had enough. Managing the team is becoming a personal and very public embarrassment, so he pays another visit to the owner.

At this point the first two acts are simply repeated. The manager's resignation is refused a second time and he returns again to lose even more games.

On the manager's third visit to the owner, the action picks up somewhat:

MANAGER: I really think this has gone far enough. I am asking you to accept my resignation. Please.

OWNER (*leans back in chair and stares at ceiling in deep thought*): You know, manager-*san*, timing is very important. I think perhaps we owe your problems some serious consideration, but I personally do not feel that this is the right time to discuss them. Perhaps I'm too optimistic. Perhaps you're too pessimistic. Who knows? I still think you should give it another try.

The manager goes back to the team once more, and the drama moves swiftly toward its inexorable conclusion. Suspense builds for a few days while the owner meets with the front office management for elaborate talks. Finally the owner, "unable to stand selfishly in the way of the manager's wishes," grants permission for a *kyūyō* "with deepest heartfelt regret."

At this point all concerned can breathe a sigh of relief. Since everyone has acknowledged his duties and responsibilities not once, but several times through the resignation-refusal procedure, the owner can now announce the manager is leaving and name a replacement without serious loss of face for anyone. The official resignation of the old manager can wait for the end of the season.

A resignation *kyūyō* is such an emotional ordeal that Shigeru Sugishita certainly deserves a prize. The malfortunate Sugishita's managerial career was marked by not one but two *kyūyō*'s of the resignation variety.

Called in to take over the Hanshin Tigers in 1966, Sugishita was expected to give the formidable Tokyo Giants a run for the pennant. But, plagued by injuries, the Tigers soon fell far out of contention. Reports of friction between Sugishita and his players began to circulate. "The manager behaved too much like a feudal lord," complained one. "He didn't try to be a part of us."

The more games the Tigers lost, the more sullen Sugishita grew. Once he reportedly grabbed a player who had been called out on strikes and chided him angrily for not arguing with the umpire. "What good does that do?" asked the player afterwards.

Sugishita's team responded to their manager's hostility in kind. On the train to Hiroshima after dropping three straight games, Sugishita called a council of the team elders—coaches and senior players. What could be done to improve the club? he asked. Sugishita's plea met with cold stares: "It is the manager's responsibility when the team loses," he was told curtly.

Strategy is discussed by the Giants in a pre-game meeting

In desperation Sugishita requested a *kyūyō* twice during the season and twice he was turned down. Finally in mid-August, after a disappointing loss to the Giants, his wish was granted. Sugishita typically assumed all the blame: "This season the Tigers were expected to put up a fight for the pennant. That I failed in my responsibilities is a big disappointment. The main reason I am leaving is because the Tigers were toothless against the Giants. There were too many injuries. I tried my best, but even so the Tigers couldn't win. I became mentally tired and asked General Manager Tozawa to let me rest."

Tozawa tried to soften the blow: "The present poor state of the team is not solely the manager's responsibility. There were many injuries and the players didn't hustle enough. We accepted Sugishita's request because he was mentally tired. The owner agrees that this is not Manager Sugishita's responsibility."

Sugishita's departure triggered a wave of guilt on the Hanshin team. The new manager led off by calling on everyone associated with the team to share in the blame. Now that Sugishita was no longer a thorn in the side of the Tiger organization he was back in good graces.

Two years later Sugishita got another crack at managing, this time with the Chunichi Dragons. By the end of June his team had lost 19 of 20 consecutive games, and another rift between Sugishita and his players was developing. Finally Sugishita was ordered to take a rest for an "indefinite period of time" in order to "create a fresh atmosphere" on the team and end the lengthy slump. As he took a painful last look at the Dragon dugout, Sugishita may have consoled himself with the knowledge that he had already survived one such circuitous sacking.

The many advantages of *kyūyō* notwithstanding, there do exist maverick owners who refuse to bow to convention. Unfortunately for Takehiko Bessho, manager of the 1970 Yakult Atoms, the Atoms' owner was one of these. Bessho was winning only one game in four his second year as manager. After a calamitous 10-game losing streak, he pleaded with the owner for a rest. Bessho was told that he could stick it out or quit altogether.

To quit outright would have been unthinkable. Bessho stayed and the Atoms went right on losing. This time, though, the owner spoke up in his manager's defense, reciting the usual platitudes about how the team must share in the blame, how Bessho had made a great contribution to baseball in his playing days, and so on. Two farm team coaches were brought up to help Bessho devise a new "dual strategy" for ending the Atom slump.

For a short time things did seem to improve, as the team won five of its next eight games. But then the roof caved in: The Atoms suffered 11 consecutive defeats. On the day of the 12th game, the Atoms' owner reached a decision. The manager would have to go. That afternoon, Bessho visited the Atoms' executive offices and formally submitted his resignation. "I am sorry I was unable to satisfy the fans' expectations," Bessho told the owner, and bowed from the waist in apology.

The owner accepted Bessho's resignation along with his apology and Bessho thus became the first Japanese manager to resign—officially—in mid-season. The head coach took over as manager and Bessho was offered a trip to the U.S. to "study major league baseball." As for the Atoms, they went on to set a league record with 16 straight losses.

Perhaps the most unusual example of *kyūyō* was the one involving Minoru Murayama and the 1972 Hanshin Tigers. The Murayama affair shows what happens when the Japanese must face conflicting obligations. It is a classic case of Japanese-style intergroup diplomacy.

As the Tigers' leading pitcher for more than a decade, Murayama had a glorious career that included three "Best Pitcher" awards, one MVP, more than 200 wins, and the lowest lifetime ERA in Japanese baseball history. His appointment as player–manager in 1970 at the age of 32 was a rare tribute, and came as an appropriate climax.

Murayama got off to a brilliant start as manager, narrowly missing the league championship. Rebounding from three years of sub-par pitching due to injuries, he showed some of his old form while logging a 14–3 mark and setting a Japan record with his league-leading ERA of 0.98.

The next year, however, Murayama's luck began to sour. Plagued by a sore arm and a bad knee, he won only seven games. The rumors were out: "Murayama's pitching days are over." What was worse, it was becoming painfully evident that his managerial abilities did not match his earlier brilliance as a player. An explosive, fiercely proud competitor, Murayama once cried on a teammate's shoulder after a bitter defeat.

As a pitcher, Murayama had inspired his team, often providing the extra spark that turned defeat into victory. But when he donned his manager's cap, his temper was a liability. He expected other players to match his own fiery intensity and he played favorites, openly criticizing players he did not like. It wasn't long before dissension arose. The Tigers slipped from contention at the beginning of the season and struggled through a dismal year.

By the start of Murayama's third season as manager, it was evident that the situation was not going to improve. Murayama was not pitching at all. He explained that he wanted to devote more time to developing young pitchers and managing the team.

With the season two weeks old and the Tigers once more in the second division, Murayama called a press conference and made a surprise announcement. He would, he told the startled reporters, turn the team over to Head Coach Tomeyasu Kaneda in order to devote himself to pitching. Murayama accepted complete responsibility for the team's predicament. He vowed to do his best to regain his old form, take his regular turn on the mound, and help the younger pitchers.

At a press conference the next day, the team owner confirmed what Murayama had said. Murayama would concentrate on pitching while Kaneda filled in as acting manager. "Can this be considered a managerial *kyūyō?*" asked one reporter. "Yes, it can," the owner replied. "It is a mental *kyūyō.*"

In response to another question, the owner verified that Murayama himself had asked for the *kyūyō* in order to jolt the team out of its rut. When it came to the question of Murayama's return, however, the owner equivocated. "Murayama will come back when the team reaches .500 perhaps—or maybe even higher. When we reach the point where we feel it is all right for Murayama to handle two responsibilities, we will evaluate the situation and make a determination at that time. Perhaps the team will ask Murayama to come back and we'll make a determination then." (This translation of an exchange quoted in *Baseball* magazine retains the ambiguity of the original.) Murayama kept the title of manager.

Nothing quite like this had ever happened before. Pretending not to notice that the Tigers now had two managers, the front office praised Murayama's courageous decision. The acting manager promised to do his best to win more games so the manager could return to his rightful place. The pitchers wailed that the miserable showing was their fault. They solemnly promised to pitch better and move the club up in the standings so Murayama could end his self-imposed exile.

Privately, no one had any illusions about Murayama's comeback. He had vowed to start and pitch in relief as often as possible, but he was not the Murayama of old. His arm was gone, he was out of condition, and an old knee injury forced him to pitch with his leg wrapped from ankle to thigh. He had to take painkillers to ease his suffering.

In the weeks that followed, Murayama's appearances on the mound were rare. When he did pitch, the results were unimpressive. The Tigers, however, began to jell under the firm guidance of the acting manager, and improved their standing. After each victory, Kaneda would join the owner and the players in alluding to the day, near at hand, when the manager could return to the team.

Unfortunately for Murayama, it was all a show—another act in the kabuki drama of baseball—scripted and performed to save the manager's face. With each passing day, it became more obvious that the Tigers had no intention of giving the manager's slot back to Murayama. Seven times Acting Manager Kaneda submitted his resignation, and seven times it was refused. Yet no announcement concerning Murayama's status came from the front office.

By August the Tigers were in second place, only two games behind the league-leading Giants. Everyone still called Murayama *kantoku* (manager) and the head coach *kantoku dairi* (acting manager). Murayama was included in all the strategy meetings, and Kaneda made certain to mention to the press at every opportunity that he was directing the club with the help and guidance of Murayama. Except for a small faction of players loyal to Murayama, everyone was pleased

400-game-winner Masaichi Kaneda, manager of the Lotte Orions, surveys his charges

with the way Kaneda was handling the team.

When rumors of a rift between Kaneda and Murayama reached the press, both refused comment. But no one who saw Murayama sitting alone at the end of the dugout game after game could fail to understand what was really happening.

The season drew to a finish with Kaneda still in command. The Hanshin team finished second. They had kept the outcome of the pennant race in doubt until the last few days of the season. Tiger fans were delighted. So were young Tiger players who had warmed the bench under Murayama—Kaneda had given them a chance to play and develop. The future looked bright.

The problem of Manager Murayama still remained, however. The team had done so well under the acting manager that the logical thing to do would be to promote him to manager. After all, the club had an obligation to its fans who wanted to see winning baseball. But, then again, what about the great pitcher who had contributed so much to the team over the years? The Tigers owed a tremendous debt to this proud, easily misunderstood man and could not casually discard him.

If he were replaced as manager, it would represent a devastating blow to his pride.

The Hanshin front office did what most Japanese will do when faced with a difficult decision. Nothing. They stalled for time. The owner of the Tigers—chairman of the board of Hanshin Railways (the team's parent company)—left responsibility for the decision up to two people: the president of Hanshin Railways and the president of the Hanshin Tigers. The president of Hanshin Railways, whom outsiders speculated held the real power, begged off. "I'm just a committee member," he protested. "This is a problem for the team owner to handle." The Tiger president also insisted that the owner make the decision since it was he who had originally lobbied for Murayama's installation as manager three years earlier. A spokesman for the owner, however, announced that the owner was ill—too ill to even discuss the problem. And so it went.

Days passed, then weeks; still no announcement from the front office on the fate of the "Two-Headed Tiger"—as the Hanshin club was now known. "Perhaps it would have been better if the Tigers had just fired Murayama in the first place," one reporter observed sadly. "He's a man who values honor, but to be left hanging this way . . ."

Finally, the expected happened. Murayama came in, stoically submitted his resignation, and then notified the club of his retirement as a player. The owner, after "realizing" that Murayama could not be persuaded to change his mind, quickly offered the post to Kaneda. Kaneda said he needed time to think and then accepted a few days later. Murayama refused a job in the Tiger organization, ignored overtures from other teams, and dropped quietly out of baseball.

This whole chain of events may seem bizarre to Americans, who are used to seeing managerial heads roll with complete disregard for feelings (more than one major-league manager has learned of his dismissal from the morning newspaper). But in Japan, where the human values of duty and personal honor are all important, any change in the status quo is a serious undertaking. For Murayama, Kaneda, and the front office executives to have behaved in any other manner would have been—in Japanese terms—dishonorable.

3 BASEBALL SAMURAI STYLE

The batter knocked the dirt from his spikes and stepped back into the box to a count of three and two. Taking his stance, he eyed the pitcher evenly. It was a tense moment: In the stands the fans craned their necks to see whether a hit, or even a walk, might help lift the home team out of its dismal slump. Play for the past few weeks had been so uninspired that the night before the club owner had seen fit to comment about the team's poor performance to the manager. The manager in turn called a special pre-game meeting of players and coaches. Whether the pep talk would inspire the flagging players remained to be seen.

The pitcher went into his windup and fired a fast ball. Thousands of fans sighed in relief as it sailed past the plate, high and outside, and the umpire called "ball four." Then something incredible happened. Dropping his bat, the batter broke into a sprint down the first base line and slid headlong into the bag amid a cloud of dust.

Had the batter mistaken the last pitch for a called third strike? Had the summer heat gone to his head? No, he was merely following orders. At the pre-game meeting, the manager, after delivering a sound verbal thrashing about responsibilities to the fans and the club ownership, ordered every player to slide head first into *every* base until the team regained its fighting spirit.

There is an old saying that goes something like this: 'Put one Japanese against one Chinese and the Chinese will win. Put two Japanese against two Chinese and the Chinese will still win. But put three Japanese against three Chinese and the Chinese don't have a prayer.' Whether or not this bit of folk wisdom is valid, it is certain the Japanese have mastered the art of group cooperation with a social philosophy that subordinates individual desires to the collective good.

Sometimes Japanese "groupthink" can be downright frightening, for it is this kind of mentality that makes otherwise sane adults risk bodily injury by sliding into base headfirst to prove their loyalty to the team (although such cases are admittedly rare). Many American managers ban the headfirst slide—the danger of serious injury is too great. But the Japanese manager, no less aware of the risk, knows that some things are far more important than avoiding injury.

Headfirst slides are just one of the many extreme demands that may be made on a player under a set of strict unwritten rules that might be called the *Samurai Code of Conduct for Baseball Players*.

This code has roots in *Bushido*, a warriors' mode of behavior dating from the 13th century. Bushido means the "Way of the Samurai," referring to the armed retainers who did battle in the service of the great *daimyo*, or feudal lords. It sets forth rules of conduct that developed out of the intimate relationships between sword-wielding sa-

Giant star Sadaharu Oh poses with sword

murai and their masters. Incorporating elements from Confucianism, Buddhism, and Shinto, *Bushido* stresses such values as loyalty, self-discipline, reverence for nature, simplicity, modesty, and unquestioning obedience. In addition, it connotes a strong love for Japan and devotion to the idea of being Japanese.

Bushido, in modified form, is still a force in Japanese life. Its influence is greatly felt in the most traditional, least westernized institutions like *sumo* wrestling and the criminal underworld of the *yakuza*. It has also helped shape the everyday world of education, business, politics, and, of course, baseball.

The Samurai Code of Conduct for Baseball Players has been refined and developed over the years—even to accommodate the influx of Western ideas. Although it is not always strictly adhered to (especially by members of the younger generation) it has nevertheless had a profound influence on the game of baseball. Strict, demanding, and believed to be full of wisdom, this code, though unwritten, is understood by everyone.

Its preamble stresses duty, honor, and the value of being a "team player"—summed up in another proverb: "The nail that sticks up will be hammered down." And the various articles then extend over those rules a Japanese player is expected to observe on and off the field.

Article 1. The player must be a total team member. In America a player is on his own from early October to the middle of February, but the Japanese ballplayer has far less time to himself. The official opening date for spring training in Japan is February first, but the Code suggests a player would be wise to report for "voluntary training" one or two weeks in advance. Failure to do so will brand him as not serious about his job even though training in advance to get a head start is against league rules. (A few teams even hold "voluntary training" sessions in December and January, and one manager, nicknamed "the drill sergeant," once began "spring training" in November.)

Not only is a player expected to report early for spring training (usually leaving his wife behind) but when the regular season and the Japan series are over, he can still look forward to the fall series of

Tsuneo Horiuchi, a pitcher, stays fit in the off-season

show fans and the opposition that the team is united and unshakeable in its determination. They also make a favorable impression on the owner.

Along the same lines, it doesn't hurt to eat a lot of Nippon Ham if you are a Nippon Ham Fighter; to carry the *Yomiuri Daily News* around in your back pocket if you play for the Yomiuri Giants; * or to chew Lotte mint gum if you are a Lotte Orion. And it won't go unnoticed if you are careful to say "I'm proud to be a Kintetsu Buffalo" (or whatever) whenever a reporter is within earshot.

Article 2. The player must follow established procedure. In America, many batters step up to the plate and swing away without regard to form or style. A number of pitchers do the same when they throw. Joe Morgan flaps his arms like a chicken; Louis Tiant turns his back to the batter while winding up; Stan Musial with his famed "peek-a-boo" stance, and Juan Marichal with his high-kick delivery are only a few of the American players who have developed highly individualistic styles that have brought them great success. "Form is only the look of things," an American coach will argue. "Getting results is what counts."

Not so in Japan, where the rule of established procedure is supreme. The canons of baseball form are drummed into every player's head from his little league days on. The Code teaches that the "masters" of baseball, just like the high-ranking masters of judo, karate, or swordsmanship, know the best way to prepare the player for combat. They are older, wiser, and more experienced.

According to the batting masters, for example, the batter must stand at the plate with his elbows close to his body and his feet not too far apart. He must have a sharp, even swing that just meets the ball as it comes over the plate. He must never "bail out," or swing from the heels like Bobby Bonds, Dave Kingman, and many American long ball hitters. That leads to too many strikeouts. Making contact is the most important thing. Swing only at strikes, work the count, and try for a base hit.

The pitching canon dictates that the pitcher throw with a deliber-

---

* The name the Tokyo Giants adopted in 1947.

ate, uniform motion and a balanced follow-through which leaves him ready for fielding. Speed is sacrificed for control. Strikeouts are dramatic, but it is better to let a batter hit the ball than it is to walk him.

This obsession with form has its basis in the Japanese belief that form has a reality of its own. There is a right and wrong way to attack an opponent with a sword, to arrange flowers in a vase, to construct a garden, to make and serve a cup of green tea and to throw a curve ball. The correct form, which is the most economical way of doing anything, has been discovered and refined sometimes through centuries by the great masters of the past. A good player is one who can merge his own movements with correct form; everything else will follow in time.

In America, excellence is equated with getting results no matter how unorthodox the form. In Japan, it is more important to conform to the set way of doing things. The batter who looks good striking out is praiseworthy, while the stubborn individualist who insists "I know what's best for me" is not tolerated.

The difference between Japanese and American attitudes shows up dramatically in the different ways the ballplayers train. A Japanese camp is tightly organized while an American one, by comparison, is not. In the United States, a player is left largely on his own to devise a program that will work for him. He loosens up, takes defensive practice and batting practice with the team, but most additional training is tailored to individual needs. Coaches and trainers will help, but the feeling is that every player knows what he must do to stay in shape and keep his position on the team. It's up to him.

In a Japanese camp, the coaches make the decisions—how many miles a player must run, what exercises he needs to do, how many practice swings a batter should take, and how many pitches a pitcher will throw. Everyone trains together, following identical procedures with martial precision. Seldom is anything left to the player's imagination.

The spring training schedule for a Japanese baseball team is nearly as complex as a Japan National Railways timetable—and followed just as strictly. One American who has played in Japan remarked: "You can set your watch by it."

Oh stretches his back early in the spring

Shown below is a typical daily schedule for infielders and out-fielders at one Japanese camp.

7:30	Morning wake-up call
8:00– 8:30	Meet in hotel lobby for "speed walk"
8:30– 9:30	Breakfast (menu: fish, rice, *misoshiru*)
9:30– 9:50	Rest period. Prepare for practice
9:50–10:10	Team meeting. Review of practice.
	Walk to stadium
10:20–11:15	Exercise and running

            1) Ten laps around the field (2½ miles)
            2) Calisthenics
                a) Situps 200 (4 sets x 50)
                b) Back arch 200 (4 sets x 50)
                c) Wind sprints (100 m. x 10)
                d) Jumping sprints (50 m. x 10)

11:15–11:25	Catch
11:25–11:35	Pepper drills
11:35–12:00	Defense practice

            1) IF—ground ball, DP
            2) Catchers—pop flies, wild pitches
            3) OF—fly balls

12:00– 1:30	Batting practice. Divide in three groups

        Group A—Batting cages
            Batting cage #1—right-handed
            pitcher: 6 min.
            Batting cage #2—left-handed
            pitcher: 6 min.
            Batting cage #3—breaking-ball
            pitcher: 6 min.
        Group B—Pitching machine
        Group C—Ground ball practice
        (Note: Groups rotate on the half hour)

1:30– 1:50	Lunch on the field (menu: rice balls)
1:50– 2:00	Loosening up
2:00– 3:15	Intrasquad game
3:15– 3:45	Defense practice

            1) 3B pick-off play (with runner on first)

3:45– 4:00	Baserunning

            1) Sliding

4:00– 5:00	Special batting practice and defense practice (For players with problems)
5:00– 5:30	Running. 10 laps around the field (2½ miles)

5:30– 7:00	Dinner
	Group A: Chinese buffet
	Group B: Western buffet
	Group C: Japanese restaurant
7:00– 7:30	Rest
7:30– 8:30	Team Meeting. Review day's practice
8:30–10:30	Massage (every player, three trainers)
	Toss batting and shadow pitching areas
	open
10:30	Curfew
11:00	Lights out

Article 3. The player must undergo hard training. This means practice, practice, and more practice. And if you look closely at the above training schedule you will begin to appreciate the grueling pace followed for six weeks beginning on January 15. The first two weeks are usually devoted exclusively to physical conditioning. Most players don't even touch a ball until February 1. And so by March 1 when the exhibition season opens, Japan's professional ballplayers are probably the most superbly conditioned group of athletes in the world.

American players report to camp in mid-February and spend an average of three hours or less at the park each day, a schedule that leaves plenty of time to bask in the Florida or Arizona sun. While some work hard to get into condition, others simply play their way into shape.

In Japan, the latter is heresy. Players are on the field anywhere from five to nine hours a day, often in near freezing temperatures. Coaches, who huddle over bonfires to ward off the cold, conduct punishing drills reminiscent of Marine Boot Camp. One team, for example, starts the day at 8:30 with a five-mile run. Between normal baseball drills, the players will run up and down the 275 steps leading to a nearby shrine several times and then do 20 laps around a quarter mile track. Later, a second five-mile run will conclude the day's training (although pitchers may also be required to run the ten miles from camp back to the hotel). Another team makes its pitchers run up and down the stadium steps with 50-pound sacks strapped to their backs.

The Japanese ballplayer is proud of his ability to take this kind of

The Taiyo Whales run the
steps of a nearby shrine

Hanshin Tiger pitchers work
the stadium seats carrying
extra weight

punishment. He reasons that if he trains hard for nine hours a day in the spring, then a three-hour game during the regular season will be easy. He also knows that by devoting almost all his waking hours to the pursuit of perfection he is emulating the great masters of the past—the swordsmen who spent countless hours practicing 'kata' (forms) against the day when their skills would be needed in battle. According to Japanese folklore there were samurai who could draw their swords and quarter an apple tossed into the air before it fell to earth.

Like the ancient swordsman who stood blindfolded on a high pedestal for hours to develop his balance, the Japanese ballplayer spends endless time in the batting cage. A typical day might see him taking 50 swings against a right-handed pitcher, 50 against a left-hander, another 50 against breaking pitches, 50 in the toss batting circle, and final 50 against the pitching machine. Later at the hotel he will find time for another 100 shadow swings. (Just try swinging a bat as hard as you can 40 times to see how tiring this can be.) Some batters start training each morning with an incredible 500 shadow swings, while others flail into a heavy sand bag.

Pitchers train with equal zeal, throwing as many as 300 pitches a day. American pitchers claim this is bad for the arm, but the Japanese feel it helps make control razor sharp. They reason that if practicing everyday helps the batters maintain their edge, the same must be true for pitchers.

During the season, this hard training continues. In grueling 4-hour pre-game workouts batters take nearly three times as much batting practice as their American counterparts, while pitchers throw with similar dedication. Between games, in the clubhouse before the mirror, back at the dormitory or at home in stocking feet on the straw mat floor—a batter or pitcher never stops trying to perfect his form. (Players in a batting slump will often get up in the middle of the night to shadow swing.)

Hard training goes beyond the physical level, for masters of the martial arts taught that with sufficient powers of concentration the mind can make the body do almost anything. Consequently, a player's mental health is regarded just as important as his physical

Pitchers practice control at Giant camp

shape. During the off-season it is not unusual for players to study at a Zen temple, where they develop, through meditation and rigorous spiritual discipline, the calm to help them in a tight game. Purified and strengthened through spiritual practice, the mind can easily order the body to pull every outside low pitch or punch every inside delivery to the opposite field.

Another technique for sharpening a player's mental powers is known as *yamagomori* (retreat to the mountains). Like the Swiss, the Japanese believe they can draw strength from the mountains that cover most of their country. Particularly Mt. Fuji, which holds a sacred place in their hearts. Former Tokyo Giant star Shigeo Nagashima once described what a *yamagomori* near the majestic mountain did for him:

A major turning point in my career came after my fifth year in professional baseball. It was the first year I had finished under .300. It was a painful time, and the struggle I had that year was a bitter memory.

I thought I had hit a wall but then I realized that it was because I was getting tired of playing baseball. It was affecting me physically and mentally.

I really like Mt. Fuji. Perhaps people will say that I am childish, but when I see the outline of that mountain against the sky, I feel my heart is purified and everything becomes well with me.

So that year, two weeks before the New Year, I packed some food and went to Sengokubara (at the base of Mt. Fuji). I forced the trainer to come with me. After two weeks there, I recovered from my fatigue. I could just look at myself and see that I was better. And I thoroughly changed my thinking about what a professional baseball player is.

I stopped smoking and I regained my top physical condition. The mountain helped me see myself again.

Article 4. The player must play "For The Team." The Code says that the player must not concern himself with individual records such as batting averages, home runs, wins, or saves. There is no room for attitudes like that of one American major leaguer who announced that he "didn't get any satisfaction" out of his team's 10th inning 1–0 win because his relief pitcher had received credit for the victory.

Players should not dwell on personal illness or fatigue. Those who are tired or injured must do their best to play at peak efficiency anyway, for nothing is as important as the success of the team.

This article of the Code takes a special toll on the pitchers. For despite the professed regard of most "enlightened" Japanese managers for the American rotation system, they still are tempted to use a pitcher who is going well, without regard to the amount of rest he has had. In a crucial mid-week three-game series, for example, a Japanese manager will often start his top pitcher in the opening game on Tuesday and then use him again in relief in one or both of the next two games. The same pitcher can also expect to start the following weekend.

This, of course, is hard on the player. An American would refuse to submit himself to such abuse since it might hurt his arm and shorten his career. But the Japanese has to comply.

Article 5. The player must demonstrate fighting spirit.

> *No matter how tough the pinch you're in*
> *You will not give up or lose heart*
> *The will to win the title always in your breast*
> *You will seize and hold fast the pennant flag.*
>
> *Fighting nobly unto death*
> *Yea, even in death you will stand firm*
> *With a strategy keen as a glittering gem*
> *Thirty thousand clapping hands will blossom*
>
> *Your back to the wall, about to breathe your last*
> *A sayonara home run turns the tide*
> *In the corners of every fan's eyes*
> *Hot tears will glisten again.*
>
> *Dragons, Dragons, Dragons*
> *Chunichi, Chunichi, Chunichi*
> *Guts! Thrust and advance with guts! ***

This rousing fight song, written for the Chunichi Dragons, illustrates the importance the Japanese place on "fighting spirit," the

* *The Chunichi Song* by Masanosuke Yamamoto. ©1974 Toshiba Records.

quality most admired in a baseball player. While most Americans hold that skill, conditioning, and experience make a winning athlete, many Japanese believe that deficiencies in any of these areas can be compensated for by the kind of fierce competitive drive that leads a player to disregard his own safety and health. The winner of the 1974 Japan Series "fighting spirit" award, for example, played with a broken ankle.

According to the Baseball Code, a mediocre player with fighting spirit can become a good player, and a good player with fighting spirit can become a great one. For a player with fighting spirit has more than just his ability and ordinary hustle. He has a will to win and a spiritual strength that enables him to perform at top level, regardless of his physical condition. An outfielder may be taped from his ankle to his thigh, but if he has fighting spirit, he will chase down and catch that long fly ball. An overworked pitcher may lose physical strength and speed on his fastball, but if he has fighting spirit, he will rise to the occasion and defeat the opposition. A player's will is considered supreme to his infinitely teachable body.

The ability to overcome bodily discomfort comes only with much practice and discipline. The samurai, for example, used to fast for days while walking around with toothpicks in their mouths to look as if they had just eaten. They were practicing to overcome hunger.

Accordingly, "suffering" is an integral part of a Japanese baseball player's training and to this end the Japanese have designed the "1000 fungo drill," a diabolical exercise in which a coach or crew of coaches hit ground balls to a player—first to his left, and then to his right before he has a chance to resume his position, and then back to his left again—perhaps 300 times or until the player drops from exhaustion.

A variation is the "100 fly-ball" drill, the outfielders version of the 1000 fungo drill. Wally Yonamine, a Hawaiian of Japanese descent who joined the Tokyo Giants in 1951, describes what it was like for him.

When I first came to the Giants I was really lazy. I lacked self-discipline. The Giants worked me hard. They put me in center and began to hit the ball

Former Giant star Shigeo Nagashima goes through the 1000 fungo drill

to me. First to the left, then to the right, then back to the left, then up in front of me, then way back over my head. Man, after chasing 35–40 fly balls, I was flat on my back. The coach told me to get up, but I couldn't move. Then they started to hit me with the ball. The coaches are that good.

I'm grateful I got that training while I was young. It made me a better ballplayer. It gave me discipline.

The manager never praised me. That's not the Japanese way, but he really changed me.

Still another variation is what some call the "Ole Infielder's Drill"—named for young infielders who are prone to jump out of the way of wicked line-drives, matador style. In this drill, a coach will stand the player on the third base line about twenty feet away and begin to hit bullet-hard line shots at him. Thirty minutes later the player's body is black and blue, one or two fingers are bent back, and, more often than not, he is on the verge of tears.

These drills are not to improve fielding. The Japanese refer to them as "Guts" drills. And they are intended in the main to show the younger player that baseball is not an easy game.

Coaches have modified these drills over the years to accommodate "softer" generations. Twenty years ago the 1000 fungo drill was just exactly what the name implies. Coaches counted every ball hit to make sure. It took three hours. One manager made his players use their bare hands, while another forced several batters who were afraid of the ball to stand in the box and "practice" being hit by them.

The aura that surrounds these drills reflects the romantic attitude Japanese take toward sports. For a young player, his first professional training camp is almost a modern day puberty ritual. Each season newspapers dramatize these rites of passage with such headlines as MUD, SWEAT AND TEARS. SPRING CAMP: THE SONG OF MAN! and I'LL BECOME A MAN.

Article 6. The player must behave like a gentlemen on the field. In America, beanballs, collisions on the basepaths and the resulting sprains, bruises, and broken bones are an integral part of the game. In Japan, such injuries are rare. The Baseball Code of Conduct prohibits the brushback pitch and the spikes-high slide. They are not *fea purē*—"fair play." If a Japanese pitcher should accidentally hit a batter, he will more often than not tip his cap and bow in apology. Similarly, if a baserunner should knock a fielder down, he will say "Excuse me."

The Code also prohibits displays of temper on the field. It is bad manners to break bats or helmets or to argue with the umpire. Expressions of anger and sorrow are considered un-Japanese. In addition, it is poor taste to spit or chew gum at the plate. It doesn't look good. Aspiring youth is expected to emulate Japan home-run king Sadaharu Oh, who, as one paper pointed out, conducts himself like a gentleman: "When he strikes out, he breaks into a smile and trots back to the bench."

Although violence is forbidden by the Code, occasionally tempers flare and things get out of hand. When this happens, Japanese players will lash out with an intensity seldom seen in American ballparks. Angered at an accidental brushback pitch, a player once attacked the pitcher with his bat. While an irate team manager responded in like fashion when a cup of sake was poured on him by a hostile fan. And there have been numerous times when players, suddenly enraged by an adverse call, have ripped off the umpire's mask and actually punched him.

In cases like these, the player apologizes profusely after regaining his composure and the league officials are surprisingly lenient. The penalty is typically a small fine of one or two hundred dollars and a stern lecture—with an apology to the fans from the league commissioner for the disruption of the game. A value system that places such a premium on suppression of rage does not seem to grade degrees of violence. Bumping an umpire is almost as serious as putting him in the hospital. Violence just isn't supposed to happen in Japan.

The need to maintain poise is one reason a Japanese player will smile when he commits an error. If an American player grinned after booting an easy grounder, he would probably be yanked from the game, given a thorough chewing out by the manager, and a fine for his improper attitude. But, for the Japanese, the smile means something else. It is a defense mechanism intended to show the opposition (and reassure his teammates) that the player is not bothered by the error. The smile says: "Everyone makes an error once in a while. My confidence is not shaken. Just watch what I do with the next ball that comes my way."

Article 7. The player must not be materialistic. This article is usually invoked at contract time. The player must enter into negotiations in the spirit of compromise and not make unruly demands. The Japanese have traditionally viewed themselves as a poverty-stricken people. Even today, they are likely to remark that "Japan is a poor country." As justification, they are quick to point out that Japan is dependent upon other nations for its natural resources, while disregarding measures like GNP and foreign currency reserves.

It is easier to understand these views if one realizes that even in modern Japan, the notion of poverty retains its traditional historical virtues. Poor people are believed to be hard-working and honest. Materialism somehow clouds the purity of the spirit. And many Japanese would be quick to agree that a desire for wealth is the foundation upon which corruption rises.

The professional ballplayer in Japan should not allow ideas about money to pollute his mind. He should be flexible and always available to discuss contractual terms for the coming season—face-to-face. Refusing to answer the telephone when the front office is trying to reach him (as some American players do to express their displeasure with the team's offer) is taboo. Playing hard-to-get is a childish and disruptive tactic.

The Code explains that money is the least measure of a man's worth. Money cannot give a man stature and respect. Only his family name, his school, or his profession can bring that. Players who hold out for a higher salary prove only one thing: They are thinking of themselves and not the team.

Thus the player usually winds up taking whatever the club feels like giving him. In 1966, for example, the Taiyo Whales had financial problems and the players accepted twenty percent across the board salary cuts. The front office may plead a bad year at the gate or money problems in the parent organization. "This is all we can give you. We're sorry. We know you are worth more than this. Please understand." And all the Japanese player can do is bow and sign his contract.

Shadow swings late at night

The minimum wage for a major-league baseball player in Japan is $7200 (it's $18,000 in the States) and only a handful of players per team make as much as $30,000 a year. Approximately half the players on each team make less than the average "salary man" who, in inflation-ridden Japan, earns somewhere in the neighborhood of $10,000 annually, including bonuses. Yet holdouts are nonexistent. The player who hasn't signed his contract by December 31 (like all Japanese organizations, the team tries to have its business taken care of before the New Year) is a rarity indeed. Pressures to conform and sign are simply too great.

Article 8. The player must be careful in his comments to the press. Players in the U.S. are inclined to speak out. In the great American tradition of "telling it like it is," they will often make public their feelings about anyone or anything they don't happen to like: "I'd have a better ERA if it weren't for those clowns at short and second." "The general manager knows as much about baseball as my seven-month-old kid." "The owner is a menace to the game."

In Japan such talk is socially unacceptable. It not only disrupts team harmony but also upsets the fans. A player should never criticize his comrades, his coaches, his owner, the organization he plays for, or even the game of baseball.

Here are a few comments, only too familiar to fans in America, that would be found unacceptable in Japan.

1. Play me or trade me.
2. I'm tired of sitting on the bench.
3. The owner is a cheapskate.
4. I'm sick of playing baseball. There are other, more important things in life.
5. I know better than anyone else how to get myself in shape.
6. Either he goes or I go. (Alternate: This team isn't big enough for both of us.)
7. I hate Cleveland, Chicago, etc.
8. I'm only playing for the money.
9. No one talks to me like that. I don't care if he is the manager.
10. For the life of me I can't understand why he took me out. Sometimes the decisions he makes are ridiculous.
11. Sore feet, my ass. The guy is jaking it.

Anyone who makes such comments to the press that are detrimental to the team image can expect reprisals (anything from a fine or temporary suspension to trade or outright release).

Article 9. The player must follow the rule of sameness. This flows from the wisdom that states: "The nail that sticks up will be hammered down." Thus such "colorful" players as the American who used to bring his pet chicken to games only make waves. Nor should any player be misled by the hirsute world of the Oakland Athletics. There shall be no long hair, no goatees, no beards.

A Japanese who reports to camp with a handle bar mustache and hair down to his shoulders would immediately be accused by the manager of having an "unsportsmanlike appearance" and ordered to report to the nearest barber shop post-haste. As Nankai Hawk Manager Katsuya Nomura in a lecture on long hair explained (with typical Japanese incisiveness):

> As far as musicians, artists, and writers—that is to say "contemplative" people—are concerned, it seems that long hair suits them. But, as far as we sportsmen go—and this includes psychological effects—it is not good for us. Furthermore, from the fans' point of view, it doesn't look good when there is a lot of long hair sticking out from under the baseball cap.

Another manager put it more succinctly perhaps, after ordering all players to cut their hair short for a forthcoming team trip to the States: "We don't want the Americans to think we're a bunch of wild men."

The Japanese feel that short hair and a clean-shaven face are more "practical" for an athlete. But there is more to it than that. A player whose appearance is extraordinary might start to act in a manner different from his teammates. And that would raise the danger of upsetting team unity. Too much individuality is generally considered dangerous in Japan.

Article 10. The player must behave like a good Japanese off the field. What a player does off the field reflects upon his ball club. He is expected to conduct himself with the dignity befitting his status, and as Article 17 of the Japanese Uniform Baseball Player's Contract requires: ". . . exert his best efforts in his personal conduct, fair play and sportsmanship so as to be an example for the Japanese people as a whole." This means among other things that there should be no carousing at night in bars and cabarets, no fooling with girls, and no gambling. Players who get into street fights or cause traffic accidents can expect to be fined and suspended.

The player must bear in mind that he is being watched by the youth of the nation. He is expected to lead a model life. He should be a faithful, obedient son to his parents and remember his high school teachers. He should be like the player who when asked what his dream in life was replied: "I want to get married and live together with my mother and my wife." He should be married by the time he is 29 and have a child, preferably a son, within the first year of marriage. Furthermore, the player must love baseball, love his team, and, above all, love Japan. This is so important to some clubs that they will conduct "character" investigations of the new players they have drafted just as a precautionary measure.

Article 11. The player must recognize and respect the team pecking order. Like most organizations, baseball teams in Japan are characterized by an ordered vertical structure. Everyone on the team from owner to batboy has a well-defined position. One's "rank" in this hierarchy depends on age and experience with the team.

At the top of the pyramid is the owner—the chief of staff—who oversees the whole operation. He is not as accessible to the players on the team as his American counterpart, but his presence is strongly felt. Most Japanese owners don't know much about baseball but that does not stop some of them from trying to run the team. One owner, known as "The Trumpet," had a telephone installed in the dugout and would call the manager an average of twenty times a game to offer his advice. A second sat in the stands and religiously noted which infielders failed to attend the conferences on the mound, which batters spat on the plate, and so forth. While during a particularly acute energy crisis another held regular meetings to urge his team to win in order to help the parent organization and to improve the national economy. It was their "patriotic duty." The one that tops them all, however, was the owner of a perennial last-place team who, in desperation one year, hired a baseball "critic" to manage. The critic fared no better than his predecessors.

Former Manager Tetsuji Kawakami lectures at training camp

The manager is the general who runs the overall campaign. In addition to those responsibilities outlined earlier, he conducts strategy sessions. And this he does with a vengeance. The Japanese are noted for their love of meetings. Their penchant for endless discussion, consulting, conferring and achieving group consensus before the man at the top hands down his "decision" is well-known.

A baseball team is no different. The manager will meet with his coaching staff every day to pore over the mass of data the team has assembled (collecting data is another great Japanese love) checking, testing, comparing, analyzing, shifting, ad infinitum, to find the combination necessary to produce a winning team. Some teams use computers and others have charts with which to analyze every conceivable aspect of a player's performance. A batter's chart will record every pitch thrown to him in previous games—noting whether it was inside, outside, or waist high, whether it was a curve, fork or fast ball, and whether the batter swung and missed, took the ball for a strike, grounded out, popped up, or whatever. The chart also shows how many runners were on base, how many were out, what the score was, etc. Similar charts are made up for pitchers. All this data is grist for the daily meeting.

The manager also conducts a meeting of the players before each pre-game practice where he announces fines, hands out praise, and goes over the opposing lineup. American teams usually hold such meetings just once before each series during their first swing around the league. After that, a meeting is held only if new players appear on the opposing team. In Japan, there is a meeting before every single game.

After pre-game practice there is also a short huddle in the dugout where the manager reminds his players of what he told them earlier and offers such last-minute advice as "Watch out for the wind" or "The catcher has a good arm." He may even assemble them again in the 4th or 5th inning to assess the opposing pitcher.

Of course the manager must also manage, and this he does more than his American counterpart. He calls more special plays: steals, the hit and run, the squeeze, the sacrifice, pick-offs. In fact his coaches give so many signs that they're often more tired than the players by the end of the game. The manager gives his batters less freedom at the plate and shifts his defenses more. Sometimes all this activity seems to be nothing more than to remind everyone who is in charge. On occasion, for example, he may walk out on the field for no apparent reason, stand there a few minutes surveying the situation and then return to the dugout without so much as a gesture.

The manager also seems to find it necessary to 'punish' his charges if they play poorly. He may fine a pitcher who gives up a hit while ahead on the count or a batter who fails to drive in a runner on third with one out. Others will remove a fielder after an error—grandly waving the player out of the game in full view of the crowd, perhaps simply to appease the unhappy fans. And woe be the man who hits into a double play with the bases loaded in a close contest. The manager might find it necessary to bench him for a few days as "disciplinary action" for his transgression.

Among the original strategies that the Japanese managerial mind has devised is the practice of keeping his starting pitcher (as well as the rest of the starting lineup) a secret until game time. Every manager follows this rule. American pitchers are announced at least a day before so the fan will know whom he is coming to see. In Japan, the manager reasons that this is giving the other team too much help. In another strategic ploy, a manager will start his worst pitcher, allow him to throw one pitch, and then replace him with a regular. This is known as "fooling the opposition."

The Japanese manager plays every run as if it were a matter of life and death.* The big inning that many American managers play for is usually accidental in Japan. (Rarely does a Japanese manager gamble on the double steal or the suicide squeeze.) The result is a much slower, step-by-step brand of ball with a focus on the immediate present. "I've seen Japanese managers make moves an American would never make," says one American ballplayer. "Why I saw a guy take his clean-up hitter out of the outfield in the 7th inning with the score tied and the bases loaded—for defensive purposes. An Ameri-

---

* Approximately 75 percent of all games in Japan are won by the team that scores the first run. Scoring the first run is so important psychologically that many teams seem almost to give up after falling behind in the early innings.

can manager would be thinking ahead to getting back the runs sure to score."

This "here and now" philosophy manifests itself in other ways. A Japanese manager will, for example, go with a pitcher who is "hot" until he is too tired to lift his arm but, conversely, allow a first year hurler who is fresh from the farm team only a single failure. (One bad game and the newcomer is considered "not hot.")

An American describes what he once saw on his Japanese team:

We had a 19-year-old kid on our team who would throw batting practice every day for about 20 minutes. His arm was so sore that touching it was like touching a boil. Yet they still made him go out there and throw. One night we were losing 10–0, so the manager decided to put him in the game. At that time the kid had been pitching two weeks straight without any rest, but he turned in two solid innings of relief. The manager was pretty impressed with him. "Nice ball," he said. "I'll use him as my secret weapon." The next day, in a key situation in the third inning, the manager put the kid in. He threw three pitches and gave up three hits. The manager was pretty mad, and the next day the kid was back throwing batting practice. That was the last chance he got all year.

Managing by inspiration is another tactic invented by the Japanese. In one game, for example, a manager elected to remove his starting pitcher who was leading 3–0 with two out in the 9th inning. This, after he had struck out the two previous batters. The manager apparently "saw" something that no one else did and called on his ace to garner the final out.

Here a coach elaborates on an unusual managerial insight he witnessed in another game:

For a week prior to our 1971 Japan Series our team was sequestered in a hotel. We were totally secluded. No one was allowed to go out. No one was allowed to see his wife. The managers and the coaches went through stacks of manuscript with the players dealing with the strengths and weakness of the Giants. We saw countless movies and video tapes. One of the things the manager emphasized time and time again was that no one steals with the Giant ace Horiuchi on the mound. He had too good a move to first and Mori, their catcher, had too strong an arm. Yet, in the 9th inning of the first game trailing 1–0, with one out, a man on first and Horiuchi pitching, the manager gave the steal sign. The runner was thrown out and we lost the game. All because the manager had had an inspiration.

It is also the manager's job to keep up team morale. Many managers actually place blame for a team's poor performance on low morale. If a team gives up five runs per game, it is "poor morale"—not poor defense. To improve team morale, at the start of the season, the manager can do a number of things. He can risk his job by publicly "vowing" to win a championship. (This puts pressure on the players.) He can trade for players noted for their fighting spirit in the hopes that some of it might rub off on the other players. He can extract "promises" or "vows" from certain men to bat .300 or win 20 games, and he can come up with catch-phrases or slogans designed to unite or inspire—of which these are but a few.

> Running Baseball
> Protect the One Run
> Bold Baseball
> Conquer with Youth
> Action Baseball
> Living Baseball
> Hit and Win
> Dynamic and Precise Baseball
> Burning Baseball (an old favorite)
> Courage Baseball
> Crush the Giants
> Get Brainy and Brawny
> Clean Baseball
> Jump, Jump Whales
> Go, Go Giants

The coaches are the staff officers. Their duty is to impart the wisdom of the batting, fielding, and pitching masters to the players, to run them ragged in training, to check up on their private lives to make sure they're behaving, to advise the manager at the many strategy meetings, and to "take action" when the players fail to perform. If a player goes 0–10 at the plate, it is time for the coach to take him aside and tinker with his batting stance—nothing outside the confines of batting orthodoxy, of course, just move the elbow in a bit, open the stance an inch or two, and that's it. A week or two of special batting practice and his mission is accomplished. The important thing is that the coach has done something. The American idea that a player can work himself out of a slump has not caught on in Japan.

In the United States, the coach is more like a teammate. He works "with" the players. He answers questions. He offers suggestions. He tries to help each man find his own rhythm and style. And that's it. Often, his function is nothing more than batting practice pitcher or gin-rummy partner.

A coach in Japan has more power and authority. He is more aloof from the players. His word is law. His opinions are revered. Reporters actively seek out his views. Weekly sports magazines carry such articles by coaches as "What Batting Is All About" and "How I View The Giants."

If a man does not do well, the blame falls on the coach as much as it does on the player. If the pitching staff loses its effectiveness, the pitching coach might be demoted to the farm team. Similarly, when a batter is having a hot streak, the coach often shares in the glory. It is

A meditation session

not uncommon to see a coach call a streaking hitter aside on his way up to the plate and whisper in his ear. Thus, everyone will know that the "mysterious advice" the coach is whispering is somehow responsible for the player's success.

Another part of the coach's function is to help the manager maintain discipline and to mete out punishment where due—especially to the younger players. A youngster who misses a sign or makes an error must be reprimanded—not by just a fine or extra training, but also by a verbal dressing down—"What the hell do you think you're doing out there?" "Are you blind, you idiot?" (The "shake-it-off" school of psychology has not been well-received in Japan where a public embarrassment is a more memorable lesson than anything else.)

The coach also helps maintain discipline off the field. A young player on the Yakult Atoms (now the Swallows), once made the mistake of appearing in the dining hall clad only in a towel. A coach gave him a savage slapping for this indiscretion in front of the rest of the team. The player offered no resistance. He took his beating, bowed and apologized to everyone, and went to put his clothes on. Such is the power of a Japanese coach, for Japan is a country where age and rank must be served.

American coaches have been known to talk themselves blue without visible result. That problem doesn't exist in Japan. The "You can't talk to me like that" attitude has not yet taken hold. This is not without its adverse effects, however. For rarely does one see a Japanese player display initiative—the diving catch over the wall or a baserunner gambling and taking the extra base. The chance of failure and incurring the wrath of the manager and the coaches is too great. "Japanese just aren't used to thinking for themselves," one Japanese coach admitted candidly. "They're too used to being told what to do." And he then went on to tell the following story:

Once I was in the Winter Instructional League in the U.S. with some of the younger players on the team. I was standing with Duke Snider watching one player take batting practice. He was pulling the ball foul every time he swung, so finally he turned and asked me what to do. I told him to ask the Duke—that was what we came for. He did and Duke said: "Try to figure it out for yourself," and walked away. The player still kept on pulling the ball and so finally, at his insistence, I told him what to do—to pull in his elbow. He did and his batting improved. A while later Snider-*san* came back, saw that the player was doing better and asked him: "Did you do that all by yourself?" The player said no, and Snider just shook his head and said: "You'll never be any good unless you can do things for yourself."

The older the player on a Japanese team, the more deference and respect he is given. Senior veterans are the noncommissioned officers and are usually allowed to take it a little easier in practice (although most won't).

A shortstop with nine years experience outranks a second baseman with seven, and thus has the edge in being chosen for positions like team captain or player representative.

American team captains are usually selected because of their playing or leadership qualities. In Japan, however, the team captain is more a status title, and the feeling is that the player with the most experience deserves it, regardless of his ability to lead. In Japan, there are few "natural born leaders." Eligibility for a leadership position is automatic as a player progresses up the chronological ladder.

One advantage of being an "elder" on a Japanese team is that the older player can occasionally hold onto his position slightly longer, even though a younger player who is better may be sitting on the bench. This is a privilege of seniority in Japan, and although the younger, more qualified player may not like it—and it may not even be good for the team—it certainly helps keep the social order stable.

A rookie in Japan is equivalent to the basic trainee and, of course, life is hardest for him. He has to be first on the field and the last to leave. He must fetch the balls and carry the equipment. He is the last in line to use the team bath. If the team bus is scheduled to leave at 9:00 in the morning, the rookie must be on it by 8:40. He also has to bow a lot and keep his mouth shut.

Years ago, life was even rougher for the rookie. If an older player asked him to go buy some noodles or some cigarettes, he had to do it. He had to clean the team bath, and give massages to the older players. He had to shag balls in the outfield until practice was over and, finally, the coaches had time for him.

Things are changing, of course. A Japanese baseball team is not what it used to be. American influence has worked its way into the system, so there is more equality. Still, the player can never forget his position in the pecking order, and this is reflected in his manner of speaking to superiors. The Japanese language has several levels of politeness, ranging from that used in the Emperor's court to the language on the docks in Yokohama. The level of language used is one of the most obvious and important ways to acknowledge respect for another.

Thus, the younger player must address veteran players, coaches, the manager in the proper way. To a veteran, he would say *Suzuki-san* (Mister Suzuki). To use the team captain's first name would be too familiar. When he speaks to the manager, he says *Kantoku-san* (Mister Manager). He does not address him by name, for that implies a lack of respect for the position. (In like manner, a company president is addressed as Mister President, and a police officer as Mister Policeman.)

Japanese who go to the States to train are continually amazed at the way even the rawest rookie addresses the manager. "Hi, Red. Hey, Lefty." "What's happening, man?"

In return for the homage paid older players, the Code teaches that with age and authority comes a certain responsibility to those below. The team should function as a family. The manager should look after his players with fatherly concern and the veteran players should be like older brothers to the younger ones. This applies not only on the field, but off it as well. Take them to dinner. Loan them money. Counsel them on their problems. Be a guiding light and point the way.

Article 12. The player must strive for team harmony and unity. According to the Code, a team can operate at maximum efficiency only when all concerned know their jobs and function together as one harmonious unit.

Emotional types have no place on a Japanese team. Those who get into fights in the clubhouse or enjoy practical jokes may be "relieving tension" on an American team, but are only contributing to it in Japan. The good Japanese team is composed of players who never

Sadaharu Oh relaxes after practice

argue, never complain, and never criticize others. Leave that to the coaching staff.

The good team is like a beautiful Japanese garden. Every tree, every rock, every blade of grass has its place. The smallest part ever so slightly out of place destroys the beauty of the whole. The rocks and trees viewed individually might be pleasing to look at, but, when organized properly, the garden becomes more than just the sum of its parts. It becomes a work of art. It becomes perfection.

When each player's ego detaches itself and joins twenty-five others to become one giant ego, something magical happens. All the efforts and sacrifices the players have made at last become worthwhile. For they are now a perfect functioning unit. Nothing can match the pride that comes from being able to say: "I am a Yomiuri Giant."

4 the super samurai

October 11, 1958. Whitey Ford and the New York Yankees have just beaten the Milwaukee Braves in the World Series.

On the same day, in Tokyo's Korakuen Stadium, 35,000 fans are settling down to watch the opening game of Japan's version of the World Series—the Japan Series. It is a crisp autumn afternoon; an azure blue sky with not a cloud in sight—a welcome relief from the sweltering Tokyo summer.

The contestants are the Yomiuri Giants, the Central League flag winners, and the Nishitetsu Lions, Pacific League champions. The two teams are meeting in the series for the third straight time. The Lions have won the previous two years.

On the mound for the Lions is Kazuhisa Inao, a chunky 20-year-old right-hander who had 31 wins during the regular season. Pitching in the last 9 games down the stretch, he is the main reason the Nishitetsu club has won its fourth pennant in five years.

The Iron Man didn't have it that day. He was knocked out of the box early and wound up on the losing end of a 9–2 score. He watched from the sidelines the next day, as the Lions lost again 7–3. Two days later, at Heiwadai Stadium in Fukuoka, Inao was back on the mound and dropped a narrow 1–0 decision. Nishitetsu had lost three in a row.

In Game Four Inao relieved in the 4th inning and his home run in the 10th clinched a 6–4 Lion victory. The next day Inao pitched the whole game and led the Lions to a 4–3 win. With the Giants lead in the series now cut to one game, Lion fans began to take heart.

A day of travel back to Tokyo and a day of rain gave Inao two days rest. This was all he needed to shut out the Tokyo team and deadlock the series at three games apiece.

The stage was now set for the seventh and deciding game. The next day, given the ball for the third time in a row and the sixth time in the series, Inao stopped the Giants 6–1 and lifted the Lions to their third consecutive Japan crown.

In the space of eleven days, Inao had started five of the seven games and won all four of his team's victories. He pitched a total of 47 innings, 26 of which were *consecutively* scoreless. This truly incredible feat earned Inao the nickname "Iron Man" and a permanent place in the annals of baseball.

The superstar pitcher of postwar Japan is a throwback to the days of Cy Young and Christy Mathewson, with a dash of the old samurai spirit thrown in for good measure. Needless to day, Iron Man Inao was one of the greatest. He won over 20 games in each of his first eight years in baseball, including a three-year streak of 30 win seasons. In 1961, he won an incredible total of 42 games (a Japan record and a figure not approached in the States since Jack Chesboro's 41 wins in the early part of the century).

In an eight-year span, Inao appeared in more than half of his team's games. He hurled over 345 innings a season, including an exhausting total of 404 one year. His eight-year ERA was an amazing 1.82.

There were a few others in Inao's class. In 1959, sophomore Tadashi Sugiura of the Nankai Hawks posted a 38-4 record (371 IP) and pitched *all* four games in a Hawk sweep over the Giants in the Japan Series. And in 1961, rookie Hiroshi Gondo of the Chunichi Dragons won 35 games and hurled an astronomical 429 innings—second only to a ridiculous 542 innings one pitcher threw in the talent depleted war year of 1942. Several other pitchers have put together seasons of 30 or more wins and logged close to 400 innings in a single campaign.

In the U.S., records even approaching that have not been seen for more than half a century. During an average year, a leading big-league pitcher wins from 20 to 25 games and works less than 300 innings. He sticks to a schedule of pitching only after three or four days rest and seldom, if ever, relieves. No American has pitched two nine-inning games back-to-back in the last forty years. And only a few—Wilbur Wood, Stan Bahnsen, Robin Roberts, Curt Simmons—have experimented with a three-day rotation.

"Iron Man" Inao

Inao and the other Japanese super samurai never knew the luxury of so much rest. There were pennants to be won, and their managers leaned on them hard. They would start one game, relieve in one or perhaps both of the next two, and then, with but a single day's rest, start again. In a critical three-game series, they would often start two of them.

Many great major-league pitchers such as Bob Gibson, Warren Spahn, Early Wynn, Juan Marichal, and Whitey Ford were still pitching good ball in their late 30s. Spahn and Wynn lasted until the age of 43. Each believed the old adage that "a pitcher only has so many pitches in his arm." By carefully adhering to a schedule that gave them proper rest between starts, all were able to prolong their careers, as well as their big money days. And no manager would have been so foolish as to ask a Spahn or Gibson to break that routine.

The Japanese pitcher, unfortunately, is bound by the samurai code. He must go whenever the manager calls. And for those who are called too often, the consequences can be disastrous. Inao, for example, developed a sore arm in his eighth season. He was 25 years old. He won 28 games that year, but his arm gave out in the following season and he dropped to a record of 0–2 with a horrendous 10.64 ERA. Inao struggled through five more mediocre years before retiring at the age of 31 in 1969. Sugiura, who turned professional at age 22 after finishing college, had six super seasons before arm trouble set in and sealed his fate.

Gondo was finished as a star pitcher by 24. He had followed his sensational rookie year with a strong second season, but then his arm went bad. He dropped to ten wins, and his pitching days were over. Many other top Japanese hurlers have come to the same sad end. They lose their effectiveness prematurely and bow out of baseball an average of five years before their American counterparts.

The Japanese pitcher simply has no choice. If he refused to pitch for fear of shortening his career, he would be branded by the fans, the press, and the management as being selfish, rebellious, and even cowardly. As Gondo described his situation: "In those times, there were pitchers like Inao and Sugiura. It was impossible to refuse to pitch if the manager asked you. Many times, my fingers and arm hurt, but I pitched anyway. If I had refused, the manager and the fans would say: 'You're not a man.' The *Bushido* code was very strong."

One exception was Masaichi Kaneda, considered to be the greatest pitcher in the history of Japanese baseball. He dared to rebel. In a fabulous 20-year career, "Golden Arm," as he was known, won 400 games and amassed a grand total of 4490 strikeouts. (As the Japanese press is fond of pointing out, this surpasses Walter Johnson's major league mark.) * Kaneda, a temperamental Japan-born Korean, pitched his first 15 years with the old Kokutetsu Swallows of the Central League. After a modest rookie season in 1950 when he joined the

* During the New York Yankees' 1955 visit to Japan, Kaneda once struck out Mickey Mantle three times in a row.

team in mid-season, the 6'2", 170 pound speedballer went on to win more than 20 games a season for the next 14 years. Twice he won 30.

Kaneda was a workhorse in the real samurai tradition. He averaged well over 300 innings per year, with a very low ERA of 2.24. In a Central League season of 130 games, Kaneda would start 25 times and relieve 25 more.

After logging a 30–17 mark in his fourteenth year, the outspoken southpaw announced that beginning the following season he would not pitch without three days rest after each start. He did not want to risk damaging his arm and his career, since he was closing in on 400 wins and 4000 strikeouts.

This declaration of independence, even from one of Kaneda's great stature, caused quite a stir. The Swallows' front office was infuriated. They called a press conference and blasted their star southpaw as being "bent on bettering his individual records."

Kaneda remained unfazed by the public uproar. With characteristic aplomb, he sailed to a 27–12 mark in 1964 and declared himself a free-agent. For under the Japanese rule in effect then, a player with ten years service became free to negotiate with other teams.* He quickly signed with the Yomiuri Giants, the glamor team of the league, who put him on a four-to-five-day rotation for the next season. (The following spring at the Giant training camp, the independent Kaneda promptly caused another scandal by deciding to train "his own way"—a direct violation of the Code. This earned him the nickname "Emperor" Kaneda.)

But the Kanedas in Japan are extremely rare. Few have what it takes to so flagrantly violate the Code. With samurai stoicism, the Inaos, the Gondos, and the Sugiuras, humbly answer their master's call. In the great tradition of the samurai warriors and such Japanese soldiers as Lieutenant Hiroshi Onoda (who spent thirty years after World War II in a Philippine jungle carrying out a commanding officer's order to stay behind and spy on the enemy) they answer the clarion call to duty—performing heroic feats of courage and valor—until the last pitch is squeezed out of their arms.

* Kaneda was one of the very few to take advantage of this rule.

"Emperor" Kaneda

In recent years, wiser heads have advocated adopting the American rotation system. They argue that the tortuous overwork of the team's top pitcher is grossly unfair to him and in the long run hurts the team as well. They note that the manager's penchant for using his best pitcher almost exclusively in crucial contests is detrimental to the development of other pitchers on the staff. The younger ones, in particular, lack the experience and confidence so vital to a pitcher's growth.

They suggest that perhaps second-line throwers feel left out and are losing their interest in helping the team. And they point to the 1963 Japan Series between the Giants and the Lions in which Inao was removed from the game early in the seventh and final contest. According to one report, the second, third, and fourth pitchers on the

staff were convinced their services would not be required since the
Iron Man was on the mound (he had appeared in "only" four other
games and was no doubt well-rested). Therefore, they spent the evening just before the game touring the cabarets of Tokyo's Ueno district until the wee hours of the morning. When called from the bullpen the following day, they were, needless to say, in no condition to
pitch. The Lions lost the game (and the Series) 18–4.

To their credit, Japanese managers are gradually moving to the rotation system, developing three or four starting pitchers as well as
relief specialists. Such an enlightened approach has virtually eliminated the 400 inning-a-year pitcher, but the memories of pennants
won on the strong arms of those like Inao linger in the minds of many
managers. Life can still be very difficult for a young pitcher with superior talent.

When a manager embroiled in a pennant race is faced with a choice
between giving his star adequate rest or succumbing to the tempta-
tion of using him as much as necessary down the stretch to secure a
championship, he will usually take the latter course. Indeed, most
Japanese managers still cannot understand why top pitchers in
America are given three days rest even in the final weeks of a close
pennant race. They find it difficult to comprehend why Americans
make such a fuss about starting a Koufax or a Gibson in the seventh
game of the World Series with only two days rest. What is so heroic
about that?

Once a pitcher has shown he is of superstar quality, he is pigeon-
holed. The manager will make extraordinary demands on him. The
pitcher has, in a very real sense, been "promoted" or "appointed" to
the office of "ace," and removal from office does not come easily.

Team players in Japan are often "assigned" to win a certain number
of games. Batters may be requested to hit for a specific batting
average or for a designated number of home runs.

Similarly, players will "promise" their managers to accomplish certain goals in the coming season. One manager, for example, when
called on to quiet a skeptical press doubtful over a trade that sent the
team's number two pitcher away in exchange for a younger first base-

Hanshin Tiger rookie Kazuyki Yamamoto looks somewhat stunned after pitching his first major-league win. Tiger Manager Tomeyasu Kaneda, however, appears quite pleased

man of unproven ability, assured everyone that the recent trade was a good one because the newcomer had "personally promised" to hit 30 home runs and drive in 100 runs.

An ace's assignment is, simply, to carry the team. The meaning of "ace" in Japan is very different from what it is in the United States. In Japan, it has a strong, emotional, almost mystical connotation. The idea is that once a pitcher has performed superhuman feats, he is expected to keep repeating them when called on to do so. If he falters, there is something wrong with his spirit.

A case in point is the story of Yutaka Enatsu. What happened to Enatsu underscores the plight of a superstar pitcher who became the victim of rising expectations. In 1967, fresh out of high school, Enatsu stepped into a starting role for the Central League Hanshin Tigers of Osaka. He had a respectable 12 win rookie season. But in his second year Enatsu achieved superstardom. With an explosive fast ball and a murderous curve, he shattered the single season strikeout record with a total of 401. He won 25 games and was voted the Sawamura Award as baseball's best pitcher. (This is Japan's version of the Cy Young Award, named in honor of former pitching great Eiji Sawamura who was killed in the Battle of the Ryukyus during World War II.)

Moreover, Enatsu was the only pitcher in the league who could consistently defeat the powerful Giants of Tokyo and handle with ease their two batting stars, Oh and Nagashima. In nearly every three-game series with the Giants, Enatsu would do the bulk of the pitching. He would often start the first and third games and win both. Once in a crucial September series at Koshien Stadium in Osaka, he shut out the Giants twice in three days. His pitching kept the weak-hitting Tiger team in the pennant race until the final Giant–Tiger game of the season, a 10-inning contest that Enatsu lost by a 2–1 margin with *no* day's rest.

The Hanshin front office was ecstatic. Osaka fans were ecstatic. Here was a real superstar—another Inao; a second Kaneda; a match for the mighty Giants. Here was a pitcher who might provide the impetus for the Tigers to break the Giants' perennial stranglehold on the Central League crown. Even American observers recognized Enatsu's ability. Red Schoendienst, the St. Louis Cardinal manager, remarked upon watching Enatsu pitch: "He is one of the best left-handed pitchers I've ever seen."

The next season Enatsu continued his brilliant pitching and Giant-killing ways. He defeated the Giants six times and at one point ran up 34 consecutive scoreless innings against them. But he missed a good part of the year because of elbow trouble and finished with only 15 wins.

The young speedballer was back at full strength for the 1970 season. His arm was sound again and his strikeout pitch as good as ever. He took his regular turn on the mound and relieved in close games. But something was wrong. He began to tire more easily. With one day's rest the zip on his fast ball was gone, and by the fifth inning—after giving up five or six runs—so was Enatsu.

While it was obvious that Enatsu was not Superman and that 18 innings of first-class pitching in three days was too much to ask, the obvious was not apparent to the Tiger management or to most of the press.

They did not ask, "Is he overworked?" or "Is there something wrong with his arm?" or "Is he getting tired?" but rather, "What's wrong with his fighting spirit?" and "He's an ace. Why doesn't he act like one?"

In mid-season it was revealed that Enatsu had been given an expensive watch by an admirer with gangster connections. The previous year six players had been banned from baseball for life for rigging games, and the Baseball Commissioner was determined to avoid further controversy. Enatsu was suspended under an article of the Professional Baseball Regulations which prohibits "association with habitual gamblers." An investigation was launched and within two weeks the Commissioner's office decreed that the gangster was not a "habitual gambler" and Enatsu was reinstated.

But the seeds of doubt had been planted. Heads began to nod and tongues began to wag. "Enatsu is morally and spiritually weak." "Yes, Inao would never accept a watch like that." "That's the trouble with this younger generation. They're all too selfish—no values." "I hear Enatsu doesn't train like he's supposed to." "Yes, did you know he has been spending a lot of time at the Princess Night Club in Osaka and that he smokes a hundred cigarettes a day?" "No, really? A hundred?"

The stories flew. Enatsu was just not serious enough about baseball. Even the Tigers' own manager expressed open concern that his star pitcher's will-to-win was less than it should be. The Tigers were embroiled in another heated pennant race with the Giants, and it was agreed that Enatsu would have to show more fighting spirit if his team hoped to capture the Central League flag.

Enatsu returned to action and continued to give more than any reasonable person could ask. With enough rest, he was the Enatsu of old. With one day's rest, he had trouble.

The Tigers and the Giants went through the long, humid summer months in a neck-and-neck battle for first place. The Tigers' "aging" (32) but still fiery Player–Manager Minoru Murayama placed himself in the starting rotation in mid-season and put on a brilliant display of stretch-drive pitching. He had a string of victories and a microscopic ERA of 0.98, a Japan season record. He and Enatsu headed up a strong pitching staff that carried the Tigers in their drive toward the pennant.

During September, Enatsu pitched superbly. He lost one heart-breaking game—a 14 inning, one hit, 1–0 contest in which he retired 33 batters in a row from the 3rd inning to the 13th. After losing another close game a short time later, he announced in frustration and disgust that he was sick of baseball. A blatant violation of the Code. Promptly suspended for his improper attitude, he was not reinstated until he delivered the perfunctory apologies.

In early October, the Giants rolled into Osaka on the bullet train from Tokyo for an all-important three game series with the Tigers. The two teams were in a virtual tie for first place with only a handful of games left to play. This series would decide the pennant. Even though "strategy" prohibited managers from announcing their pitchers until 30 minutes before game time, everyone knew that Enatsu (21-14) would be starting the first game.

Pitching with two days rest, Enatsu lost. But, the next day, Player–Manager Murayama brought the Tigers back with a near-perfect two-hit shutout. The stage was set for the crucial third game. The remaining games both teams had were against far weaker opposition. The winner of this game would have the inside track to the pennant together with the tremendous psychological lift that a victory would bring.

There was really no question who would pitch the third game. Enatsu was tired, obviously. He had not started and won a game against the Giants with one day's rest all year. The Tigers did have several well-rested back-up pitchers who could be counted on for a solid inning or two. Perhaps they would divide mound duties, with Enatsu and Murayama ready for relief. But, no, as happens so often in Japan, emotion once again triumphed over reason. The Tigers decided to use their ace.

It was typical Japanese baseball theatrics. A must-win game and the Tiger ace was on the mound, with only one day's rest. Could his fighting spirit prevail over his weary body?

The first three innings it appeared that it might. The Tigers took a 1–0 lead and Enatsu, pitching carefully (he went the full count on nearly every batter), held the Giants to a hit and a walk. In the fourth inning, however, he showed signs of weakening. Two Giant hits and a Tiger error tied the score at 1–1. The Tigers quickly got the run back, but in the top of the fifth, Enatsu was in trouble again. He surrendered a hit and a walk with none out. Enatsu bore down and worked his way out of his second crisis, but he had already thrown over a hundred pitches (120 is average for an American major-league game) and was visibly tired. He was taking far too long between each delivery and TV camera close-ups showed him breathing heavily. The strain of so much pitching was taking its toll. There were still four more innings to go, but there was no indication that Murayama was going to take Enatsu out. The bullpen was quiet. This was Enatsu's game to win or lose.

The Tigers lengthened their lead to 3–1 in the bottom of the 5th, and the 55,000 Tiger fans in ancient Koshien Stadium began to see victory and a pennant looming on the horizon. What they didn't see was that their hero was nearing the breaking point.

The 6th inning found Enatsu in hot water once more, as the Giants quickly put two men on base. Enatsu reached back for what was left of his fast ball, and with some fine defensive help escaped. But that was as far as he could go. In the 7th inning he cracked. A walk, a single, and a bunt that Enatsu was slow fielding, loaded the bases with one out. And home-run king Sadaharu Oh—on his way to his ninth straight title with 47 round trippers—stepped to the plate. If there was ever a time to bring in a fresh pitcher, this was it. Yet the Tiger manager remained motionless in the dugout.

Enatsu managed to get two straight strikes on Oh, but then, to the dismay of everyone in the stadium, threw four consecutive balls! Enatsu slumped dejectedly to his knees, as the runner on third trotted slowly home with the run that cut the Tiger lead to 3–2.

The next batter was Shigeo Nagashima, "Mr. Giants,"—regarded as the most dangerous clutch hitter in Japan. Out on the mound, Enatsu looked as though he had neither the strength nor the will to throw another pitch. Murayama began to loosen up on the sideline. A

Scorekeepers also manage to keep an eye on the action

weary Enatsu slowly, reluctantly, went into his windup and delivered a fast ball with nothing on it that Nagashima lined into left field. Two more runs came across and the Giants took the lead 4–3.

Only then did Murayama make his move. He brought *himself* in to relieve. A thoroughly beaten and humiliated Enatsu handed the ball to his manager and, head down, trudged off the mound.

Murayama quickly retired the side, but the damage had been done. The momentum had shifted to the Giants. The collapse of their star seemed to take the fight out of the Tiger team. The Giants scored twice more and went on to win the game—and, subsequently, the pennant.

Question: Why didn't the Tiger manager take Enatsu out earlier? A U.S. manager would never have waited so long, especially with Enatsu so visibly exhausted. But then a U.S. manager would never have started him in the first place.

The young left-hander's failure to win that final game proved only one thing: not that Murayama was a bad manager, but that Enatsu's spirit was not yet strong enough. Too bad the Tigers lost the pennant as a result.

Enatsu finished the season leading the league in wins, strikeouts, and shutouts. He was fifth in ERA. A dream season for any other pitcher, but for Enatsu, the Tigers, and Hanshin fans, a bitter disappointment. Murayama had asked Enatsu to perform superhuman feats, and Enatsu had failed to rise to the occasion. It was a costly failure.

The attempt to cultivate proper attitudes in the young pitcher continued. He was given a part-time job in an Osaka department store during the off-season to help develop his sense of responsibility. And a new manager whisked him off to the mountains for some meditation, soul strengthening, and spiritual guidance.

But the following season Enatsu continued to falter after one day's rest and, in time, began to have trouble beating the Giants at all, even though he still handled the rest of the league with ease. Enatsu also developed periodic arm trouble and a minor heart condition (he had to cut down on his smoking). His old fast ball now gone, his strikeout totals diminished accordingly.

Tiger management finally got the message and began to use him a little more sparingly—often with three days' rest between starts, only occasional relief appearances, and no more Iron Man stints expected against the Giants. Although he had two more 20 win seasons, it was a case of too little too late. In 1974, Enatsu's seventh year, he fell from his average of 20 wins a season to a mediocre 14–15 mark. The next year he dropped to 12–12 and his inability to pitch a complete game relegated him to the bullpen by season's end. At age 27 Enatsu appeared to be burned out, his status as a top pitcher gone. Sadly, he is now surrounded by an aura of failure and disappointment for his inability to become the superman he was expected to be.

Sore arms and abbreviated careers have been accepted with a characteristic lack of bitterness by Japan's star pitchers. When Sugiura retired he made this touching comment: "I want to assume responsibility for the two defeats I suffered in the 1965 Japan Series with the Giants. I am also doubtful about my future. . . . Younger pitchers will not make headway if an old player like me continues to pitch."

Sugiura, 30 when he made that speech, was persuaded to come back. He remained a fringe pitcher for a few more years and then retired permanently.

Gondo, whose salary had risen to $30,000 by his second year, had a brief stint as a commentator and then took a factory job paying $150 a month. He admitted that his career might not have ended so soon had he been used more carefully. "My arm still hurts when I try to raise it a certain way," Gondo told a reporter. "But," he added, "even now, if I were able, I would pitch any time I was asked."

At least it can be said that the pitcher's efforts are not usually forgotten by his old team after he retires. Sugiura became a coach with the Hawks, and Gondo, at 33, was finally called back to coach the Dragon's farm team. Iron Man Inao was named Lions' manager when he retired as an active player; and he went on to pilot the club through five straight second-division seasons before he submitted his resignation. Obviously the Lions' organization did not retain Inao for his managerial prowess—the club was simply repaying its debt to a man who had contributed immeasurably to the team during his eight-year tenure as baseball's best pitcher. Losing seasons notwithstanding, Lion fans would have it no other way.

5 the REBELS

The third baseman sat in front of his dressing area and gingerly tested his swollen left hand. Although suffering from a severe sprain, the player would play again today as he had for the past few days—with the help of painkillers.

Three games were left in the season and his team needed only one win to clinch the league championship. He was not about to sit this game out. Swallowing a tiny pink capsule, he grabbed his cap and glove and made his way out of the locker room. As he reached the ramp that led out onto the playing field, he began to feel better. Perhaps it was the pill taking effect; whatever the reason, he was proud to be part of a team on the verge of winning a pennant. He was proud to be leading his team in home runs and RBIs again. Most of all, he was proud to have spearheaded the drive to two critical wins in the past two days.

Pausing inside the dugout, the third baseman routinely scanned the lineup card posted on the wall. Suddenly his forehead wrinkled in a frown—his name was not there in the usual clean-up slot. He read the card again carefully; perhaps his position in the batting order had been switched. But no, his name was missing. Then one of the coaches told him. "The manager's taking you out today. He doesn't want to take a chance with that hand of yours. Take a rest."

"Take a rest!" The player felt rage boiling up inside him. "What the hell do you mean take a rest?" he stormed. "I can still play. I can help the team; my hand doesn't hurt that much." With that he slammed his glove to the ground and, pouring forth a volley of curses, savagely kicked the dugout bench.

The third baseman's outburst lasted only seconds. For the remainder of the afternoon, he sat in glum silence on the bench, watch-

Chunichi Dragons go through pre-game warm-ups

ing his teammates win a pennant. But the manager, aware of the effect such displays can have on team morale, did not overlook the show of temper. During a lull in the victory celebration after the game, he called his star into his office for a brief closed door session.

Just before practice the following day, the manager announced that one of the infielders had a few words to say. Wearing a grim expression, the third baseman stepped forth and spoke: "I am sorry for my childish actions yesterday. I have upset our team spirit, and I apologize deeply. I am truly sorry." He bowed, then returned to his place. The meeting continued and the incident was immediately forgotten. All was well: team harmony had been restored.

In Japan, even a star is expected to conduct himself properly. No matter how valuable a player may be to his team, he must follow time-honored rules and regulations and do his best to preserve harmony on the club. The Japanese word for individualism, *kojinshugi*, still carries a strong negative connotation—despite the influx of western values. The individual, the Japanese reason, is nothing without the team; and egocentric behavior that disrupts the team will not be tolerated.

At contract time, for example, a rookie pitcher who leads the league in wins would never and could never demand a 600 percent increase in salary as Vida Blue did after his dazzling first year in 1971 when he won 24 games and led the league in strikeouts. Nor would great Japanese players ever make such a spectacular demand as Sandy Koufax and Don Drysdale did when they held out for a quarter-million dollar "joint" pact.

Holdouts by big-name players are commonplace in America, but in Japan they are virtually unheard of. There is simply too much pressure on the player to sign early and show he is "with the team." Talk about his individual accomplishments is considered conceited and selfish. While the Japanese star may envy the independent spirit of the American, he is much too timid to emulate it.

The Japanese player coming off an exceptionally good year is thus in a quandry. Hesitant to hold out for what he believes he is worth, he has little choice but to accept what the club offers him—although he may be unhappy about it. "Well, I thought perhaps, that . . . er . . . I don't mean to be rude but . . . uh . . . I was hoping for something slightly. . . . If you would please consider . . ."

To which the owner or general manager might reply: "I see. I hope that we have not insulted you too much by offering you such a low and worthless contract. Why don't you go home and think about it. And I, myself, will personally give this matter some further consideration. I will talk to our accountants and see what can be done."

At the next meeting, the owner might up his offer a little more and say, "This is all we can give you. We are very sorry. We know you are worth more. But we had a bad year at the gate and we have to pay the foreigner we are bringing over a lot of money. Please understand. We value your contributions to the team very much. Perhaps if we have good attendance next year, we can afford to pay you more. We will try our best."

These "negotiations" normally involve two or three conferences until finally a meeting of the minds is achieved. The player will then sign his contract—reluctantly in many cases—and convey his happiness to the press that the contract "war" is behind him so he can "devote his every thought to preparing for the upcoming season and winning the pennant for the fans."

Often the player must agree to terms unheard of in the States. Nankai Hawk catcher Katsuya Nomura won his second consecutive home-run and RBI title in 1964, yet the club forced him to take an eight percent cut because his batting totals were slightly lower than the year before. And Iron Man Inao saw his salary reduced by more than half in the three years following his decline as a leading pitcher.

Now and then a player will make a stand as Isao Harimoto did in 1968. Harimoto, a Korean outfielder on the Toei Flyers, had just won his second straight batting title and was asking for 30,000,000 yen (then about $88,000) as his ten-year bonus. Such a bonus enabled the established player to align his income with the exorbitant sums then being paid rookies to sign contracts. The practice was ended with inauguration of the draft system, but in the mid-1960s, Harimoto was one of the players still eligible. The Flyers offered him 12,000,000 yen. Harimoto was indignant. He put himself in the same class as Yomiuri Giant stars Oh and Nagashima who had each received about 40,000,000 yen. Harimoto threatened to leave the club if they didn't show more "sincerity" toward him. He said he would rather return to Korea than have his services valued so lowly. (Harimoto was also eligible to declare himself a free-agent under the rule that a player with ten years' service could negotiate with other teams.) The Flyers and Harimoto eventually reached an amicable agreement at 25,000,000 yen.

But the Harimotos are very rare. The individual star would rather sign his contract unhappily than risk a confrontation. Contract squabbles just create bad feelings all around. And players who do refuse to take cuts are usually traded. This is one reason the average salary of the Japanese star is so much lower than his U.S. counterpart. Oh and Nagashima of the Giants reached the $200,000 class and Player–Manager Katsuya Nomura of the Nankai Hawks hit the $150,000 mark in his 20th year. But, except for them, only a dozen or so others make over $50,000. In the States, nearly half the players in a starting lineup make that much.

An American star will often use his status to gain special treatment. He may show up late for training, openly criticize his manager, and violate team rules. Often those at the top will look the other way.

"Stars are different," they reason. "They contribute more. They face more pressure. They have to be kept happy."

Because of Japanese feelings about *kojinshugi*, however, the Japanese who steps out of line is usually dealt with swiftly and harshly. The third baseman who vented his anger over being benched, for example, was the most important player on his team. Yet, he was forced to apologize the following day.

Another infielder—the leading hitter on the Taiyo Whales—disliked the team's new manager. One night in a bar he expressed his feelings. A reporter, who overheard the player's tirade, told the manager. The manager benched the player and used him only sparingly for the rest of the season. He saw to his release at the end of the year.

Takenori Emoto, the number one pitcher on the Nankai Hawks, tried to defy his manager's edict against long hair. The handsome 26-year-old let his locks grow long and became a big hit with teenage fans around the country. His manager, Katsuya Nomura, warned Emoto to get his hair cut short or be fired from the team. The warning came at the end of the 1974 season. By January Emoto decided that his baseball career was more important than his good looks. (It was a traumatic experience for the young ballplayer. "I don't think I look good with a short haircut because of my poorly shaped head," he moaned when the ordeal was over. "Perhaps I should grow a mustache to make up for it. But I suppose the manager would then issue a ban on mustaches.")

On rare occasions, however, a player will refuse to knuckle under, as Shinichi Eto did in 1970. Eto had been the mainstay of the Dragons for 11 years. He was the league's perennial All-Star left-fielder—a distance hitter and two-time batting champion—and he didn't like it when Shigeru Mizuhara instigated a curfew and practice regulations as the Dragons' new manager. Mizuhara naturally expected everyone on the team to obey his regulations, but Eto had other ideas. He was often late and objected loudly to fines levied on him for his tardiness. But Mizuhara and the Dragon front office stood firm. Eto refused to give in and "resigned" from baseball. He didn't play again until the Dragons traded him to the other league where he promptly won his third batting title.

Yutaka Enatsu, the Hanshin Tiger left-hander who had trouble with his fighting spirit, was unhappy with the severity of the training he was expected to undergo each spring. Enatsu reasoned that since he would be pitching all the time during the regular season, it was foolish to wear himself out in camp. So to demonstrate his feelings, he took the bold step of going to sleep in the outfield while his teammates were running. (When a Japanese does rebel, he tends to be a little extreme.) The manager was not pleased with this show of independence, but Enatsu played his superstar status for all it was worth—to the chagrin of everyone connected with the Tigers. After a feud that lasted all through a second-division season, the manager left the team. The Tiger front office threatened loud and long to trade the rebellious pitcher. But the new manager and coaching staff, after numerous conferences on what to do with their problem boy, smoothed things over and Enatsu stayed on.

Another star, pitcher Seiji Hiramatsu of the Taiyo Whales, refused to pitch late in the 1974 season because of a painfully sore elbow. His manager openly attacked him as being lazy, but Hiramatsu held firm. He was not going to risk injuring his arm any further. Although not traded for his insubordination, due to a slightly sub-par record he was forced to take a big salary cut.

These incidents are exceptions. Whether or not they reflect a trend toward American individualism is hard to say. But many feel the radical notion that a baseball star does what he wants is simply more evidence that the younger generation of Japanese has lost its appreciation for traditional values.

Professional baseball, in many ways, is an anomaly in Japan. Business firms, for example, hew to lifetime employment and promotion by seniority. There are no stars akin to the glamorous junior executive types fought over by American companies. A young engineer who designs mammoth supertankers earns only slightly more than a clerk of the same age at the same firm.

In the sports world, however, the Japanese tradition of irreplaceability and equal treatment for all is harder to uphold. First of all a top ballplayer gets more attention and earns many times more money than most young men his age. Second, his contribution to the

The Hankyu Braves' top pitcher Hisashi Yamada demonstrates the submarine delivery so popular in Japan

team is highly visible and dramatic compared to the white collar world of business. Yet, the baseball player does not enjoy the same kind of security most others do. He can be traded or released, his salary may be cut in a bad year and, if he is a pitcher, his career may even be shortened by the demands of an overzealous manager. No wonder, then, that some successful ballplayers are beginning to feel that they owe it to themselves to rock the boat upon occasion.

The younger a star, the more scandalous it is if he rebels. Such was the case of Yomiuri Giants' pitching phenomenon Tsuneo Horiuchi.

Horiuchi burst into pro baseball at the age of 18. He won his first 12 games, led the league with a 1.39 ERA, and was voted co-recipient of the 1966 Sawamura award for best pitcher in the league. But his performance seemed to distort his perception. He made the mistake of equating brilliance on the mound with equality to his seniors. He was, as one baseball writer described him, ". . . disrespectful to his elders and often rude. He seems unable to say 'good morning' with the kind of smart bow that a young player should execute. For Horiuchi it is always a nod of the head and a casual grunt containing a tinge of arrogance that is unhealthy for young Japanese players. Occasionally, he is even openly defiant toward his superiors."

To make matters worse, Horiuchi displayed his bad manners on the field as well. "He is one of the cockiest players in the country," wrote another reporter. "What disgusts me is the way he catches the ball when it is thrown back to him by the catcher. He does this with a most haughty sidehand or backhand flip." Horiuchi's critics also complained about how he spit so often on national television and how his cap would flop to one side when he threw his fastball. In fact, the size of Horiuchi's cap was a hotly debated issue for a time.

But most important to the Giants was Horiuchi's constant violation of curfew and training rules. One writer described Horiuchi's penchant for sneaking out after hours:

Horiuchi was very clever at this. He would stay in his dormitory room until the lights went out. Then he would change into his suit for a night of fun in the nearest entertainment area. When he stole from the dormitory, he would always walk backward. If he was discovered, he would say: "I'm sorry. I'm late. I've just returned." In this way his punishment was lessened.

The other players in the dormitory said: "We warned him over and over not to break the rules, but he wouldn't listen to us. We didn't know what to do."

Horiuchi, characteristically, never made any excuses for his violations. If he were caught, he would accept his punishment without saying anything, even if one of the coaching staff would strike him for his insubordination, as was sometimes the case.

The Dormitory Superintendent, who has caught Horiuchi sneaking out after curfew many a time and who is known by the players as "The Ogre" because he is so strict, says of Horiuchi: "Horiuchi is a good fellow. He is only trying to impress the others. He wants the other players to respect him, to think he is a man. That's why he breaks the rules. The other players don't have the courage to do what he does. You can't dislike Horiuchi. He has a good heart, inside."

Horiuchi also felt that he could handle such unimportant matters as getting into shape, all by himself, without the wisdom of his coaches to guide him. As he was fond of explaining: "I am the ace. I am a pitching genius. I can win without training." This was blasphemy, of course.

At the beginning of Horiuchi's second year, he was woefully out of condition and he found himself down on the farm team when the season began. There Horiuchi solidified his reputation once and for all as the black sheep of the Giants when he staged the "Tamagawa Revolt"—known to every baseball fan as the most infamous rebellion in the history of the Yomiuri Giants. A writer for *Baseball Magazine* described the incident.

THE TAMAGAWA REVOLT

When the rainy season began that year, Horiuchi was pitifully out of condition, so Giant manager Kawakami dispatched him to the farm team camp along the Tama River just outside Tokyo. This, of course, was very upsetting to the proud, rebellious youngster. He comes from the economically poor mountain region of Yamanashi Prefecture where people are famous for having the "stubbornness of a weed."

Young Horiuchi demonstrated just how much he was disturbed shortly thereafter in an intra-squad practice game. He was named the starting pitcher for the Red Team in a match against the White Squad. He was obviously not in the mood to pitch in such a lowly game, as his listless pitching revealed. He surrendered hit after hit to the batters on the White Squad. His pitching was hideous, to say the least. The coach of the Red Team became angry. And this is when the "Tamagawa Revolt" began.

Red Team Coach Kitagawa was furious. He strode out to the mound to confront Horiuchi. He angrily grabbed Horiuchi's glove off of his hand and shouted: "If you can't show more enthusiasm than this, then don't pitch." The irate Kitagawa then took the ball and assumed mound duties himself. Horiuchi shrugged nonchalantly in the irritating manner that has become his trademark, and strolled leisurely back to the bench. He sat down and leaned against the dugout wall in a relaxed manner, with his arm over the back of the bench, and gazed absentmindedly at the sky.

Coach Kitagawa, himself a former pitcher, glared at Horiuchi as if to say: "Even though I'm old, I can pitch better than you" or "What difference does it make whether you throw or not?" Unfortunately, Coach Kitagawa was out of practice. He tried desperately to pitch well, in order to shame Horiuchi. But, despite his gallant spirit, he gave up more hits than Horiuchi.

Assistant Coach Machida, alarmed at what was happening to Coach Kitagawa, became angry himself. He turned on Horiuchi who was sitting calmly on the bench as if he didn't have a care in the world. "Get up, Horiuchi. Get out there and pitch again!" he ordered. But, Horiuchi simply shrugged in defiance, and with a slight sneer, turned and looked the other way.

Batting Coach Minamimura, who had been observing the whole situation closely, came flying over, eyes flashing. "What the hell do you think you are doing?" he stormed. "Who the hell do you think you are? Get out there and pitch. What do you mean sitting here on the bench? It doesn't matter whether you are the rookie king or the lowest person on the farm team. The Yomiuri Giants will not allow this rebellious attitude. If you want to be a Yomiuri Giant, you must behave like one!" Horiuchi, however, remained motionless. He refused to pitch. So the matter was duly reported to the head manager of the farm team.

Horiuchi, after cooling off and thinking about his atrocious behavior began to realize that he was jeopardizing his career as a Giant. He subsequently repented. That night, he paid a visit to the farm team manager's office. He entered the room, walked over to the manager's desk and got down on his knees on the dirty floor.

With both hands placed inward on the floor (i.e., in the formal bow position), he lowered his head and said: "I deeply apologize for my actions today. I deeply regret doing what I did. I know I was wrong, but I just couldn't help myself. Please forgive me."

The farm-team manager was moved by the apparent sincerity of Horiuchi's apology. And, as a result, he didn't hit him, didn't fine him, and didn't file a report on Horiuchi's insubordination to the Giant varsity Manager Kawakami. The case was then closed. The "Tamagawa Revolt" became history. But, from that day on, Horiuchi was known as "Bad Boy Taro." *

Horiuchi has generated other controversies. Midway through one season, the brash youngster announced that he was not going to lose any more games that year. This pompous proclamation, of course, upset just about everyone and when Horiuchi proceeded to lose his next two games, the reporters observed "These setbacks should cause Horiuchi to reflect on his humility."

They didn't, however. Some time later, after defeating the lowly Yakult Atoms for the umpteenth time, Horiuchi declared in disgust: "The Atoms are nothing but a bunch of amateurs." His insult won headlines in the sports papers the next morning. The Atom players were incensed. Not only was it a brazen sign of disrespect by such a young player, but the slur was delivered in public. The insult strengthened the Atoms' resolve, and from that day on they became a

---

* Taro is a common Japanese first name.

painful thorn in the young pitcher's side.

Horiuchi survived as a Giant and has had many good seasons since. The Giants were patient with him because of his outstanding talent and potential. A lesser player with Horiuchi's attitude would undoubtedly have been traded or released.

Off the field, the Japanese baseball star is a very different person from his U.S. counterpart. The American feels that his private life is his own, and leads it pretty much as he pleases. A bachelor may boast that he sleeps with a different girl every night and likes his women "warm, wet and wild." He may divorce and remarry or swap wives and even families as Fritz Peterson and Mike Kekich of the New York Yankees did in 1973. In short, he doesn't give a damn what anyone thinks.

The Japanese star, however, is expected to set a good example for his young fans. He must follow certain rules of conduct which can, in American terms, assume ridiculous proportions.

A handsome, young catcher—the heartthrob of thousands of female admirers—once took the bold step of getting his own apartment in Osaka where his team played. This was cause for concern to his fans,

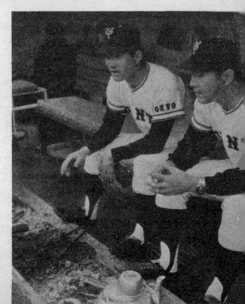

Nagashima (left) and teammate ward off early season chill over hibachi in dugout at Korakuen Stadium

since a "serious" player should be living in the team dormitory or at home under the guidance of his mother and father. With such freedom, wouldn't this unattached star be tempted to sin? After all he was only 25, his parents were in Tokyo, and who would watch over him? But the press, guardians of public morals that they are, filed a report on the catcher's new lodgings along with a photograph of the place. This picture showed the apartment's proximity to the stadium and reassured his followers that the player would never be far from the positive influences of baseball and his teammates.

Whenever the catcher came to Tokyo to play against the Giants, the TV cameras would always manage one or two shots of his beaming, kimono-clad mother watching from the reserved section and waiting to take him home after the game. The fears of the fans that their hero would stray too far from the path of righteousness were thus allayed.

It is permissible for a baseball star in Japan to have a girl friend. And he may date her. But he has to be careful not to put his arm around her or kiss her in public—both brazen displays of affection. In fact the more shy and ill-at-ease he is around her, the better. This helps to show that he seldom strays in his thinking to things unrelated to baseball.

The girl should giggle shyly, which is quite natural for the Japanese female. This demonstrates that she does not know how to behave around men and also implies the proper lack of experience. It shows that she is modest and a "good" young Japanese lady.

If the star is planning to marry, it is important that the girl be of "good character." In Japan, this normally involves the following: college education, knowledge of one foreign language, plus proficiency in the tea ceremony, flower arranging, and calligraphy.

After completing her education, the girl may work in a company to gain "experience in life." But she should not stay past the age of 26 or 27. If she works longer than that, she might get "too much experience" (i.e., she will become too familiar with men). She should also live at home with her parents and spend a lot of time with her mother, learning how to be a good Japanese wife. She should learn how to cook, clean the house, sew and make clothes—all minor Japanese arts.

She should not be of foul temper. She should not seem too intellectual. She should not be too quick to express her opinions. She should not argue with a man. And above all, she must have the qualities of patience and endurance. These are necessary because once married she will be spending all her time at home—cleaning house, taking care of the children, and watching her husband on TV. (Unlike America, where players' wives form a rooting section at home games, there is still a large segment of the population adhering to the tradition that a wife should not come to her husband's place of business.) Any questions regarding an intended's character in Japan can be resolved by hiring one of the many detectives who are in business just for that purpose.

A star must not spend too much time with his girl friend. Maybe once or twice every two weeks during the off-season, but less frequently during the season. This shows fans that his mind is strictly on baseball and that there is no funny business afoot.

The engagement is announced when the player feels his future is relatively secure and when he is "mature" enough to accept the responsibilities of marriage. Typically, this is between the ages of 24 and 28. Of course, the player will wait until both sets of parents have given their consent.

The engagement of a superstar is a big event and the wedding is an even bigger one. Home-run king Sadaharu Oh's wedding in 1966, for example, was an exercise in regal splendor. After a traditional Shinto marriage ceremony in Tokyo's Meiji Jingu Shrine, Oh and his bride held a reception at the lavish Hotel New Otani that was attended by 1200 guests and cost more than 20,000,000 yen ($60,000). Oh's bride wore a kimono created by Japan's renowned designer, Eisuke Koda, who had been designated a "living national treasure" by the Japanese government. The kimono reportedly cost three million yen ($10,000). More than 100 reporters covered the event and the Ambassador from Nationalist China was a principal speaker. (Oh is Taiwanese.)

Marriage is considered a "good thing" for the baseball player. It brings order and a sense of responsibility to his life. Oh remarked that he thought he would "play better as a result of marriage, because a married sportsman has a better life and inspiration." When Bad Boy Horiuchi finally tied the knot, his nuptial bliss engendered a change of heart in his attitudes toward training. That following spring he worked harder in camp than ever before. Horiuchi assessed the reason for the new leaf he had turned over: "When I was a bachelor, I did whatever I wanted. I ate when I wanted to. I slept when I wanted to. I went out and came home when I wanted to. Now there is order in my life. Life is worth living. I feel more responsibility now that I am married."

Horiuchi's bride commented on the remarkable change in her husband: "He seems very content now. He is master of this house. He is a good traditional Japanese husband. He orders me around and tells me what to do. I bring him tea and things like that and he seems to be relaxed. He doesn't talk to me about baseball around the house."

Many bachelor players carry on clandestine love affairs. And more than one married star keeps a mistress. There are even "secret" second wives and families that first wives may or may not know about. These second wives are not all that unusual in Japan and they underscore the dichotomy between a person's public and private lives. The same double standard that exists in most countries is more marked in Japan. The operative philosophy seems to be: "What the public doesn't know won't hurt them." The important thing is to maintain the image of purity, so as not to damage the family name or that of the team. A photograph of a popular player emerging from a Turkish bath with a contented look on his face, for example, might cause his fan clubs to disband overnight.

As always in Japan, there are notable exceptions. A former star used to brag that once the game was over, he would head for the nearest geisha house and spend the night. One manager scandalized the baseball community when he announced that during spring training he periodically sent his players to the Turkish bath—at team expense. And a star catcher once shocked his fans a few weeks before his wedding when he admitted openly that he was the father of an illegitimate child by another woman. Players who own up to such scandalous behavior, however, are usually cast as heavies in the black and white world of Japanese baseball.

The player desiring to maintain his image as a "good Japanese" would be wise to be seen doing one or more of the following:

1. Tending the bonsai trees in his garden

Japan's first streaker bows to the fans

2. Practicing with a rare old samurai sword
3. "Viewing" cherry blossoms
4. Gazing serenely at Mt. Fuji
5. Sweeping the grounds around a Buddhist retreat
6. Praying for grace at a Shinto altar
7. Bringing his mother to a game
8. Encouraging rookies on the team
9. Visiting his old hometown at least once a year where he should:
   a. Go to the cemetery and pray to the souls of his ancestors
   b. Visit his former high school teachers and thank them for their guidance

A star may write stirring tales dealing with fighting spirit or the resolution of personal crises, but he would be unwise to consider anything like *I Can't Wait Until Tomorrow 'cause I Get Better Looking Every Day* by Joe Namath or Jim Bouton's controversial *Ball Four*.

A player must also be careful about endorsing products in advertisements. Vitamins, health foods, milk, and baseball equipment are acceptable. But any ads involving, God forbid, panty hose or sheets are better left to others.

Of course Japan is changing. People are more open; and the younger generation is more cosmopolitan. Maybe the day will even come when a swinging young Japanese star will be able to announce to his adoring public that he likes his women "warm, wet and wild" without scandalizing the entire baseball world and doing irreparable damage to his reputation.

6 "BURNING MAN" and OTHER HEROES

The tiny auto wove through sluggish mid-afternoon traffic en route to the Korakuen sports complex on the north side of Tokyo. Sullen clouds still blanketed the sky, but the threat of rain had disappeared. "At least the game will be played," thought the anxious driver, Tetsuhara Kawakami, the bespectacled coach of the Yomiuri Giants.

Kawakami turned to his passenger. "Did you sleep well last night?" he asked.

"Not very well," the young ballplayer replied. "I couldn't sleep until four this morning. I'm just too tense. I guess I'm old fashioned—with the Emperor coming to the game and all."

The passenger's name was Shigeo Nagashima. In his second year as a pro, this young power hitter was already the darling of the sports world. Nagashima had won rookie of the year honors the season before and was now headed for his first batting crown. But on this particular day, he was unabashedly nervous. Nagashima, worrying about this game for a week, had worked himself into a batting slump.

The parking lot at Korakuen Stadium was always crowded, but today was obviously special. The main entrance was heavily guarded by police, struggling to stem the tide of camera-toting fans who were waiting to catch a glimpse of the Emperor and Empress. This was the first time in history that the Imperial couple would attend a professional baseball game, and baseball officials were praying for a good contest.

In the clubhouse after batting practice, Nagashima stood with his teammates as Manager Shigeru Mizuhara addressed them. "The Emperor and Empress are attending today's game," Mizuhara said agitatedly. "You were all swinging well in batting practice. If you all play as though this were just another game, the results are sure to be good. It's just that—well, we have to win today. In order to win we'll all have to do our best. We're all excited about their Majesties being here, so let's try to put our excitement to work to win the game."

As Mizuhara spoke, the Emperor and Empress had entered the stadium and, waving to the cheers of the capacity crowd, took their seats in the royal box. Down on the field the air was electric—this would be no ordinary game.

The last strains of *Kimigayo*, the Japanese national anthem, faded into the Tokyo dusk and the umpire called "play ball"—in a voice more solemn than usual. Nagashima's appointment with destiny had commenced.

From the start it was a closely fought match. The Giants and Hanshin Tigers were locked in a 1–1 tie when Nagashima came to bat in the 5th inning. His anxiety about his recent slump began to disappear in the 3rd inning when he had slammed a drive down the third baseline for a hit. Whatever remained of it was eliminated entirely as he clouted a 1–1 pitch into the stands to give the Giants a 2–1 lead. Nagashima was living up to his reputation as a pressure player.

In the 6th inning, the Tigers struck back for three runs, taking the lead 4–2. But in the 7th, a promising rookie named Sadaharu Oh plunked a two-run shot into the rightfield stands to tie the game again.

In the 8th inning with the score still at four apiece, the Tigers brought in a new pitcher, an intense flame-throwing youngster named Minoru Murayama. Giant fans groaned, for Murayama was the hottest thing in baseball. The day before, pitching in relief, he had struck out the side—Nagashima included—in the 9th inning. Now, as he took his place on the mound, Murayama appeared full of confidence. This was his golden chance to pitch before the Emperor, and he was going to make the most of it.

Murayama was flawless as he set the Giants down in the 8th; and in the 9th the Tigers failed to score. With Murayama at the peak of his form, it was beginning to look like extra innings. If so, the Imperial Couple, whose scheduled time of departure was 9:30, would miss the end of the game. No one wanted that to happen.

The Emperor stayed to see Nagashima bat one last time. He only had to watch five more pitches. With the count at 2–2, Nagashima took a deep breath as Murayama went into his windup and threw the most famous pitch of his career—an inside fast ball that Nagashima saw coming all the way. The Emperor leaned forward in his seat and watched the ball sail ten rows into the leftfield stands. Rounding second base, Nagashima glanced up at the royal box and then trotted on to home plate to be mobbed by his teammates. Everyone wanted to touch him, as if some of his incredible magic might rub off on them.

The Emperor and Empress stood in their box and smiled. Then, bowing ever so slightly toward the players milling around home plate, they prepared to leave the stadium. The scoreboard clock read 9:40. The greatest game ever played in Japan was history. And Shigeo Nagashima had won it for his team.

To describe exactly what the name Shigeo Nagashima means to the Japanese would be impossible. Although it is probably safe to say that the Yomiuri Giants Manager and former star third baseman is the best loved, most admired, and most talked about figure in the history of sport. The adulation accorded to Nagashima is unequalled even by Babe Ruth fans in his years with the Yankees. Of all sports heroes in the world, only Brazil's Pele can approach Nagashima's stature. Not since the days of Joe DiMaggio has there been an American athlete in any professional sport who has come close to capturing the public imagination the way Nagashima has in Japan. Joe Namath and Muhammed Ali have their detractors. But Nagashima has none. In fact there has been no American figure since John F. Kennedy, at the peak of his popularity, who could be compared with Nagashima as a symbol of national pride.

When Nagashima joined the Giants in 1958, he was already a national hero. He had rewritten the home-run record book during his college days at Rikkyo University (one of Tokyo's classy Big Six conference schools) and signed with the Giants for a record 17 million yen (then $48,000). Nagashima was so popular that in his rookie year he drew overflowing crowds to exhibition games. He lost no time in establishing himself as the best in the pros, racking up averages of

Shigeo Nagashima practices at the batting tee

.334, .334 and .353—three straight batting crowns—after a stunning rookie season.

Nagashima had charisma Japanese style. Tall (5'11", 175 pounds) and good-looking, he was quickly dubbed "Golden Boy" by the press. On the field he could run, throw, and hit with power (a rarity in those days); and he displayed a youthful exuberance seldom seen among players who, with samurai stoicism, kept their emotions under tight control. As a third baseman, Nagashima had no peers. He had the cat-like quickness of a Brooks Robinson plus a lightning arm. At bat, his timing was superb. He was an aggressive hitter who thrived on pressure. When there was a crucial game to be won, it was usually Nagashima's bat that powered the Giants to victory in the late innings.

The "Emperor's Game" in May 1959 solidified Nagashima's reputation as a pressure player. It is regarded by many Japanese as the greatest game ever played in that country. His *sayonara* home run is to the Japanese what Bobby Thompson's "shot heard round the world" or the one Babe Ruth supposedly called at Wrigley Field in the 1932 World Series are to Americans. That game earned Nagashima another nickname—"Burning Man." It was a tribute to his fighting spirit.

Nagashima represented a whole new breed of ballplayer for Japan. He was openly coveted by American teams, and his superstar image symbolized the new superpower status Japan was acquiring after a post-war decade of harsh struggle. The Japanese public had never had a hero quite like Nagashima and they worshiped him with unprecedented zeal. Until Nagashima married at age 29, for example, the identity of his future bride was a matter of national concern. Reporters were assigned specifically to track down the fortunate young lady.

When Nagashima finally announced his intention to marry a pretty hostess for the 1964 Tokyo Olympics, it was the biggest sports story of the year. To the question on every reporter's lips at the time—"Have you kissed her yet?"—Nagashima would reply with a blush and a mumbled non sequitur. To the Japanese, the Taylor-Burton and Princess Anne-Mark Phillips courtships were as nothing compared to the romance of their idol. The wedding was the most publicized event since the marriage of Crown Prince Akihito to a commoner he met on the tennis courts.

For 17 years, this Giant clean-up hitter reigned supreme as the acknowledged king of Japanese baseball. By the time he was through, he had amassed six batting championships (a Japan record), two home-run titles, five RBI crowns, 444 home runs and a lifetime batting average of .305.

Nagashima was chosen the Central League's most valuable player five times and voted Japanese All-Star third baseman every season he played, even in the final years of his career when age had diminished his considerable skills. To the end, annual surveys showed him to be the favorite of an incredible 40 percent of the fans.

Nagashima's prowess as a player earned him the highest salary in baseball until the year of his retirement. The ten-year bonus he received in 1967 was a staggering 40 million yen ($110,000) and in his last year of play his pay was nearly $200,000. When he left the team the Giants gave him a special bonus of $65,000.

Nagashima formally announced the end of his playing career on the last day of the 1974 season before 50,000 tearful fans at Korakuen Stadium. The moment was reminiscent of Lou Gehrig's "luckiest man alive" speech at Yankee Stadium and the Japanese nation came to a standstill as "Mr. Giants" spoke his parting words.

Nagashima stood on the pitcher's mound with tears flowing down his face, a display of emotion rarely seen in Japan. He was joined by many of his teammates, some of whom burst into tears as Nagashima shook their hands. "Don't quit. Please don't retire," shouted the fans as Nagashima walked off the field for the last time to assume his predestined role as Giant manager. Nagashima's retirement, acknowledged as one of the top ten news stories of 1974, was in many ways the most important event of all to the Japanese.

In 1975, the year he took over as manager, Nagashima and the Giants continued to dominate the media. When he took a squad of some forty players and coaches to Florida to train with the Dodgers,

Left: The marriage to end all marriages Right: A tearful farewell to the game

no fewer than fifty newsmen went along to cover the event. For even in retirement Nagashima was by far the most popular figure in sports. He had become a national symbol along with Mt. Fuji, the bullet train, and the GNP.

Fans advance a variety of reasons for Nagashima's popularity. "He was the first great all-around player Japan ever produced." "He always hustled." "He hit in the big games." "He was cute as a younger player and handsome as an older one, he's *otoko rashii* (manly)," female fans add. "He was colorful for a Japanese. He was one of the first players to really show his feelings on the field." "He trained harder than anyone else in camp." "He's like a country boy. If he met a movie star or some other famous person, he'd act just like you or me." "He's a nice guy."

A nice guy. This simple phrase probably sums up Nagashima's appeal as well as any. In short, he was—and is—a Japanese for all seasons.

The following excerpts from interviews convey some of the essence of Nagashima.

Nagashima at 26:

Q. What kind of girls do you like?

A. Clean, sincere. That kind of girl is very good.

Q. Have you had an *omiai* (an interview for arranged marriage) yet?

A. Not yet. I'd like to do that at least once, but I'm kind of shy about it.

Q. What would you do if there was a power failure when you were talking with your girl friend?

A. I would not take advantage of the darkness. I would never grab her hand, because I'm a gentleman. I would wait quietly until the lights came back on.

Q. What are your hobbies?

A. Baseball. Baseball is my hobby as well as my profession. There is nothing as enjoyable as baseball.

Q. If you appear in a movie, what movie actress do you want to appear with?

A. I don't think I want to appear in a movie yet. Now I am thinking only of baseball.

Q. Whom do you respect most?

A. Napoleon and Manager Kawakami (the Giants' manager). The two of them were an inspiration to me in my boyhood.

Q. How much can you drink?

A. I can only drink a little and that's all. I'm weak at alcohol.

Nagashima at age 32:

Q. Who is the master of your house?

A. I am the master.

Q. How do you intend to train your children?

A. I intend to train them strictly.

Q. Do you want your son to be a baseball player?

A. Yes, I would let him be a player. There is no world cleaner than baseball. It is a world of real ability. It is not necessary to flatter anybody.

Q. What do you expect from younger players?

A. It was their parents who gave them their talent and character; and they should repay them with great efforts.

Nagashima on meeting the Emperor:

The honor I thought was more than I deserved, but I accepted it. I purified myself for the day of the meeting, selected the best suit I had and then presented myself at the palace. I was extremely nervous. When the Emperor and Empress finally appeared, I felt so much in awe. I introduced myself by saying "I am Nagashima of baseball." I felt a combination of awe and fear in my body. There I was, just one baseball player standing in front of the Emperor. They spoke of the game the Emperor had attended at Korakuen. They praised me for the *'sayonara'* home run I had hit. I was deeply moved because the Emperor remembered a home run I had hit six years ago. Then the Empress, who was standing next to me, smiled gently and congratulated me on my recent marriage. I couldn't have been more moved at that point.

As a Japanese, I have never been so moved as I was on that day. As far as my pride is concerned, it is a memory I will cherish always. The photograph I received from that meeting is now a family treasure.

Nagashima's farewell speech to the fans:

During these seventeen years as a baseball player, I have experienced many things. When I think about each one of them, I cannot deny that I owe you for your passionate support in everything. When I was in good condition, your support further strengthened my fighting spirit. When I was in bad condition, your support encouraged me a great deal. I would like to thank all of you for your encouragement. I believe my achievements have greatly depended on them.

Nagashima on becoming the Giants' manager at 38:

This is a task I do not accept lightly. I will never disgrace the tradition and the honor of the team. A manager's job is different than that of a baseball player. If you are a man, you have to face adversity and pain and do your best. On the diamond during my last games as a Giant, I heard cries of the fans. "Thank you for your trouble. Please, by all means win the pennant next year." In answer to that I will just say this: I shall desperately try to do my best. I might make mistakes, but that is the privilege of youth. Most importantly a man should not have any hesitation at any time. I will try to do my best so that I won't have any regrets. I have learned well from former Manager Kawakami's instruction. I only hope that I shall be able to carry out my full responsibilities.

The fact that so much attention can be focused on one man underscores the hero-worship syndrome in Japanese society. Most Japanese are forced to submerge their identities in one or more groups, gaining prestige, for example, from belonging to a glamorous supergroup, like Mitsubishi and the other giant conglomerates. One adverse result is that the average Japanese gets lost in the crowd—a crowd of thousands of co-workers, all wearing identical dark suits and white shirts with the company pin affixed prominently to the lapel of their jackets. The idea of an individual performing superhuman feats appeals to the Japanese since the individual gets so little recognition. They take particular pleasure in following a star like Nagashima who made it big outside the normal path of success and yet still retained his Japanese values.

Nagashima is not the best player Japan has ever produced, just the most popular. The only major record he holds (aside from his five Japan Series MVP's and 25 home runs) is that of six batting titles—and teammate Sadaharu Oh is threatening to demolish that. Others have outshone Nagashima; but for a variety of reasons including personality quirks and accidents of fate, no one has ever matched his popularity.

Tetsuharu Kawakami came closest. He was Nagashima's predecessor and is known in Japan as the "God of Batting." Kawakami played first base for the Giants from 1938 until 1958 (with a break for the war) and was recognized throughout the country for his famed red bat, which he used to establish a Central League season high of .377, and the league's highest lifetime batting average of .313. Kawakami won five batting titles. He then went on to manage the Giants for 14 years and lead them to 11 league championships.

But Kawakami was a lone wolf who stood aloof from the crowd in a most un-Japanese fashion. His heart was in the right place, however; to prepare for the task of managing he spent more than one freezing winter at a Zen temple strengthening his mind. (Zen temples are not noted for their heating facilities.)

Then there was Giant pitcher Eiji Sawamura, who won a permanent place in the nation's heart for a game he pitched in 1934. Sawamura was 19 at the time, and still an amateur, when he faced an American all-star team headed by Babe Ruth and Lou Gehrig. Sawamura went the distance, losing 1–0 on a 9th inning home run by Gehrig. But in the process he performed a feat that had been thought impossible by his countrymen. He struck out Charley Gehringer, Ruth, Jimmy Foxx, and Gehrig in succession. Japanese sports fans still talk about that game. Sawamura became the Giants' first 30-game winner with a 33-10 mark in 1937, and he starred for several years before joining the Imperial Army to fight in the Pacific War. Sadly, he died in the battle of the Ryukyus. To honor Japan's first great pitcher, the commissioner's office established the Sawamura Award to be given each year to the best pitcher in the game.

The Nankai Hawks' rugged backstop Katsuya Nomura was certainly in Nagashima's class. Nomura was Japan's greatest catcher. During a career that began in 1954 and spanned more than two decades, Nomura rapped a record 2500 hits and knocked out over 600 home runs. But, Nomura did play in the smallest park in Japan, Osaka Stadium, which measures a scant 280 feet down the lines and 350 to dead center—a fact that tends to detract from his performance. In addition, the Nankai parent organization did not own a nationwide TV network, so Nomura did not have the benefit of the same nightly exposure that Nagashima did playing for the Yomiuri Giants.

Stocky Korean slugger Isao Harimoto is unquestionably a better hitter than Nagashima. Harimoto first appeared in 1959 with the Pacific League's Toei Flyers (later the Niitaku Home Flyers and now the Nippon Ham Fighters) and he set two important records: the highest single season batting average (.383) and the highest lifetime mark for Japan (.325). Harimoto also hit over 400 home runs. But there were complaints that he did not hustle enough and that he spoke his mind too freely, habits that did not endear him to the baseball establishment. Nor did the fact that Harimoto once beat up a taxi driver and two fans in a drunken brawl that cost him a $300 fine and a two-week suspension.

Wally Yonamine, a second generation Nisei from Hawaii who came to Japan in 1951, has baseball's third highest lifetime batting average at .311 and is regarded as the finest lead-off hitter ever to play the game. Wally's blood may be Japanese, but his heart is American as he demonstrated by introducing the hard slide. This breach of etiquette was not accepted kindly by opposing basemen or fans.

Hanshin Tiger Tomio Fujimura was Japan's first authentic home-run king. In 1949 he broke Kawakami's record of 25 by belting a then incredible 45 out of the park—seven more than Nagashima's best year. He set a league batting mark with .362 in 1950, only to be passed the following year by Kawakami's .377. A flamboyant competitor who would field line drives barehanded (to demonstrate his fighting spirit), Fujimura won the lasting affection of Tiger fans in 1950 when several of his teammates jumped to the newly formed Pacific League for more money. The loyal Fujimura stayed on. And though his powerful bat tailed off somewhat, having lost many good years to World War II, he finished with 224 career homers.

Still another early home-run king was Kaoru Betto, a college star who did not turn pro until he was 28. Like many Japanese in the 1940s, Betto held playing professional baseball in low esteem; but a fierce, competitive pride eventually made him change his mind. As Betto put it: "When I saw how well Kawakami and the others were doing, I said to myself, 'I can do better.' So I returned to baseball." *
Betto nearly fulfilled his own prediction. In 1950, for example, he hit 43 home runs and won the Pacific League's Most Valuable Player award. His marriage to a glamorous beauty queen in Japan's version of the Joe DiMaggio–Marilyn Monroe liaison focused even more attention on Betto, but, unfortunately, he lasted only ten years.

Kazuhisa Iron Man Inao and Masaiichi Kaneda were certainly su-

---

* Betto reportedly once claimed: "There's not a pitcher alive I can't hit."

perheroes to the Japanese—but of a very different kind from Naga-shima. Inao is Japan's favorite "tragic hero"—his end came too soon. And Kaneda, the 400-game winner and Japan's "God of Pitching," is the rebel hero who dared break the rules by refusing to pitch without proper rest. Fans admired his courage—perhaps even secretly envied him—but their affection was for Nagashima and his homespun style.

Among hurlers, there were a number of 300-game winners. A 6'4" 230 pound White Russian from Hokkaido named Victor Starfin, for example, won over 300 games from 1936 to 1955. Takehiko Bessho (1942–1960), was a 300-game winner for the Giants, and his 42 wins in 1939 left him tied with Inao for the Japan single season record. Then there was Hanshin Tiger Masayaki Koyama, a pitcher whose control was reputed to be so good he could hit a 10 yen coin in the strike zone blindfolded. Koyama pitched over 20 years (1952–1975), winning 320 games. While Tetsuya Yoneda of the Hankyu Braves (1956–1976) was the second all-time winningest pitcher with 342.

Others include 5'3" Yoshio Yoshida (Tigers, 1952–1969) who was Japan's first real shortstop; Shigeru "Buffalo" Chiba (Giants, 1938–1956) Japan's greatest second baseman; and Hiroshi Oshita (Flyers, 1946–1959) who held the highest season average with .382 until Harimoto edged him out. Oshita's well-known penchant for geisha houses, however, disqualified him as a candidate for Japan's fa-vorite Knight in Shining Armor. Futoshi Nakanishi (Lions, 1952–1969) was another all-time great. Nakanishi, a 5'8" 180 pound slugger who could hit the ball 500 feet, won four straight home-run titles, and as playing manager, led his team to a pennant in 1963. But after his retirement, Nakanishi's image lost some of its luster in a curious incident.

Nakanishi had gone on to become a baseball commentator in 1969, when three of his former charges were suspended permanently from baseball for participating in a fix. (This was the *yakuza*-inspired "Black Mist Scandals" in which a total of six players were banned for life for rigging games.) Nakanishi assumed responsibility for the illegal activi-ties—although he had already severed ties with the team—and there-upon vowed not to speak or write about baseball until he had discov-ered through "self-reflection" wherein he had failed as a manager.

There is one player whose performance at the plate is outstanding compared to all others including Nagashima's. His name is Sadaharu Oh, and he is the most prolific home-run hitter of all time. The son of a Chinese emigrant, Oh signed with the Giants in 1959 for a $60,000 bonus. He was then a 19-year-old pitching whiz, but Giant coaches recognized his power and shifted him to first base. It took him three years to reach his stride, but since then he has been hitting home runs at an incredible pace. From 1962 to 1974, the left-handed slugger won the home-run crown every single year, averaging over 45 a year. Oh, whose unusual foot-in-the-air stance enables him to lean into each pitch, holds the Japan single season record of 55. Oh has passed the 714 career home-run mark and is closing in on Henry Aaron's world title. ("800 is my target," Oh says.) Appropriately, Oh's family name means "king" both in Chinese and Japanese.

Oh has also won five batting titles, more RBI crowns (nine) and more Most Valuable Player awards (seven) than any other player in Japan. His lifetime batting average is .306. In 1974 and 1975, the 5'10" 175 pound Oh did something no American player has ever done: he won back-to-back triple crowns (1974: .355/51/114; 1975: .332/49/107).

Through the 1960s and early 1970s, Oh and teammate Nagashima formed the most devastating clean-up duo Japan has ever seen. The "O-N Cannon" as they were sometimes called held a visegrip on league batting honors. They were to the Giants what Ruth and Gehrig were to the Yankees of old. The "pride of the Giants," as well as the pride of all Japanese baseball, were the primary reason for the Giants' "golden era" when the team won nine straight Japan Series from 1965 to 1973.

Throughout those incredible years, however, Oh always played in the shadow of Nagashima. In annual "favorite player" surveys, Oh usually polled around 20 percent, miles ahead of anyone but Nagashima, though still far behind the master. Oh surpassed his famous teammate in every aspect of the game. Yet, any Japanese who was asked to name the best player in the land would more often than not reply Nagashima.

It wasn't so much Oh's Chinese blood as it was Nagashima's charisma and his "seniority."

But with Nagashima no longer active as a player, Oh is unquestionably the top player in the game. He has all the credentials: he is modest, hard working,* unassuming, and a first-class gentleman. The media, which played such an influential role in Nagashima's rise to glory, have done as much for Oh—recording every available detail of his life style and passing it on to hungry fans. The whole nation knows that Oh is an amateur pianist, that he takes "batting practice" with a sword, that he doesn't read much for fear of straining his eyes, that he drinks a secret blend of Korean ginseng herb to vitalize himself before games, and that his golf handicap hovers around nine. (Subway posters with his smiling face proclaim "Eat Navona Cake"—"the 'home-run king' of cakes.")

Oh's prowess on the diamond has made him rich as well. His annual salary now exceeds $200,000 a year. At the end of 1974 the Giants added a $33,000 bonus as reward for his winning a second

* On the average, Oh will take an incredible (in American terms) 30 to 40 minutes of batting practice before a game.

Nagashima hangs up his uniform for the last time

straight triple crown. Oh's salary is reportedly matched by fees for public appearances, endorsements, and outside investments. Oh is typically blasé about all the money he is making. In traditional Japanese fashion he is reported to give his monthly salary check to his wife and mother. "I don't know how they are spending it," he says.

That Sadaharu Oh would be a star on any team in the States is clear to all who have seen him play. Of course some Americans downplay his home-run heroics because of the inferior pitching he faces and the smaller parks in which he plays,* but, in Oh's defense, he hits his home runs in a 130-game season (compared to 162 in the U.S.) and he is also walked as many as 150 times a year. This appraisal by Clete Boyer, a former New York Yankee (now with the Taiyo Whales), is typical:

I think he's super. He's one of the best ballplayers I've ever seen. If Oh played in the U.S., he'd be a superstar. He'd probably lead the league in home runs and would hit with the best of them.

People say they'd brush him back in the States because he crowds the plate so much, but he'd learn fast. He's got great reflexes. He's got a perfect swing and the perfect mental attitude. I'd compare him to Hank Aaron. And, in his own way, he's like Ted Williams. His eye is that good!

Besides Oh, there are perhaps ten pitchers and twenty other players who could step into the starting lineup of any major league team. Koji Yamamoto of the Hiroshima Carp, for example, can run, throw, and hit as well as most major-league outfielders and his teammate Yoshio Sotokoba is a pitcher with an excellent fork ball and control to match. A third "Carp"—infielder Sachio Kinugasa—might give Sal Bando a run for his money.

Hanshin Tiger catcher Koichi Tabuchi, at 6'3" 210 pounds, is as strong as an ox and could hit the ball out of any major-league stadium.† In 1975, with seasons of 37 and 45 home runs under his belt,

---

* The average ball park in Japan is about 300 feet down the lines and 350 feet to dead center—about 40 feet shallower than those in the U. S.

† Tabuchi hits most of his home runs at Osaka's cavernous Koshien Stadium. The largest park in Japan, it measures 375 feet down the power alleys and 400 to dead center.

Home-run king Sadaharu Oh, in the throes of a mid-season slump, works on his form under the scrutiny of Giant Manager Nagashima (90)

the 29-year-old catcher walloped a league-leading 43, putting an end to Oh's 13-year reign as home-run king. (Oh "slumped" to 33.)

Shigeru Takada, the Giants' leftfielder and sometime third baseman, runs like a deer and has a slingshot arm. Perhaps the best outfielder in Japan, Takada would probably hit .300 on any team in the world. At 6′3″ and 195 pounds, Michio Arito of the Lotte Orions hits with great power and fields so well that he has been coveted by U.S. teams for years. And Yutaka Fukumoto, a fleetfooted centerfielder for the Hankyu Braves, stole 106 bases (in 122 games) in 1972 and 95 the following year. The list goes on, and grows longer each year.

Unfortunately, it is extremely unlikely that any of them will ever play on an American team. For just as there has never been an appreciable Japanese "brain drain," there is not likely to be a "talent drain" involving athletes. Leaving one's team to play in America would be regarded as an act of national disloyalty—even if there was no sanctity of contract agreement between the U.S. and Japan. (And any Japanese owner who attempted to trade one of his stars for an American would probably be shot by the fans.)

One young Japanese player who had the opportunity and opted for America soon learned the folly of his ways when he found himself in the middle of a battle-royal of such proportions that it threatened to destroy baseball relations between the two countries for good.

His name was Masanori Murakami and he was a 20-year-old left-handed pitcher who belonged to the Nankai Hawks of the Pacific League. In 1964, the unproven farm team hurler was sent to America, along with two other young players,* to spend the season with the San Francisco Giant farm team at Fresno. It was part of a player exchange agreement approved by both the Japanese and American baseball commissions that the Hawks had signed with the San Francisco club.

Besides being simply a good-will gesture, the Giants hoped that some day they would be able to send players from their farm system to train in Japan. There was a standard option clause in the agreement that allowed the Giants to purchase the contract of any player who made the parent team for $10,000, but the Hawks' management felt certain that no player would ever make it that far. After all, they were not even good enough to make the Hawks' roster. A season or two in the U.S. would be good experience, however, and they would return to Japan better players.

Young Murakami had a particularly promising summer with the Fresno team. Not only was he the club's most effective relief pitcher, compiling a strong 11-7 record, but he became an instant hit with the fans one game when he walked over to the third baseman who had just saved a run from scoring, doffed his cap, and bowed deeply from the waist.

That September the San Francisco Giants unexpectedly called him up to face the New York Mets at Shea Stadium in New York. In the clubhouse before the game, he responded to reporters' questions.

"Yes, I am a little nervous, but I think I will like it here. . . . I

---

* Catcher Hiroshi Takashi and third baseman Tatsuhiko Tanaka. Both were sent to Twin Falls, Idaho. Neither one lasted but, along with Murakami, they became the first Japanese to play professional baseball in America.

hope I will please Mr. Manager. . . . No, I have not told my family yet. I will write them tomorrow; I'm sure they will be very happy." And then to his interpreter: "Shouldn't I be out on the field now taking practice with the others? . . . Is it really all right with Dark-*Kantoku* (Manager), if I stay behind to speak with the press? . . . Are you sure he won't object?"

Later that night, before 50,000 screaming Met fans, Murakami was called from the bullpen. He pitched one inning of scoreless relief and became the first Japanese ever to appear in a major-league baseball game.

"Mashi," as he was dubbed, could not speak English well, but he had a friendly manner and a winning smile.* (Although there were some who wished he would not bow and say "Excuse me" so often.) He became an overnight hit in San Francisco, especially with the large Japanese-American segment of the bay area population. His own countrymen were also tremendously proud of him. He had given an enormous boost to the prestige of Japanese baseball.

"Mashi" appeared in eight more games that season. He hurled 15 innings, won one game, and had a glittering ERA of 1.80. The Giants were delighted with Murakami's performance. They offered him a contract for the 1965 season and "Mashi" promptly signed. He wanted to stay in America and play in the majors, he declared. San Francisco sent $10,000 to the Hawks for Murakami's services. The Hawks gratefully accepted the money and all seemed well.

In December of that year, however, things began to happen. After a stint in the Arizona Instructional League, Murakami returned to Japan to visit his parents and almost immediately the pressure was on from all quarters—the Hawks' management, the press, his family. They wanted him to stay in Japan. He was Japanese, an only son whose place was with his family. It was his duty to play at home.

On February 1, the Nankai Hawks' front office announced that Murakami had signed a contract to play with them for the 1965 season. They stated that Murakami had (mysteriously) "lost his desire" to

---

* San Francisco Giant Manager Alvin Dark called Murakami "one of the most considerate and well-mannered rookies" he'd ever seen.

play ball in the United States, and thus the Hawks wanted to keep him in Japan.

To U. S. Commissioner of Baseball Ford Frick, this was a clear violation of baseball's hallowed reserve clause. Murakami had signed a contract with the Giants and he and the Hawks were obligated to honor it. If they didn't, any other major league player would feel free to leave his team whenever he wanted. Frick dashed off a letter to Japanese Baseball Commissioner Yushi Uchimura urging that, in the best interests of baseball, the Hawks honor their agreement with the Giants and send Murakami back to San Francisco.

The Giants, as Frick reminded the Japanese commissioner, had an option in the initial training agreement with the Hawks to buy any one of the players' contracts. When they sent the $10,000 to Nankai for Murakami, they were exercising that option.

The Hawks countered by claiming that all along they had no intention of selling Murakami's contract to the Giants for a paltry $10,000. After all, they themselves had given Murakami a $30,000 bonus just to sign with them upon graduating from high school. The Hawks' front office explained they had only "loaned" Murakami to San Francisco and interpreted the $10,000 as a bonus for Murakami's services.

This explanation didn't wash with Frick, however. He insisted that the Giants had a valid contract and demanded Murakami's return. The Hawks, perhaps realizing the futility of their position, turned to more devious ploys. First they claimed the club signature on Murakami's release—which accompanied the $10,000 check—was a forgery. When Frick refused to swallow this, they tried to get their erstwhile pitcher back via the "homesick clause" in the initial agreement which provided that a player unable to adapt to the American way of life be released immediately and allowed to return home.

Frick didn't buy this either, in light of Murakami's earlier eagerness to stay with San Francisco. When Nankai still refused to return Murakami, Frick took drastic action. He immediately suspended baseball relations between the two countries and instructed the Pittsburgh Pirates, scheduled to visit Japan that fall on a good-will tour, to cancel their trip until the matter was resolved.

The President of the Nankai team was indignant: "Even if the

Pirates do not come to Japan, Japanese baseball will not suffer," he declared. "Frick's statement is proof that he is holding Japanese baseball cheap and it certainly is regrettable." He was clearly upset over Frick's "unwillingness" to appreciate the "moral rightness" of the Hawks' position.

Commissioner Uchimura suddenly found himself in a very difficult position. Primarily a figurehead responsible to the owners, he was reluctant to rule against the Hawks. But, on the other hand, he did not want to damage relations with America because Japanese baseball would only suffer in the long run.

As most Japanese do when faced with a difficult decision, Uchimura stalled for time. He became ill and was "forced" to delay his decision. On March 17, six weeks after Frick had expressed his displeasure, Uchimura finally made his ruling. With the characteristic Japanese penchant for compromise, he ruled that Murakami might return to the San Francisco Giants for the 1965 season, but must return to Japan, permanently, in 1966. He judged that the Hawks had regretfully made a serious error in misinterpreting their agreement with the Giants, but emphasized that from the beginning the Nankai club had no intention of trading Murakami permanently to San Francisco.

Uchimura explained that the trouble began when the Giants claimed Murakami as their permanent property. Murakami's parents had objected strongly to this and to his subsequent return to the San Francisco team since there would be much uncertainty about his future.

Frick and the Giants were cool to Uchimura's compromise proposal. They felt that Murakami's return to Japan in 1966 would still be a violation of the reserve clause. The Giants then made a counterproposal. They said that if Murakami were farmed out after the 1965 season, he would be free to return to Japan. He would not have to stay in the minor leagues. But if they decided to keep him on the varsity, he had to remain.

Frick followed up with a ruling that Murakami had to come back to the States *before* any further settlement could be made. He decreed that the first step must be recognition of the validity of Murakami's contract with the Giants.

This did not help Commissioner Uchimura's situation at all. After a few more weeks of sitting on the fence, he drafted a reply which made it clear that Murakami would be staying in Japan a bit longer. His reply read: "I believe Mr. Frick should more deeply appreciate our position . . ." and added that he would have to discuss the matter further with Murakami's parents.

Murakami, meanwhile, had been working out at the Hawks' training camp. Opening day was less than two weeks away and he was undoubtedly disconcerted by the war raging around him.

Murakami's parents gave him permission to return to San Francisco on the condition he would play for the Hawks in 1966. His father felt strongly that his only son should play for Nankai.

On April 28, three weeks after the season had begun, the matter was finally resolved. Frick and the Giants relented, and wearily allowed that Murakami could return to Japan after 1965 if *he* still wished to do so. In their reply, they felt obligated to remind the Japanese that ". . . in any international agreement, sanctity of contract is the most essential feature." Frick then lifted his suspension.

The relieved Japanese commissioner issued a statement of gratitude to his American friends: "I feel the elder brother has given in to end the family dispute." The Hawks returned the $10,000 to the Giants and Murakami caught the next plane to California.

The basis for this bizarre dispute went far deeper than just a misinterpretation of words. It arose out of very different attitudes Americans and Japanese have toward contracts. The Japanese believe more in the spirit than the letter of a contract. In fact intercorporate transactions involving millions of dollars take place regularly in Japan with no written contract whatsoever. The Hawks' management seriously believed that the Giants would never expect them to give up a promising young pitcher so easily. They never anticipated upon signing the agreement that one of their players might be good enough to make it to the majors. Since they did not expect the situation to arise, they paid no attention to the option clause in the contract. Undoubtedly they reasoned that the clause was a standard part of American contracts and, regardless of its presence or wording, assumed the San Francisco organization understood their feelings.

San Francisco, however, had not understood. For them, "an option clause was an option clause" and $10,000 for a pitcher who spent most of the season in Class C baseball was fair compensation. They fully expected the option clause would apply if they ever sent any player to Japan and the Hawks decided to keep him.

Murakami pitched the 1965 season for San Francisco and finished with a 4-1 record and an ERA of 3.50. He was given a "day" by Japanese-American fans in the bay area on August 15, which, significantly, was the 20th anniversary of the end of World War II. During the season, Murakami also received an unusual telephone call from Nankai batting great Katsuya Nomura that was broadcast over nationwide radio. Nomura urged the wayward pitching star to give up any further aspirations of playing in America and return home to his rightful place on the Hawks.

At the end of the season, Murakami did return to Japan, but announced that he was still undecided as to which team to play for. The Giants had offered him $15,000 and Murakami indicated he would like the Hawks to pay him a comparable figure. When he paid a visit to the Commissioner's office and asked what his status would be in Japan if he played in San Francisco for two or three more years, he was told he would still remain Hawk property and could not negotiate with other clubs. Murakami raised the ire of *Hōchi Shinbun* which ran a story entitled "Selfish Murakami," criticizing him for business techniques he had obviously learned abroad.

Of course, there was never any real doubt as to what Murakami would do. Under the Code he had no choice. In December, he announced he would play for the Hawks. He said his decision to remain in Japan was primarily due to his parents' wishes. Murakami's father worked out a formal agreement with the Nankai general manager, in which Murakami would be paid an estimated $13,000. (The club said it could pay no more because Murakami had yet to prove himself in Japanese baseball.)

The Hawks, naturally, were elated to have him; here was a young, strong, 22-year-old pitcher with two years' experience as a successful American major leaguer. They looked forward to his getting an "early start on the all-time wins record."

Murakami's first season as a Hawk received mixed publicity. *Hōchi Shinbun* reported that he had learned some "bad things" overseas. He had, for example, acquired the habit of throwing his glove at the bench and kicking things when his pitching was off. More than once Murakami heard cries of "Go Back to America" when he was knocked out of the box.

The paper also noted that Murakami was "morose" and didn't seem to be a good mixer with his teammates. He ate alone at a separate table in the team dining hall and was always the last player to leave the field, after the others had departed.

Sadly, Murakami never fulfilled the dreams of glory that the Japanese baseball world had for him. Forbidden by his coaches to throw the feared brushback pitch—a technique he learned in the U.S.—he lost much of his effectiveness. He won only nine games his first two years, his ERA sagged to 4.05, and he suffered an overall 60 percent salary cut. He did have one good year of 18-4 with a 2.38 ERA in 1968, but then faded into mediocrity. The whole distasteful episode ended in bitter disappointment for Murakami.

For those in Japan who fought tooth and nail over him, his failure to "break the all-time wins record" was just further evidence that Japanese baseball was gaining respectability. The day was approaching when Japan could take on the Americans in their own game.

7 a game for the fan

The new manager of the last-place Yakult Atoms signalled an end to the pre-game warmup. He called his players together and began to deliver some last-minute instructions for the evening contest with the league-leading Tokyo Giants.

The crowd that swelled the stands of Tokyo's Meiji Jingu Stadium was growing restless. "Let's get on with it," yelled a young construction worker clad in undershirt and baggy work pants. He took a swig from his disposable plastic bottle of *Ozeki sake* and flashed a grin at his friends, displaying one brilliant gold tooth. "Let's see how badly you can lose this one," he shouted. "C'mon, what's holding you up—afraid of losing again?"

The woeful Atoms were in the throes of a record-breaking losing streak. In the last game they had suffered their eleventh straight defeat, passing their earlier season high of ten. That same afternoon, in a desperate effort to "change the mood on the team," the Atoms' front office had taken the radical step of accepting the manager's official resignation in mid-season, the first time such a thing had ever happened.

The Atoms' cheerleader, a portly middle-aged man, clambered wearily atop the first base dugout. Dripping with perspiration, he picked up his huge Atom pennant and began to wave it. "Go, Atoms!" he yelled halfheartedly, "Break that streak!"

"Go, Atoms! Break that streak!" The crowd along the first baseline picked up the rhythmic chant as the cheerleader pulled out a silver whistle and began to blow in shrill, cadenced notes. "Gooo, Atoms! Break that streak!"

Reports from the clubhouse claimed the Atoms were "full of fight" and in a "bright mood" for the game. And the somewhat skeptical

121

fans at the stadium were indeed hopeful that such might be the case. When the Atoms surrendered two runs and four hits in the first inning, the mood on the Atoms' bench still seemed confident. "I thought we would soon get them back," the manager later remarked. Even when the Giants struck once again for five hits and three more runs in the third inning, the Atoms did not give up hope: "Let's raise our voices and fight to the end!" cried the players.

The Atoms held the Giants the rest of the way but, unfortunately, were unable to mount any sort of attack. The game ended with the Atoms on the short end of a 5–0 shutout—their twelfth humiliating loss in a row. The opposing manager made the candid observation: "I didn't notice any particular change. I feel sorry for their former manager."

"You're hopeless," shouted the construction worker, who by now was rather drunk. "I've never seen such lousy playing."

His words were cut short when the Atom players, instead of hurrying inside the clubhouse as usual, lined up alongside their manager facing the home stands behind first base. And as the startled fans watched, the Atoms removed their caps in unison and bowed deeply in apology for the defeat.

Japan may be the only place in the world where a losing team feels obliged to offer its followers an apology. But what else would you expect in a country where a team sent out thousands of New Year "apology" cards as the Yomiuri Giants did in 1975 when they finished in the cellar?

Such behavior reflects the deep sense of responsibility Japanese teams feel toward their paying customers. This attitude has elevated the team/fan relationship to an almost personal level. When the home team wins a game, one of the first things the manager might say is: "I'm glad we won for our fans. We're happy that so many of them came to support us." By the same token, when a team loses, a manager is quick to acknowledge his team's failure to satisfy its supporters: "To our fans all over the country, I am sorry that we were unable to bring you victory tonight. We are trying to do our best. Bear with us and we will bring you a winner."

This sense of responsibility goes far beyond winning or losing. Fans

The Yakult Atoms (now the Swallows) remorsefully acknowledge their 12th straight defeat

deserve the best possible show, as one fan put it: "A professional player is, more than anything else, supposed to entertain us by performing good plays and exciting home runs. After all, he is being paid to do so." If the team plays poorly, win or lose, the manager will offer his regrets: his team made too many errors, the batters struck out too often, nobody hustled enough, and the game was dull. Contrast this to what an American player or coach might say: "I don't give a damn what the fans think. Our job is to win. So what if the game was slow. Winning is what counts, isn't it?"

Players in Japan apologize for getting hurt, batters apologize for batting slumps, and winning pitchers apologize for not throwing a shutout. Veteran players even apologize for playing too long and not giving younger players a chance; while retiring players apologize for retiring too soon. (Imagine Henry Aaron apologizing for playing too long, but in Japan he probably would.)

The apology is Japan's most useful social tool. A manufacturer will apologize to an angry public for a defective product, pledge to rectify the situation, and so avoid a costly lawsuit. And a prime minister may even survive a series of earthshaking scandals in his administration by apologizing to the nation on TV.*

In Japan, the group is all important. And in baseball, the team's fans are a very important part of the group. Announcers in pre-game talk shows, for example, will often say: "If the manager is thinking of the fans, he will start Yamaguchi. This is a big game and everyone wants to see him pitch." Or: "If Manager Nantoka wants to please the fans, he will put Enogawa into the game tonight." (Though Enogawa's batting average at the time was less than .100, he had been an extremely popular college player.)

Teams will often keep a popular rookie on the varsity who should be down on the farm, if he was a star in high school or college. A manager may not like having to spend extra time smoothing out the rough edges of an inexperienced player, but he has no choice. And if the pressure from the public is strong enough, the rookie may even get into a game. This practice is known as *fan sābisu*, "fan service."

Nothing holds fan interest more than the drama of *shōbu. Shōbu* is an encounter between combatants to determine individual superiority. It has all the romance of a samurai swordfight or a shootout between two top gunfighters. On the diamond, *shōbu* is a showdown between a top pitcher and a top hitter. When it occurs, the team concept of baseball often goes out the window (along with the notion that the purpose of a game is to win it).

The essence of *shōbu* requires both pitcher and batter to give all they have, regardless of the game situation. That means no intentional walks, no junk pitches, and no bunting for a base hit. The fans come to see their favorites do or die, and the players have to deliver. It doesn't matter who wins—whether the pitcher strikes out the batting king on a smoking fast ball or the batter blasts that fast ball over the fence. Either way the fans will be happy, for they have seen a "real" match between two titans.

Shōbu has given rise to some intense rivalries, and one of the most

* Such as former Japanese prime minister Eisaku Sato did when the 1967 "Black Mist" scandals involving widespread bribery at high levels threatened to topple his government.

famous involved Shigeo Nagashima of the Giants and the great Hanshin Tiger pitcher Minoru Murayama. Murayama, who appeared a year after Nagashima joined the Giants, had himself been offered around $45,000 to join the Tokyo club. Instead, he signed for half that amount with the Hanshin team, which was located in Murayama's home district of Kansai in southwestern Honshu. Murayama, a Tiger fan since childhood, had vowed at his father's deathbed to remain close to his mother.

This fateful decision eventually led to the momentous confrontation with Nagashima in the Emperor's game—the most famous *shōbu* in history. The dramatic, game-ending home run Murayama surrendered on that occasion marked him for life. Murayama's thirst for revenge became a major theme in the rivalry that subsequently developed. Murayama vowed publicly that he would get his 1500th and 2000th strikeouts against Nagashima—and both times he kept his vow. But the traumatic defeat he suffered in the Emperor's game continued to dog him throughout his career. As Murayama once put it: "I have become what I am because of Nagashima."

Unfortunately, the reputation a player establishes over the years may eventually lead to his undoing. In his first three years in baseball, for example, young speedballer Yutaka Enatsu was the only pitcher who could consistently beat Giant home-run king Sadaharu Oh. Fans packed the park whenever the two locked horns to see if Oh had finally figured out the blazing fastball and sharp-breaking curve of his nemesis.

Eventually, the inevitable happened. Enatsu began to lose some of his speed. His strikeouts against Oh came less and less frequently. Within the span of one season, Oh began to hit Enatsu's pitching with alarming regularity.

Enatsu, in keeping with the traditions of *shōbu* and face-saving, however, continued to challenge Oh. On countless occasions, in late innings with the score tied and no one on base, he would refuse to walk Oh or throw him junk pitches. This often resulted in another Oh home run and a loss for Enatsu's team.

Enatsu was in a quandary. He didn't want to throw anything good to Oh, with a game on the line. Yet, he knew in the back of his mind that the fans were measuring him against earlier performances. For in some Japanese eyes, avoiding *shōbu* is often worse than losing the game.

One could never imagine Tom Seaver challenging Johnny Bench if Seaver were not reasonably confident he could get Bench out. But then, Tom Seaver is not Japanese. In Japan, discretion is not always the better part of valor.

American baseball is a relatively simple business affair. If a team plays good ball and wins a high percentage of its games, fans will come to see it play (unless, of course, the team happens to be Oakland). If attendance is poor, the front office will try public relations' stunts to lure people to the park: Bat day, ball day, ladies day, rock concerts, cow-milking contests, and so on.

In Japan, the situation is somewhat different. The PR wing of the team does not zealously promote the club since the team itself exists mainly as a PR vehicle for the sponsoring firm. In fact a Japanese baseball club is often just a tax writeoff. Even so, teams may go to great lengths to acknowledge those fans who support them. After each game, some will have ball-throwing and base-running contests in which the younger members of the audience can participate. Others will hold annual "fan appreciation" festivals, in which popular TV and movie personalities entertain the crowd with one-legged races, potato sack races, songs, raffles, and giveaways. Then at the end of the regular season, teams will tour the country until late November to play games of "appreciation" in cities where they do not ordinarily appear—demonstrating their gratitude to those fans who have supported them from afar.

The idea is to solidify the team/fan relationship and it has its basis in the Japanese concept of "after service"—an essential feature of regular business in Japan where the word for "customer" and "guest" is the same. Japanese consumers prefer a relationship that does not end with the purchase of a product, and the club owners are simply acting in accord with this tradition.

One team, incidentally, demonstrated how seriously it took such responsibilities to its fans when the game-fixing scandals of 1969 were uncovered. The following season, the owner ordered his players to make a formal bow to each section of the grandstand and bleachers before every game, as an expression of gratitude to those fans who, in spite of the dark cloud over baseball, still supported them.

Though many Japanese team names are selected by the fans, the Hanshin Tigers chose their name in a survey of Hanshin Railway workers. (During World War II, the name was changed to Moko-Gun—"Fiery Tiger Group.") The Chunichi Dragons were so dubbed because the team president was born in the zodiac year of the Dragon. (Originally the name appeared in English on the uniforms as DRAGNS until an alert spelling expert pointed out the mistake.) The Hiroshima Carp took their name from Hiroshima Castle, which is called the "Castle of the Carp." While the Kintetsu Buffaloes were first called the Pearls because Kinki Nippon Railways that owned the team served an area noted for cultured pearls. But when former

Nagashima and Oh frolic on "fan appreciation day"

Giant star Shigeru Chiba, whose nickname was "Buffalo," became manager, the team opted for the change.

The extent to which fans influence the sport sometimes reaches almost unbelievable proportions. Koichi Ohta, for example, is one of the less inspiring hurlers ever to pitch in Japanese professional baseball. Yet, he is one of the most popular. The handsome blue-eyed offspring of a Russian/Japanese marriage, Ohta led Misawa High School #9 into the 1969 National Championship tournament at Koshien Stadium in Osaka and, single-handedly, almost won the title for his team.

The right-hander pitched every game of the ten-day tournament to put his club in the final and deciding contest. The eyes of the entire Japanese nation were riveted to their television sets that day. Housewives dropped what they were doing and workers scurried to the nearest tea room to watch the courageous young pitcher duel to an eighteen-inning 0–0 tie in a game finally called because of darkness. The next day, the game was replayed. Ohta pitched again and, as the whole country watched, lost 4–2.

In spite of the defeat, Ohta became an overnight hero. The following week, his picture appeared on nearly every magazine cover. Newspapers were filled with stories about him and he became a popular television subject. There was even a book titled *Let's Go Ohta!* His blue eyes and shy manner made him the idol of Japan's teenagers and Koichi Ohta fan clubs sprang up from Hokkaido to Kyushu.

After graduating from high school, Ohta received 20 million yen ($55,000) for signing with the Pacific League Kintetsu Buffaloes, as well as an additional 15,000,000 yen upon inking endorsement pacts with a chewing gum company and a soft-drink manufacturer. To prepare for Ohta's adoring contingent, the Buffalo management installed cushioned stadium seats and a special powder room.

In Ohta's first year as a Buffalo, he appeared in 25 games, managing only one victory against four defeats and posting an ERA of 3.86. Not very impressive statistics, but enough to boost Kintetsu's drooping attendance.

Incredibly, Ohta was the top vote-getter for the annual mid-summer All-Star Series. His youthful female following had done a good job of ballot box stuffing. In the nationally televised classic, Ohta appeared in one game and hurled an unimpressive third of an inning, surrendering two hits, two walks, and two runs. There were, surprisingly, few complaints from fans or players. Ohta seemed to have a peculiar appeal for everyone.

The next season Ohta fared no better. Enough was enough, the Buffalo management decided, and Ohta was shipped off to the farm team. He needed more work. He made a scant 14 appearances with the parent club, and his ERA ballooned to 6.84, yet he was again the top vote-getter in the All-Star balloting. Ohta hurled his perfunctory inning and returned to his duties on the farm team.

The following year Ohta pitched in 16 games, won two, and had a 3.90 ERA, but he still led the All-Star voting for the third year in a row. Naturally, Ohta was a little embarrassed by his popularity and his annual appearances with the best in the game.

But then he began to improve. In his fourth year, he won six and lowered his ERA to 3.23. And by 1975, his fifth season, he finally matured. His 12-12/3.71 record played a prominent role in the Buffaloes climb into pennant contention; and Ohta showed signs of becoming even better. Of course, he continued to lead in the All-Star tally. Apparently his fans knew a good thing when they saw it.

The Japanese fan is probably the most sophisticated in the world. He will sit through a three-and-a-half-hour game without getting bored or missing a single pitch, and complain if the game is called a tie because of the curfew. He views baseball as a series of strategic situations: will the pitcher walk the batter, challenge him, or give him bad pitches; will the opposition try a hit and run, a squeeze, a steal? He savors each moment with intense pleasure, and he knows the strengths and weaknesses of the players on both sides, and loves to play at managing. As one ardent female boasted: "I try to imitate the way of giving signs. I think of what the strategy should be in a situation and what I would do if I were running the team."

There are probably twice as many meetings on the mound and batter–coach conferences in Japan as in America. Yet the fans don't mind. These discussions are an integral part of the play. The Japanese sees the true essence of baseball as the "war of nerves" between pitcher and batter. To them, it is one of the most exciting parts of the game—like a *sumo* match, where the wrestlers glare at each other interminably as they go through their pre-fight ritual. The longer it takes before both wrestlers signal they are ready to go, the more the tension builds. (The actual fights are usually over in seconds.)

Similarly, when a batter steps out of the batter's box, confers with the coach, and knocks the dirt from his spikes or the pitcher steps off the rubber, removes a speck of dust from his uniform, and casts an evil eye on the batter, excitement is generated. Foul balls are not meaningless because the fans know the batter is forcing the pitcher to throw a better pitch. The more foul balls a batter hits, the more electrifying the outcome.

The American fan is easily bored with all this. It only delays the game. Due primarily to poor sportscasters, he has little appreciation for the finer points of baseball. He wants action—now. So the umpires speed up the play. To the Japanese, however, this takes half the fun out of the game. Like sex without foreplay.

The Japanese fan is also remarkably loyal. If his team hustles, shows fighting spirit, tries to make the game interesting, apologizes for its deficiencies, undergoes "hard training," and in general behaves properly, all is well. If the team doesn't win, well, as the favorite saying goes *"Shoganai"* (it can't be helped). Although Iron Man Inao had nothing but second-division teams in his five-year tenure as manager of the Taiheiyo Club Lions, before he resigned, there were no cries of outrage over his continued presence. Fans remembered what he had done on the field in years gone by. They respected him. If the Lions could not win, it was because the players were not good enough—not because Inao was a poor manager.

As one Giant fan commented after his fabled team plummeted to last place in 1975: "Now they're at the bottom and it will take them two or three years to rise to the top again. But I'll be faithful. I'll wait." Such devotion is typical.

Perhaps the biggest difference between Japanese and American fans is in their respective "ballpark manners." The American is loud, boisterous, often rude and indeed remarkable for the amount of noise

In 1975, the Hiroshima Carp won their first pennant

he can generate over a nine-inning span, whereas the Japanese tends to operate between the extremes of silence and explosion.

At one end of the spectrum is the average fan at a normal game. He is polite, restrained, and averse to such cries as "Kill the Umpire" and the Bronx cheer. He limits himself to an occasional "Come on, Hawks" or "Nice hit" or call to the beer vendor. Unlike the fickle American he will seldom vent his anger at his own team or boo a player who is trying. (Occasionally, a fan will climb up on the roof of the stadium or some other high place to "protest" his team's shoddy performance, but such behavior is rare.)

Relatively few Japanese women attend games and those who do are usually very quiet, quite unlike their American counterparts. Proper behavior consists of delicately mopping her boy friend's forehead with her hanky and offering up a few breathless "ooohs" and "aaahs" at the appropriate moment.

Taboos against displaying feelings in public as well as his general aversion to standing out in a crowd account for the calm the Japanese fan normally displays. But, on rare occasions—prompted by fierce loyalties, *sake*, the need to release pent-up emotions, and the presence of a crowd—the fan will make a radical shift to the other end of the spectrum. Then, as in most cases when a Japanese breaks with proper form, he literally explodes.

Those Cleveland Indian fans who stormed the field, scuffled with the Texas Rangers, and caused their team to forfeit the game on a 10 cent beer night back in 1974 have nothing on the good citizens of Hiroshima, the "city of peace." The Hiroshima Carp are the only team in Japan partially financed by the local citizens; and the fans don't like it when their team is defeated. In fact, on numerous occasions, they have lost their collective tempers and taken appalling steps to protect their investment. After one loss to the hated Giants of Tokyo, for instance, they laid down in front of the Giant bus to block its departure as well as bombarded the vehicle with beer bottles, cans, rocks, and whatever else they could find. (All just a few yards away from the peace shrine.)

Playing against Hiroshima can indeed be hazardous as one Giant player here describes.

We were playing a game in Citizen's Park one night when the stadium lights went out. I was in the outfield, so I started to walk in toward the dugout. A few seconds later, the lights came back on, so I returned to my position. There was a huge rock lying on the grass, exactly where I had been standing. If I had not moved, they would have had to carry me out on a stretcher.

Gripped by pennant fever, the citizens of Hiroshima hit their peak in September 1975, during a crucial game with the Chunichi Dragons. A Carp runner, while attempting to score the tying run with two outs in the 9th inning, was tagged in the face a bit too hard to be accidental. Both benches emptied and a flood of Carp fans rushed to the aid of their heroes. After the one-sided melee was broken up, a dozen Dragon players and coaches had to be treated for injuries. The incident prompted the Carp general manager to make a tearful public apology and to cancel the following night's game as a gesture of atonement.

Fans of the Taiheiyo Club Lions in Fukuoka also have their moments—especially when the Lotte Orions are in town. The Lions and the Orions have had numerous brawls with the Orion manager, the vociferous Masaichi Kaneda, usually right in the thick of things.

The rambunctious Kaneda has a particular talent for arousing the ire of Fukuoka fans. One night in 1974 a spectator tossed a beer bottle into the Lotte dugout. Kaneda, not one to put up with such things, grabbed a bat and repeatedly struck at the offender through the wire fence that separated the dugout from the stands. Only the presence of the park police and Kaneda's bat prevented the fans from making an all-out assault.

Fans in the Kansai region (Osaka, Kobe) have also been known to commandeer a stadium or two. In one important game between the Hankyu Braves and the Orions at Osaka's Nishinomiya Stadium, the Orion owner, angered over an umpire's decision, suddenly removed his players from the diamond. The umpires consequently ruled the game a forfeit to the Braves. But the fans, irate over seeing the game end prematurely, blocked the stadium exit where the Orion bus was waiting. The besieged team had to lie low in the clubhouse for nearly two hours before they could sneak out through a centerfield exit.

By the next day, the same fan who was thirsting for blood the night

Masaichi Kaneda discusses matters in his inimitable way with the Taiheiyo Club Lions' catcher

before, is a calm, peace-loving human being, who, likely as not, will appear at the ballpark carrying a placard calling for "good manners" from all baseball fans. Incongruous as it may seem, his "temporary insanity" is forgotten—which is all a part of being Japanese.

Oddly enough, in Tokyo there is practically no violence. The average Tokyoite, an out-of-towner with pretensions to sophistication, is simply too refined to participate in such barbaric actions. Consequently, Tokyo sets the standard for good stadium behavior throughout the country.

Perhaps the biggest complaint the Japanese baseball fan should have about his favorite game is the poor umpiring. The irrational, biased, and tremulous manner in which the Japanese umpire "controls" a game has wrought much havoc on the field and gone far to retard the development of true professionalism in Japan.

Consider what happens when a call is disputed in American major-league baseball. The American umpire will take just so much from an irate manager or player before there reaches a point, usually not more than three minutes into an argument, when one more word means ejection from the game. End of argument. The umpire may even draw a line on the ground and walk away. If the disputant dares cross it, he is out of the game.

In Japan, although calls are seldom disputed (it is considered "impolite" to argue with the umpire), when an argument does occur, it can be endless. The umpires are just not "fearless enough"—as even the commissioner's office has complained—to simply expel a manager who will not stop arguing.

The more stature a manager has, the more leeway an umpire will give him. Managers have been known to argue calls for as long as an hour and a half. Some will simply stand on the field, arms folded, and say nothing—a silent demonstration of their opposition to the call. Others will take their teams off the field and refuse to play until they feel they have embarrassed the man in blue sufficiently to resume the game. The umpire does nothing more than plead for cooperation—which can be very disconcerting to fans watching the standard one hour and 26 minute broadcast on television.

So sensitive are the umpires to their position in the pecking order that, on occasion, they can even be "persuaded" to change a decision—a display of weakness that would be considered sacrilege in the U.S. where an umpire's decision is final. The result is usually chaos.

In one game between the Yomiuri Giants and the Chunichi Dragons, a Giant batter singled, overran the bag at first on a bluff attempt toward second, and was called out by the umpire as he was trying to get back to the base. Giant Manager Kawakami and his player argued the call and the umpire, after discussing the situation with his cohorts, agreeably reversed his decision for the venerable Yomiuri pilot. This so enraged Dragon Manager Michio Nishizawa that he began shoving the umpire and then spent the better part of the next hour protesting the call, but to no avail.

Such scenarios are not uncommon in Japan. An umpire once changed his ruling over a play three times in the span of 45 minutes, while another saw fit to apologize to the fans for making an initial error in judgment after he had changed his decision. Still a third was eventually persuaded to reverse his decision on a game-ending play, and called both teams back from the dressing room to resume the game.

Typically, disputed calls require a group discussion. The umpire-in-chief will assemble the other five umpires (there are seldom more than four in the States) and together they will discuss and analyze the situation at length—taking into account such factors as which manager has more stature, who argued the hardest, and whether the hometown fans will riot if they don't like the ruling. Each umpire's opinion is solicited, with the younger ones careful not to air their views too strongly. The group will then rediscuss and reanalyze the problem until—in a way that is peculiar to Japanese group decision making—a *consensus* emerges. The umpire-in-chief will then announce the decision and make an agonizing appeal to the "losing" manager to accept the result.*

Japanese umpires are also widely attacked for playing favorites.

---

* An American umpire will ask for help only if he is unsure of the call. A quick check with another umpire nearest the play—or the umpire-in-chief—and the call is made, the decision is final. There is no further discussion.

Players and fans alike have referred obliquely over the years to the "Kaneda strike" and the "Oh ball." The "Oh ball" is a pitch on the edge of the strike zone which if Oh takes it is called a ball. The umpire appears to have reasoned that Oh, who has the best pair of eyes in baseball, only swings at strikes. And who is he to question the judgment of a great batter like Oh? The same thought process was applied to Kaneda's deliveries in his pitching days.

This may be similar to the sort of intimidation American umpires must have felt when Ted Williams brought his famed 20-15 vision to the batter's box, but it is much more pronounced in Japan. As one American player remarked after watching pitching-great Tetsuya Yoneda breeze through another winning season at age 40: "Yoneda can throw nothing but balls and still win in Japan. The umpires give him the edge." Such is the deference superior veteran ballplayers can command from the arbiters in Japan.

Perhaps Giant star Shigeo Nagashima has come closer than anyone

This unusual photo of two umpires joining forces to call a play at second base resulted from the fact that the Japanese have six umpires for each game compared to four in the U.S.

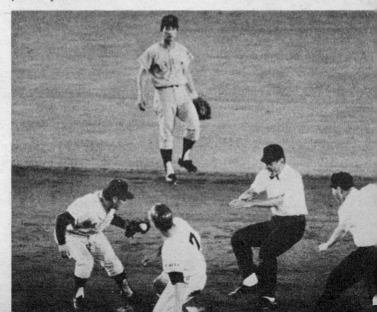

else to persuading an umpire to reverse a called third strike (something no umpire—even in Japan—has ever done). Nagashima once protested when a rookie pitcher struck him out, and the plate umpire *almost* changed his mind. In deference to the great superstar, the plate umpire held a short conference with his brethren before he confirmed that the pitch was in fact a strike and would have to stand.

Umpires hotly deny these attacks, but in the words of at least one Japanese manager: "They say they're not biased, but they are. It's so obvious. It really makes us mad." There was a player who believed this to be especially true during Nagashima's last few years. "As Nagashima's ability decreased," he said, "so did his strike zone. If I had the strike zone he did I'd bat .300 every year."

The alleged favoritism shown toward pennant winning teams— which in most years has meant the Yomiuri Giants—has been an additional bone of contention. As one player who watched the Giants sweep to pennants year after year complained: "The Giants would never swing at a near strike. They got every favorable call by the umpires." Another malcontent added: "Once I had two strikes on me in a game, and the next pitch was so far outside I couldn't have hit it if I'd wanted to. So I checked my swing. But the Giant catcher told the umpire that I'd foul tipped it and the umpire then called me out."

The story about Giant favoritism that baseball people most like to tell occurred in the sixth game of the 1961 Japan Series between the Giants and the Nankai Hawks of Osaka. The Giants were leading the series three games to two; but the Hawks were threatening to tie it all up. In the bottom of the 9th inning of that sixth game, the Hawks were protecting a one-run lead. With two out, the Giants had runners on second and third. American pitcher Joe Stanka was on the mound for the Hawks. He had worked the count to a ball and two strikes. One more strike and the game would be over; the series tied. Stanka wound up and fired a perfect strike. Everyone in the park knew it.

"Ball," the umpire intoned. "Ball?" Stanka and the Hawks roared.

When the smoke had cleared from the near-riot that followed, a disgusted Stanka returned to the mound. The Giant batter lined the next pitch into left-center field. One runner scored. Stanka raced to cover home and bowled over the plate umpire who had somehow managed to get in the way. From a prone position several feet from the plate, the umpire valiantly signaled "safe" as the second Giant runner crossed the plate to give Yomiuri the Japan Championship.

The Japanese umpire is perhaps weakest in the intricacies of the game. There are no formal umpire schools in Japan as there are in the States, so the aspirant must learn what he can through amateur, semi-pro, and minor-league competition. The resulting gaps in his knowledge have accounted for yet another contribution to the game of baseball—"creative umpiring."

A pitcher once sent his throw richocheting off home plate. The umpire's call? Foul ball. In another contest, a fielder raced back after a soaring drive to deep center. Unable to catch the ball, he managed to slap it back down onto the playing field with his glove. This time it was a home run.

The one that tops them all, however, occurred in the late innings of a closely fought match between the Giants and the Dragons at Kora-kuen Stadium in 1964. It started when Jim Marshall of the Dragons lofted a fly ball to deep left field. The leftfielder backed to the wall and leaped, but the ball tipped off his outstretched glove and into the hands of an eager fan in the first row. "Out," was the signal. "Fan interference."

Marshall and the Dragons were stupified. They surrounded the umpire and argued until they were exhausted. But the ruling stood, even after the leftfielder later admitted that it was in fact a home run.

Occurrences like these are admittedly rare, but they happen often enough to make Bill Klem's "I ain't ever called one wrong" inappropriate as an umpire's rallying cry for Japan. More fitting perhaps are the immortal words of one of Japan's own great men in blue, Nobuaki Nidegawa. His now famous decree, "I am the rule book" gave his confreres just the motto they sought.

It is difficult to remember the last time an American player laid hands on an umpire. But in Japan the expression "Kill the umpire" seems to be taken quite literally. Drunken fans, in fits of "temporary insanity," will rush on the field to assault him, only to be stopped and escorted back to their seats by the park police. (Just another aspect of *fan sābisu*.) While irate players and managers who shove, push, kick,

In Chon Paik has a slight disagreement with the plate umpire over a called third strike

and punch the umpire face only a small fine and, upon rare occasions, a light suspension.

In Chon Paik, a fiery Korean catcher for the Toei Flyers, was once so incensed over a called third strike that he pushed the plate umpire and screamed "*Bakayarō!*" (Literally, "You stupid SOB.") When the umpire ordered Paik out of the game, the ballplayer leapt on the umpire, threw him to the ground, ripped off his mask, and rained blow after blow upon the hapless official before being restrained by his teammates. Paik was fined 50,000 yen ($150) for his attack, and the incident was forgotten. By everyone except the umpire, that is.

The battle-scarred umpires find themselves in this predicament because they do not enjoy the full support of the baseball establishment. A year's suspension or a substantial fine would probably halt such incidents, but the baseball commissioner holds his position at the whim of the owners, who do not want to alienate their fans by depriving them of a popular player simply because of his "temporary insanity." Owners would rather use "friendly persuasion" to maintain peace in the park.

8 BIG FISh, LITTLE pond

The burly, hirsute American spits contemptuously into the dirt and steps into the batter's box. He towers over the frail youth out on the mound as he waves his gigantic bat back and forth. His red eyes narrow; he sneers triumphantly. Glaring out at the mound, he emits a low, menacing snarl and growls: "Come on, baby!"

The count is *tsu-nasshingu* (no balls and two strikes). The hulking foreigner lashes the first two pitches thrown to him completely out of the stadium, but foul by inches. The young Japanese hurler has been brought in to pitch relief in the 9th inning to protect a one-run lead. He retired the first two men to face him, but after now giving up two near home runs to this beast in the batter's box, he seems reluctant to pitch again.

Standing alone on the mound, he looks childlike and fragile. He stares at the massive, leering figure and pales. His knees begin to shake and he wonders if he has the strength to throw another pitch. But then, magically, the words of his high school coach come to him: "*Otoko dattara yareru*" (If you're a man, you can do it). Simple words, but they somehow strengthen his resolve.

Tightening his lips, he toes the rubber, goes into his windup and lets fly with every ounce of strength he has. Halfway to the batter the ball rises two feet, then drops sharply and does three loops as it crosses the plate. The monster in the batter's box lets out a terrible groan as he swings with all his might and misses. Spinning around, he falls to the ground with a tremendous crash.

The crowd of 50,000 lets out a mighty roar. The game is over. The home team has won. And the untried rookie has defeated the feared American. (Scene from the animated television weekly *Kyojin no Hoshi*, Star of the Giants. The American was patterned on Daryl

Spencer, former San Francisco Giant shortstop, who played a number of years in Japan.)

The American has been a big, if somewhat unnerving, force in Japanese baseball since 1951—when a young Hawaiian named Wally Yonamine first appeared on the scene. Yonamine, a Nisei, was not the first American to play in Japan,* but he was by far the most important. Because he was the first American after World War II, he became, in effect, an Oriental Jackie Robinson. Feelings still ran high against Japan's former enemy, and bringing in an American was a potentially explosive move. Opening the doors to American players, however, was a categorical imperative if Japan was to improve the level of her game, and someone had to be the guinea pig.

Yonamine, perhaps the greatest all-around athlete to come out of Hawaii, began his career as a professional football player. In 1950, the 5'9" 165 pounder starred in the backfield of Frankie Albert and the San Francisco 49er's. When an injury ended his promising career, Yonamine turned to baseball. He signed on with the San Francisco Seals of the old Pacific Coast League and was farmed out to their Salt Lake City Class C team where he promptly began hitting at a .360 clip.

That same year, the Yomiuri Giants of Japan's Central League decided to sign an American. They wanted someone who would draw fans and help the Japanese improve their game. Government officials and Occupation authorities approved the idea, hoping it would forge closer ties between Japan and the United States.

Initially it was thought best, however, to avoid the blue-eyed, fair-skinned American stereotype, since memories of the war were still fresh. Consequently, at the recommendation of San Francisco Seals' Manager Lefty O'Doul, the Giants opted for Yonamine.

Yonamine arrived in May 1951 and his first appearance proved a dramatic one, not only because of his nationality but also for what he did at bat.

---

* Pre-war foreigners included pitcher Victor Starfin (1936–1955), who won 300 games; Bozo Wakabayashi (1936–1953) a Nisei pitcher who won 240 games; Bucky Harris, an American catcher who played in the late 1930's until ordered out of the country because of the impending war; and Go Sho Shei, a Taiwanese who became the first foreigner to win a batting title—taking the crown in 1942.

Called upon for a pinch-hit sacrifice in a closely fought game, Yonamine laid down a perfect bunt and astonished the capacity crowd of curious onlookers at Korakuen by *running* furiously all the way to first base. The Japanese were not accustomed to that. No one *ran* to first on a sacrifice. The batter usually tapped the ball with his bat and then stood there. To the Japanese, that wasn't loafing; they just didn't understand the importance of hustling. The batter saw no reason to run because the odds were he'd be out. The idea of a bad throw by the fielder seemed too remote. That was percentage baseball, Japanese style.

Yonamine quickly stepped into the starting lineup and demonstrated what American hustle was all about. As the Giants' leftfielder, he was a fleet-footed ball hawk who chased down everything hit left of center—again a revelation to the Japanese who were used to staying in their own third of the outfield. As the team's lead-off man, he demonstrated time and again the importance of running out easy grounders. Yonamine was an superb batter, a .300 hitter who once amazed Giant fans by fouling off 14 straight pitches until he got the one he wanted.

Yet, it was Yonamine's aggressive style of play on the basepaths that made the country take notice. Though it nearly led to his undoing, he introduced the hard slide at second base to break up the double play. The idea was to upset the fielder or try to kick the ball out of his glove to prevent him from throwing to first. These were standard tactics in America—good, hard-nosed aggressive baseball—but the Japanese did not appreciate them. The first time Yonamine tried a hard slide, the umpire called him out for interference, and the fans grumbled that he was a dirty player.

The Yonamine experiment faced other difficulties as well, quite unrelated to his style of play. And it was not long before the Giants and certain government officials began to fear they had made a terrible mistake. They had not weighed the enormous store of resentment the nation felt toward the American Nisei. By and large, Japanese viewed Nisei as traitors because they had remained loyal to America during the war. There were many who hated Japanese-Americans passionately, and this made life very difficult for Yonamine.

Not a day went by that Yonamine did not hear the phrase *"Hawaii e kaere!*" (Go back to Hawaii) or "Yankee go home!" Since Yonamine didn't know much Japanese the fans would use what little English they knew—sometimes simply yelling "1-2-3" hoping this would upset him. They would also throw things from the stands and on one occasion, after a famous "dirty" slide, several fans actually dashed on the field and chased him into the dugout.

The young pioneer was in a delicate position. The eyes of an entire nation were upon him and Yonamine was under tremendous pressure. As he later recalled:

I went through hell that first year. I couldn't count the number of times I heard the phrase "Yankee Go Home." The Japanese didn't like me because I was a Nisei and because they thought I was a dirty player. But I knew I had to make them change their minds—for the others after me as well as myself.

I tried to do everything exactly the same way as the Japanese. I ate at the training table with them. I ate the same food they did—*tamago meshi* (a mixture of eggs and rice) three times a day. I lost a lot of weight that first year.

It was cold in the early months of the spring, especially after a place like Hawaii. There were no gas heaters in the rooms then; only a *hibachi*. And we'd have those long train rides—12 hours to Osaka, 18 hours to Hiroshima, 26 hours to Sapporo. The team always traveled third class. We'd sit on hard benches in cramped coaches, huddled around the *hibachi*. Sometimes it was so cold we had to put our uniforms on over our other clothes to keep warm.

In the summertime, it was even worse. Hot and humid. I'd get a big block of ice and put it in front of the fan and just lie there.

The players were really good to me. I remember the first night I got to Japan. I stayed up all night talking with a few of them. I couldn't speak any Japanese, and they couldn't speak any English, but we communicated with sign language and baseball terms. After three months, I could do without an interpreter.

Yonamine's forbearance paid off. He made it through his first season with an impressive .354 batting average, helping the Giants to both a pennant and a Japan Series win. And despite the dirty player tag, his overall fine play and sincere, modest manner eventually won him a large following. At year's end, team leader Shigeru Chiba approached Yonamine and said: "Wally, as a rule, we Japanese don't like Nisei. But you did what we did. You're a good man. You come back here to live and we'll back you up anyway we can."

Yonamine returned the following season, and went on to become the biggest American star ever to play in Japan. He captured three batting titles, with a season high of .361 and his rivalries with Giant first-baseman Tetsuharu Kawakami for league batting honors became legend. He was voted Most Valuable Player once, and was elected to the sportswriters' all-star team seven years in a row. His determined play on the field helped the Giants to eight pennants in his ten years on the club. He retired with a lifetime batting average of .311, and is still considered the greatest lead-off batter in Japanese baseball history.

At the end, unfortunately, the Giants treated Yonamine rather shabbily. In 1960, his tenth year in baseball, he slumped to .232 and the Giants informed him he was to be released. Retired first-baseman and Giant coach Tetsuharu Kawakami was going to take over as manager. Kawakami intended to build a team of pure-blooded and pure-hearted Japanese, and his old batting rival was not part of the plan. The Giants offered Yonamine one million yen (then $2800) as a retirement bonus if he would go back to Hawaii, but only 500,000 if he chose to stay in Japan and play for another team. Yonamine wanted to stay and made one last request to the Giants—delay the news of his release, so that he could take advantage of the rule which allowed ten-year veterans to declare themselves free-agents and negotiate with other teams. If the Giants announced his release, Yonamine reasoned, it would hurt his bargaining position and he might lose as much as $40,000. The Giants ignored his request, however, and Yonamine eventually signed with the Chunichi Dragons for $15,000. He played two more years.

In his first encounter against his former team, Yonamine hit a game-winning home run. The Hawaiian samurai had returned to haunt the master who had so thoughtlessly cast him out. It was poetic justice in the great Japanese tradition of revenge.

The successful Yonamine experiment opened the floodgates, and in poured a bevy of foreign players, including some of the blue-eyed genre. Players not good enough to make the big-leagues or even Triple A headed for exotic Japan to seek out higher salaries and a

Wally Yonamine, the Japanese-American manager of the Chunichi Dragons, just after his team won the 1974 Central League pennant to break the Giants' 9-year stranglehold on the flag

chance to star. Such unknowns as Roberto Barbon, Jun Hirota, Larry Raines, Andy Miyamoto, Carlton Hanta, Mike Solomko, Stanley Hashimoto, Bill Nishida, Glen Mickens, Jack Bloomfield, and Carl Peterson made names for themselves on the diamonds of the Central and Pacific Leagues. Raines, who went on to play for the Cleveland Indians in the late 1950s, won a batting title. And Bloomfield, a Pacific Coast League reject, won two—including a .374 mark, the highest an American has ever hit.

Needless to say, the level of Japanese baseball in those days was extremely low. In addition to their ability on the field and novelty value at the gate, what these foreign imports had to teach about the fundamentals of the game was highly valued. But as the quality of play improved year by year, the average American minor-leaguer found it increasingly difficult to make the grade in Japan.

A major turning point came in 1962, when the Taiyo Whales of the

Central League announced the signing of Jim McManus, a 6' 4" first-baseman from the Hawaiian Islanders of the Pacific Coast League. McManus was a minor-league all-star—a powerful .300, 20 home run a year hitter. He was physically the biggest American any Japanese team had ever recruited. The Whales were certain that his size and his strength—and the smaller Japanese ballparks—would make McManus a home-run king. The Whales front office confidently predicted that he would hit forty home runs in his first year. The press went even further: "Fifty," some speculated. "Perhaps he will break Roger Maris' home-run record." After all, he was an all-star in Triple A ball. Since it was the consensus of opinion that the Japanese were roughly on the same level as an American Class A team, logic had it that McManus would be nearly three times as good playing in the weaker Japanese league.

McManus's arrival at Haneda Airport was greeted with big picture spreads in the dailies, and lead stories on the TV sports news.

McManus had been signed for a figure in the neighborhood of $25,000 (a considerable sum in Japan at the time). In addition, he received a house specially constructed for him by the Whales, an automobile and travel expenses that included separate lodging at Western-style hotels when the team was on the road. McManus was an immediate sensation in Japan without having played a single game. He himself modestly predicted a season of .300, 30 home runs, and 100 RBIs. Briefly stated, McManus was a bitter disappointment. He wound up the season batting .260, hit only 12 home runs, and drove in a scant 52.

That same spring, as the Whales were pulling in their big catch, the Chunichi Dragons of Nagoya scored a coup of their own. They signed former Brooklyn Dodger pitching great Don Newcombe and ex-Cleveland Indian slugging star Larry Doby to contracts similar to the one McManus signed.

Newcombe and Doby, both in retirement, made it clear from the outset that they were coming to Japan only for "good will" purposes. Admittedly over the hill, these two made no promises or predictions of batting titles or broken records. Nevertheless, the Japanese baseball world was buzzing with anticipation. Retired or not, real flesh and blood major-league stars would be wearing the uniform of a Japanese professional team for the very first time.

Newcombe arrived in May and played first base for the rest of the season. (He had been a feared batter in his glory days on the mound for the Dodgers.) Out of shape, overweight, and running as if he were "carrying two pianos," as one team official put it, Newcombe turned in a .262, 15 home-run season. Doby, hampered by a bad ankle, was less successful. He arrived in June and batted .225 with only 12 home runs. Yet Doby once astounded everyone when he hit a tremendous 500 foot shot over the centerfield fence into the teeth of a typhoon wind. The Japanese had never seen such a blast.

Observing Doby and Newcombe in action was a sobering experience for the Japanese. Granted, the two were in retirement. Yet they had still been major-league stars! The ground did not shake when they walked and there was no lightning or thunder when they stepped into the batter's box. The McManus fiasco had shown that American Triple A stars were mere mortals; now Doby and Newcombe created doubts as to the divinity of major leaguers. Could it be the Japanese were really not so bad? Could it be that with the 1961 major-league expansion in America, they were now on par with U.S. Triple A teams?

The events of 1962 gave the Japanese pause for reflection. Perhaps it was time for a major reassessment of their game. One commentator wrote:

Importing former major leaguers and active Triple A players on the basis of past showing only serves to lower the status of Japanese pro ball. Most American players who come here are over thirty and have seen their best days. Many of them have something to teach the Japanese such as continuous hustling and abiding by the fundamentals. But there are many other things to be done to nurture Japanese players before importing American players.

Added another: "I think there is very little difference in the performance of Japanese players and foreigners who come here to play." The Pacific League Players Union went so far as to declare that it wanted the owners to stop hiring foreign players because "it takes away jobs from local players and Japan's pro ball should now be played by Japanese alone."

Early in 1963, the Japanese Commissioner of Baseball ruled that the number of foreign players permitted on each team be lowered from three to two. And at the same time the Yomiuri Giants announced that henceforth they were officially instigating a no-foreigner policy.

Other team owners were not eager to let the rising wave of chauvinism prevent them from strengthening their clubs. Rightly realizing that Doby and Newcombe were way past their prime, they decided to go after "genuine major leaguers"—which meant not those in retirement, but those who still had a few years of play left. "Let's see what they·can do," urged the owners. The word was out, however, that there would be no "baseball diplomats." * The novelty of American ballplayers was wearing thin and owners wanted only those who could help their team win a pennant.

The next few years saw the dawning of the "big-league era" in Japan. Front office officials went after the best available American talent and, at often incredible expense, succeeded in recruiting a number of "name" major leaguers to play out the remaining seasons of their careers in Japan. Two of them, Jim Marshall and Daryl Spencer, did much to brighten the tarnished American image.

Marshall, a former reserve first-baseman with the San Francisco Giants, was lured to the Chunichi Dragons by a contract most players at that time only dreamt about. He was paid a reported $40,000—more money than even Giants' stars Shigeo Nagashima and Sadaharu Oh received then. In addition, the Dragons paid his taxes, secured an expensive apartment for his family in Tokyo, installed him

---

* The tone was set before the 1963 season, when Newcombe said he would be glad to play another season for the Dragons, but stipulated that he start late and finish early because of other commitments. A league spokesman, obviously no longer in agreement with the big right-hander's view of himself as a "good-will ambassador," chided Newcombe, saying: "Newk should show more fighting spirit if he hopes to play Japanese baseball this season." Newcombe did not return to Japan.

in the most luxurious western style hotel in Nagoya, and paid all his transportation expenses. A Yankee official upon hearing of the deal told the Dragons they were crazy.

But the 32-year old Marshall—never a power hitter in the U.S.— played well. Although not in Oh or Nagashima's class, he began blasting the ball at a 30 home-run, .280 a year clip and was selected for the all-star team all three of his years in Japan.

Spencer was an even better investment. The former San Francisco Giant shortstop signed with the last place Pacific League Hankyu Braves in 1964 for $22,500 plus benefits. Spencer, though 35, quickly established himself as one of the league's most dangerous home-run threats, demonstrating the consistent and awesome home-run power the Japanese expected from Americans as he put together seasons of 34, 38, 30, 20, and 30. Spencer was twice elected to the prestigious sportswriters' all-star team. Dubbed the "monster," this 6'3" 210 pounder was credited with changing the "gray mood" of the lowly Braves. By Spencer's fourth year, the Braves had moved from the cellar to a league pennant.

Not all Japanese teams were as fortunate as the Dragons and the Braves, however. Celebrated big-league stars like former Milwaukee Brave shortstop Johnny Logan and the home-run hitting infielder of the Detroit Tigers, Chico Fernandez, signed large contracts and were abysmal failures at the plate. Logan, a perennial National League All-Star and one of the best hit-and-run batters in baseball, was signed by the Nankai Hawks. Logan was asked to bat third and expected to hit 30 home runs. He hit seven and batted a dismal .189. He also set a Japan record by going hitless 38 straight times at bat. Fernandez, playing for the Hanshin Tigers, fared even worse. He hit one home run and batted a microscopic .144. Billy Klaus and Reno Bertoia, former major leaguers of some reknown, were also signed with high expectations. Klaus batted .257 and Bertoia .175. Former Oriole slugger Chuck Essegian was expected to hit well over 30 home runs. He managed 15.

The owners who shelled out these large amounts of money were shocked. How could any "authentic" American major leaguer do so poorly in Japan they wondered. It was becoming clear that even for active big leaguers, prior performance was simply one qualification for success in Japan. It seemed to require a certain type of player to adjust. That player not only had to cope with different living conditions and the language barrier, but he had also to become accustomed to a variety of "submarine" and sidearm pitchers, a different strike zone (higher and wider), and a totally different philosophy toward life as well as sports.* It was painfully apparent that some major-league veterans found these adjustments simply too hard to make.

Furthermore, it was pointed out, there were American players with little or no big-league experience who logged impressive records in Japan while their much-ballyhooed and overpaid American counterparts were struggling to keep their heads above water. In 1964, for example, two unheralded former minor-leaguers, Gene Bacque and Joe Stanka pitched their teams to pennants. Stanka, a former White Sox farmhand in his fifth year as a Hawk pitcher, won 26 games and was chosen the Pacific League's Most Valuable Player (the only American besides Yonamine to be so honored in modern times).† Bacque, a 27-year-old ex-Detroit property in his third year as a Hanshin Tiger, led the Central League with 29 wins and a 1.89 ERA—for which he received the Sawamura award as the best pitcher in Japanese baseball.

The Pacific League Toei Flyers became the first team to really stiffen their attitudes toward the "over-the-hill boys" when they negotiated with ex-Dodger batting star Norm Larker. Larker demanded what other American big-leaguers of his stature had received—a high salary and benefits; including extra compensation for a house. The Toei front office balked. Larker would receive the same treatment as

---

* One major obstacle for the American in this regard was the way the Japanese manager used his players. The American who goes hitless in his first two or three times at bat feels more confident of getting a hit his next time up because he has a better idea of what to expect from the pitcher. For that reason, an American manager may well leave him in. The Japanese manager, however, more often regards a player's failure to perform in previous visits to the plate as evidence that he just doesn't have it that night; and so he inserts a pinch-hitter. This practice prevented many an American from ever really gaining his stride in Japan.

† The other MVPs were American Bucky Harris who won the award in 1937 and pitcher Bozo Wakabayashi who won in 1944 and again in 1947.

the Japanese players. As long as he played in Japan, they said, he would have to adjust himself to local conditions. Larker relented and signed for a reported $15,000.

The Flyers' stance struck a responsive chord in many Japanese hearts. A leading daily, *Nikkan Sports,* complaining that the clubs had been "too weak" in their negotiations with American players, happily predicted that the "celestial days for the has-been big-leaguer" were over:

Although these players are past their peak, they have received far more remuneration than Japanese players. Each year, teams pay high amounts ranging from $30,000 to 40,000 and keep our ballplayers salaries down. Japanese baseball people have been thinking that this practice of coddling American has-been players must stop. A ray of hope is seen for realization of this through the action taken by the Toei Flyers.

Nikkan Sports was wrong, however. The "celestial days" were far from over. Despite the high number of overly expensive foreign failures and the widely applauded actions of the Toei front office, the play of Marshall and Spencer was making mouths water. From the mid-1960s on, team owners with pocketsful of yen from Japan's skyrocketing GNP would continue to shell out huge salaries and benefits to active major leaguers with a few years left. They were willing to gamble that a player would turn out to be another Spencer or Marshall and not a Logan or Fernandez.

How has more than a decade of speculating on American players worked out? There have been some success stories. *Don Blasingame,* (Nankai Hawks 1967–1969) was one. The Hawks, after their experience with Johnny Logan, realized that not every major leaguer would automatically become a home-run hitter in Japan. So they let Blasingame do what he did best—bat lead off and patrol the infield. Blasingame hit in the .270's and made the sportswriters' all-star team twice.

Willy Kirkland (Hanshin Tigers 1968–1973) had a low "career" batting mark of only .246 and established a single-season strikeout record of 133, but his home-run bat still won many a game for the Tigers. He had a season high of 37, and once lashed three in a game against the

Former S.F. Giant outfielder Willie Kirkland

Left: Kirkland delivers a mock bow to rival Yomiuri Giant fans at Korakuen Stadium after hitting a home run for the Hanshin Tigers of Osaka   Right: Young Japanese fans welcome Kirkland as he takes his position in right field

hated Giants. The toothpick chewing, wisecracking American was a big hit with Tiger fans in the rightfield bleachers, with whom he would often converse in his fluent Japanese. Kirkland earned the nickname "Western Monjiro" after the toothpick-chewing TV samurai named Monjiro. *Wes Parker* (Nankai Hawks 1974) only played one season in Japan, but the former Dodger first-baseman and Golden Glove winner batted .314 and demonstrated real finesse in the field. *Don Buford* (Taiheiyo Lions 1973–1975, Nankai Hawks 1976) was known in Japan as the "world's greatest lead-off man," when he left the Orioles to take a record $80,000 contract with the Lions. Buford rebounded from a .242 "rookie" season to hit .330 in his second year and .276 in his third. He averaged 15 home runs a year. *George Altman* (Lotte Orions 1968–1974, Hanshin Tigers 1975) is Japan's grand old American. When he left the Hanshin Tigers at the age of 43 in 1975, "Daddy Long Legs," as the versatile Japanese press dubbed the high-hipped outfielder, had amassed more home runs (205) and more RBIs than any other foreigner. Former Chicago Cub Altman had the best all-around single season of any American ever to play in Japan in 1971 when he was .320/39/103. Altman is also the only American ever to win a RBI title. *Clete Boyer* (Taiyo Whales 1972–1975) was a .270/15-20 home-run man for the Whales while raising defensive sophistication to a new high in Japan. The Japanese had never seen anything like the former New York Yankee star third-baseman of the Mantle/Maris era. In fact so impressed were the Japanese with Boyer's superior knowledge of defense that they were calling him "Dr. Baseball." * *Roger Repoz* (Taiheiyo Club Lions 1973, Yakult Swallows 1974–), a former California Angel, was released by the Taiheiyo Lions after an unproductive, injury-plagued first year. But he then signed on with the Central League Swallows and has been the team's leading home-run hitter ever since, averaging nearly 30 a year.

There have also been a few surprises—unsung minor leaguers who reached new heights in Japan. *Dave Roberts* (Yakult Atoms 1967–1973) was one. Roberts, a former Oriole farmhand, holds the

---

* "I just make the easy plays look impossible," Boyer once said in appraisal of himself.

Ex-Yankee fielding great Clete Boyer makes play at third for Taiyo Whales

season home-run record for Americans in Japan with 40 (Oh hit 49 the same year). He hit 183 "career" home runs and was a two-time all-star. Former Cub property *Clarence Jones* (Nankai Hawks 1970–1973; Kintetsu Buffaloes 1974–) is the most prolific home-run hitter among the imported help. Despite an overall .248 batting average Jones has averaged 34 a year and was leading in career home runs for Americans with more than 230 at the end of the 1976 season. In 1974, Jones hit 38 home runs and became the first American to win a home-run title in Japan since American Bucky Harris won the title in the spring season of 1937 (Japan played a split season until 1939), when he walloped six out of the park. *John Sipin* (Taiyo Whales 1972–) came to the Whales at 26 from the Hawaiian Islanders and has been the Central League's all-star second-baseman ever since. A solid 30 home run, .290 a year man, Sipin is probably more popular among female fans than any other American. The press has dubbed the shaggy-maned Sipin "Lion-Man" after a popular TV cartoon hero. *Gene Martin* (Chunichi Dragons 1974–) hit 35 home runs

John Sipin, a former San Diego Padre and Hawaiian Islander, leaps for an errant throw. The young Taiyo Whales' second baseman is one of the most successful Americans ever to play in Japan

in his first year and powered his team to a Central League pennant. Formerly the property of the White Sox, he is one of few Americans to have his name immortalized in song.* And *Bo Dawson* (Taiyo Whales 1974), the 14-year-old son of a U.S. Army colonel, was signed out of Camp Zama for an estimated one-thousand yen ($3.33) a game. A virtual unknown, this hustling youngster went on to become one of

* The song in question was written to commemorate the Dragons' championship and Martin's part goes as follows:

> *In the distant night sky*
> *One can hear the cry of the Dragon*
> *Echoing in the packed Chunichi Stadium*
> *We the fans are hypnotized*
>
> *First batter Takagi—on base*
> *Second batter Taniki—sacrifice bunt*
> *Third batter Inoue—timely hit*
> *Fourth batter Martin—home run*
>
> *That's good, Come on Dragons!*
> *Burn Dragons!*

the most popular bat-boys in Whale history.

But there have been far too many disappointments. Among "name" Americans who failed to live up to expectations were Don Zimmer, Dick Stuart, Jim Gentile, Zolio Versalles, Frank Howard, and Joe Pepitone. *Don Zimmer* signed with the Toei Flyers in 1966 at the age of 34. Zimmer was small but had always hit with power as a Dodger, and the Flyers expected him to manage at least 30 home runs a year. Zimmer hit .182 and nine home runs. In 1966 *Dick Stuart* became the first "authentic" slugger to be snared from the States. Only two years before Stuart had blasted 42 round trippers and won the American League RBI crown (118) while with the Red Sox. The Whales expected the 6′ 3″ 210 pounder to give Sadaharu Oh a run for the home-run title. Instead Stuart hit 33 in his first year (Oh hit 48) and he struck out 100 times. Furthermore his fielding was atrocious. Known variously in America as "Dr. Strangeglove," and the "Ancient Mariner" who stoppeth one of three, Stuart made so many errors in Japan that he found himself on the bench his second season. The disenchanted Stuart asked for his release with more than a month left and departed for the States. After his return home, Stuart signed on with the California Angels as a pinch-hitter. Japan's baseball isolationists were delighted. Stuart had become the first "cast-off" from Japanese professional baseball to play in the major leagues. *Jim Gentile* was greeted by the Kintetsu Buffaloes in 1969 with much expectation and anticipation. Gentile once hit 46 home runs as a Baltimore Oriole, and also won an RBI title. But, alas, Gentile had knee problems and hit only eight home runs.

Zolio Versalles was another first in Japanese efforts to sign top American talent. The Carp signed this former American League MVP (Versalles had won it while playing for 1965 Minnesota Twins) in 1972 with high hopes, but Versalles batted only .189. *Frank Howard* was an even greater find. The awesome power hitter, a 6′ 8″ 275 pound behemoth who had hit 382 major-league home runs—most of them for the Dodgers—had been released by the Detroit Tigers and was enticed to Japan by the Taiheyo Lions in 1974 for $80,000. The Japanese had never seen a baseball player of his enormous size and the crowds at Lion exhibition games were overflowing. Howard injured his knee, however, and batted only twice that season—a costly $40,000 per plate appearance.

Joe Pepitone was probably the worst investment of all. In 1973 the Yakult Atoms paid $70,000 to the Atlanta Braves for Pepitone's release and another $70,000 to the former Yankee problem child for his signature on a contract. Pepitone played only 14 games and caused considerable anguish during his brief stay. But more about that later.

The list goes on and on but, suffice it to say, *Nikkan Sports* has ample reason for its editorial tirades against overpaid, overrated Americans. Of the nearly 200 American players who have tried their hand in Japan, less than half were asked back for a second year and less than one third stayed any longer than that.*

The Japanese simply have no way of knowing how an American will turn out. As one manager said: "We don't know if they're over the hill, how healthy they are, or if they can make the necessary adjustment."

In fact, most managers seldom see the player their club has signed to a fat contract until he reports to training. One ridiculous case involved Arturo Lopez (Lotte Orions 1968–1971; Yakult Atoms 1972–73). The Orions signed the left-handed Yankee farmhand thinking he was Hector Lopez, the former power-hitting All-Star third-baseman. The Orions realized their mistake when Arturo arrived in camp and was asked to play third base. The surprised Arturo replied, "If you don't mind a left-handed third-baseman, then I don't mind." Lopez wound up in the outfield, and fortunately for the Orions proved a solid .300/20 home-run a year man.

Why then do owners continue to risk big money on unproven commodities? Perhaps, as a decade before, they still like the odds. Or maybe they simply feel more important with a vintage star like Boyer

---

* This despite rare windfall years like 1976 when almost every team in the two leagues unexpectedly found itself being led by an American. To the shock of everyone, batting leader lists were suddenly inundated with a slew of foreigners: Walt (No Neck) Williams, Bobby Marcano, Gail Hopkins, Richie Scheinblum, Hal Breeden; in addition to such old standbys as Roger Repoz, John Sipin, Gene Martin, and Clarence Jones. All were flirting with either the .300 mark and/or 30 home runs a year.

or Howard on their team. Who knows?

If the highly paid American doesn't work out, however, he can at least be made the scapegoat for the club's failure. "If only the *gaijin* (foreigner) had come through. All that money we paid him, and he let us down. If only he'd done better, we might have won." In Japan, like everywhere else, having someone to take the blame is often a welcome thing.

The American in Japan has never been the object of public adulation—no matter how well he performs. He may be voted to the all-star team if he does exceptionally well, although several players with statistics in the top ten have been left far behind in the ballot count. The American is rarely asked to make an endorsement or a public appearance, and no American has ever been on the cover of *Baseball Magazine*. Some have developed a following—Buford, Blasingame, Altman, Sipin, Roberts were all well-liked by the fans. And Spencer was so popular for a while that he had to stop riding the trains to the ballpark. Yet, none has come close to matching the top Japanese on his team.

The fan has too much difficulty relating to the American. He is not Japanese. He can't speak the language and he doesn't know the customs of the land. He is just too different.*

The American seems sometimes to be nothing more than a sideshow attraction. Clete Boyer was hailed as the "World's Second-Best Third-Baseman (after Brooks Robinson)" and Don Buford as the "Greatest Lead-Off Batter on Earth." Speedy Lou Jackson was the "Black Bullet," Dick Stuart was the "Great White Whale," and 6' 8" Frank Howard replaced Daryl Spencer as the "Monster."

---

* Seldom can the Japanese pronounce the American import's name—with the result that it is often changed to suit the Japanese ear. Roberto Barbon became "Chico." Jack Bloomfield was "Bloom." Carl Peterson was "Peeto." Mike Krsnich was "Kris." Gordon Windhorn was "Windy." Chuck Essegian was "Chuck." Chico Fernandez was "Fernando" because Barbon had already laid claim to "Chico." Jim Barbieri was "Babi." Barton Shirley was "Barto." Leon MacFadden was "Mac." Richie Scheinblum was "Shane." And Roger Repoz was "Roger," but not because the Japanese had any difficulty pronouncing Repoz. One day a team official had approached Repoz in camp and asked: "What do you want us to call you?" Repoz amicably replied, "Call me Roger." And that's exactly what the team did—on the official roster.

While Japanese are becoming more accustomed to "foreign" imports, the unpleasant image perpetrated by weekly comic books and the popular animated television series of the 1960s *Kyojin no Hoshi* (Star of the Giants) still lingers. There, the former major leaguer was often portrayed as hairy-chested, unshaven, dirty, and vicious. He was a combination villain/fall guy who time and time again went down to defeat in the face of pure hearted Japanese perseverance and fighting spirit—animated enactments of the fantasy many Japanese fans have of the day when they will *rule* the world of baseball.

The average fan tends to view the American on his favorite team simply as a yardstick. If a Tiger fan, for instance, watches his team's American rightfielder strike out, he may be unhappy but he is consoled by the thought that it was a *Japanese* who struck him out. This demonstrates that Japanese pitching is improving. If an American pitcher gives up a game-winning home run and his team loses, the loss is disappointing but it shows Japanese batting is improving. And if a former big-league star comes to Japan and cannot make the grade, that is even better—Japanese baseball is catching up. Of course, when a Triple A player like John Sipin or Dave Roberts is among the batting leaders, that means the big leagues have "overlooked" his talents.

While the fans do appreciate American hustle and home-run power, they look askance at certain aspects of American play. Those who throw their bats and kick the bench after striking out lack self-control. Players who argue too much with the umpire are impolite— and the American seems to do it all the time. Brushback pitches, hard slides, or "rolling-slams"—all imported by the foreigner—are not *fea pure*, "fair play" in Japan.

As a result, Americans have gotten low conduct ratings on the baseball "report cards" issued by various sports' publications. One such report card, for example, graded Americans in the following categories: batting, defense, running, deportment, and popularity. Pitchers were rated according to: "stuff," control, technique, stamina, deportment, and popularity.

Daryl Spencer usually received high marks in all departments except deportment. The burly infielder had no compunction about flattening a second-baseman to break up a double play. To the Japanese, Spencer was far worse than Yonamine. He was half a foot taller and nearly 50 pounds heavier and when he barreled into a man, everyone in the park could hear the crunch. His style was what Americans admire: "rough and aggressive," but in Japan it lost him points.

In 1967, Spencer "hit for the circuit," so to speak. Playing first base, he started a minor brawl when he fielded a ground ball, wheeled around, and tagged the base-runner a little too hard on the face. A few weeks later, he decommissioned the opposing second-baseman with a vicious slide. Shortly thereafter, another well-aimed slide put the third-baseman out of action with a wound that required ten stitches. The spiking was unintentional, Spencer insisted, but from that time on he was labeled a dirty player. Several weeks later, Spencer roared into home plate, removing the catcher from both the play and the game.

Daryl Spencer celebrates winning the 1972 pennant with his teammates on the Hankyu Braves

When the Japanese accused Spencer of foul play, he retorted that they lacked "fighting spirit." (He had learned.) At any rate, Spencer's brand of play struck fear into the hearts of the opposition. "Our players can't perform without worrying about their safety because of Spencer's rough play," moaned one manager. Pacific League pitchers openly admitted they were throwing at the big American to get even—a breach of Japanese baseball ethics—but it did not faze Spencer in the least. "Let them throw," he shrugged. "It's all part of the game."

Spencer capped off his reign of terror that year by storming into the scorer's booth before a game and ripping the official scoresheet to shreds. The night before, Spencer had been charged with an error on an easy lob he made to the pitcher covering first. The pitcher dropped the ball, but Spencer got the error. He protested through his interpreter, who was not anxious to tell anyone as exalted as the official scorer he was wrong. So Spencer decided to take matters into his own hands. That incident cost him 50,000 yen.

Another low scorer in deportment was ex-Dodger Norm Larker, the center of the "celestial" storm, who in 1965 set the single season record for breaking batting helmets (eight). Larker's temper tantrums drew so much attention that a magazine ran a cartoon depicting him crushing a batting helmet with his foot while breaking a bat in two with his hands. Larker was nonplused. "Smashing a batting helmet or breaking a bat is better than trotting back to the bench smiling after striking out," he explained.

Joe Stanka, a temperamental 6' 3" 200 pound pitcher, had a penchant for the "shaving pitch" as the Japanese called his brushback delivery. Stanka and ex-Oriole Chuck Essegian hold the distinction for starting the only all-American fight in Japanese baseball. Stanka was on the mound and Essegian, who was fuming about an earlier Stanka attempt to decapitate him, was on second base after hitting a double. Essegian hurled an insult at Stanka and in a matter of moments the

*Former Chicago White Sox
pitcher Joe Stanka expresses
his displeasure over a call*

two were trading punches in the center of the diamond. Finally the bewildered Japanese umpires managed to separate the two slugging giants and send them to the showers.

In addition to his ejection for the Essegian fight, Stanka was thrown out of games on three other occasions, twice for "roughing the umpire" and once for "manhandling" the opposing team's manager. These incidents did little to increase his popularity.

Gene Bacque also established less than perfect marks for his conduct on the field. His crimes included making fun of the batter and throwing brushback pitches. Bacque, like Stanka and Spencer, fit the stereotype American image. Big and hairy-chested, his large hooknose simply added to the overall picture. He was one of the few who dared wear the dreaded number "four"—which in Japanese is a homonym for death. (One of the last players to tempt fate by wearing this number was a Giant outfielder who died of typhoid fever during the 1947 season.)

Early in 1965, following Bacque's memorable Sawamura award-winning year, the big right-hander accomplished a feat that no other American in Japan had ever done. He pitched a no-hitter against the mighty Yomiuri Giants. The Giants, who had the same regal pride as the old New York Yankees, were most unhappy. Nobody "no-hits" the Giants and gets away with it. Especially a foreigner.

The whole matter was compounded because Bacque liked to ridicule the batters while he pitched to them. He took particular delight in teasing Giant stars Oh and Nagashima. When they came up to bat, he would scowl, gesture in disdain, throw a strike over the plate, and laugh mockingly. Such conduct in Japan is simply not considered polite. But Bacque, a friendly, easygoing fellow, thought his act was good psychology, even though it lost him deportment points.

This gregarious pitcher also became the first and only foreign player to ignite a major riot when in September 1968 the first-place Giants came into Osaka Stadium to play a four-game series with the Tigers. Once again the Giants and Tigers were locked in one of their perennial pennant battles and, going into the series, the Tokyo team had a three-game lead. The Tigers won the first two games, and Bacque, on his way to a 20 win season, took the mound in Game Three.

Bacque began to dispose of the Giants, including Oh and Naga-shima, in his usual scornful manner, giving up only one run in the first three innings. In the fourth inning, however, the Giants mounted a scoring threat. Two runners reached base safely with none out, and the home-run hitting Oh stepped into the batter's box. Bacque promptly delivered a brushback pitch that sent Oh sprawling. Players on the Giants bench rose from their seats. Bacque glanced over, smiled with his usual disdain, and fired another brushback pitch that sent Oh to the ground for a second time.

That did it. Oh was up in a flash. He started toward the mound bat in hand, but was beaten there by Giant Coach Hiroshi Arakawa and a host of Giant players. Bacque backpedaled toward second-base, ducked one of Arakawa's swings, and launched a roundhouse right of his own that landed flush on the coach's forehead. The two were immediately surrounded by players from both teams and a 15-minute brawl ensued. Fans poured on the field to join the fray, and it was nearly an hour before order was restored and the damage surveyed.

Gene Bacque suffers the consequences of throwing consecutive brushback pitches

Bacque had broken the thumb on his pitching hand. He was out for the season.

When action resumed, the Tiger relief pitcher promptly hit Oh in the head (unintentionally) and put him in the hospital for three days. While the Tigers lost the game and eventually the pennant, Bacque lost so many points in his deportment rating that he was traded to the other league when the season ended.

Deportment also includes language, of course, and ever since the Japanese baseball community began to understand some of the more popular English expletives, Americans have had to watch what they say. Umpire Osamu Tsutsui demonstrated his grasp of basic conversational English in a dialogue with first baseman John Miller of the Chunichi Dragons in 1970. It started when Miller grounded to third and was called out on a close play at first. Miller, apparently angered at the decision, threw his batting helmet toward the umpire. After the side had been retired, Miller took his position on first and, glaring at Tsutsui, muttered, "Bullshit!" Tsutsui told Miller in English to "Be quiet!" But when Miller persisted, the umpire ordered him out of the game.

Chunichi Manager Shigeru Mizuhara, rushing to Miller's defense, insisted that the umpire had misunderstood. What Miller had really said, according to Mizuhara, was "bush." Upon reflecting for a moment Miller recalled that that was in fact the word he had used. Tsutsui, however, declared he knew what Miller had said, and it was definitely *not* "bush." So Miller thus became the first foreign player to be evicted from a game for using English obscenities.

9 ugly americans

February 1, the official opening day of spring training. The public relations director of a Central League team and a dozen or so reporters sit shivering on benches around a rusted charcoal burner in the narrow ground-level enclosure that serves as a press box. Finishing his announcement, the slightly built official turns to his American visitors and offers them a steaming cup of *Ocha*—Japanese green tea. "Please drink," he says, "it will warm your blood."

He shifts his gaze toward the group of players jogging silently around the field. It is ten in the morning, and the temperature is below freezing. The players have been running for 45 minutes. "Look at them," he says with a trace of pride in his voice, "they'll be at it for five more hours. They have been training this way for two weeks now. When our new player gets here from the States in the middle of the month, he won't be able to keep up with them."

"I hope he is a *good* American," he sighs. "I hope he doesn't have long hair. I hope he doesn't think he's something special. That just causes more trouble you know."

He reflects on his decade and a half of dealing with foreign players. "I remember the first time we signed a *gaijin*," he says. "The team appointed me liaison man. I didn't speak much English then, so I bought an English conversation book and memorized phrases which I thought would be useful: 'Your car is waiting, sir'; 'Please pass the salt'; 'Would you like some tea?' I really studied hard, but I soon found American ballplayers didn't speak that way. They would say: 'Hey man, pass the salt' or 'How 'bout a coke,' man.' And it seemed that every other word was 'son of a bitch' or 'bullshit' or 'Jesus Christ Almighty.' I didn't know what they were talking about."

"I remember one of the first Americans on the team in 1963. That

Spring training opens early and there is often a distinct chill in the air

summer, he would come to the park every day and the first thing he would say was: 'Jesus Christ, it's fucking hot today.' I thought that was the way all Americans talked, so when he invited me to his house for dinner one night, I said to his wife: 'Jesus Christ, it's fucking hot today, isn't it?' The next day he took me aside in the locker room and warned me never to use that word again to his wife. That's when my real education in English began."

"You know," he continues, "dealing with Americans has not been easy. So many of them come over here and so few try to do things the Japanese way. They don't try to learn Japanese or follow Japanese customs. They complain about everything—the practices, dressing rooms, hotel accommodations. They have to stay in the best hotel in town when we're on the road and they expect to live just like they did in America. The club pays $1500 a month or so for a western style apartment for them and some still complain it's not good enough. Do you know what $1500 a month for housing would mean to a Japanese player?

"A lot of the players who came here thought they were gods. They treated us—the team officials—like servants. I had to chauffeur one player to and from the park every day because he didn't want to take a taxi."

"Some of the Americans were prejudiced against the Japanese. They looked down on us. There was one player—a black who had been a big star in America—who used to ask me to get him a drink after every inning when the hot weather came. You know—'Hey, man, get me a coke, huh?' I did it for a while, but then I got tired of it. I was the team's business manager then, not his valet. So the next time he asked me, I told him to get it himself. He became very angry and roared, 'You fucking Jap!'

"I knew what that meant and it made me angry. So you know what I did? I looked him straight in the eye and said, 'You fucking nigger!' We didn't speak to each other for a long time after that."

The American import has often been a source of agitation to his Japanese teammates over the years, even when his performance on the field has been good. First of all, he is depriving a Japanese player of a job. Second, his higher (taxes paid) salary and the special treatment accorded him by the club cause bitter resentment among the other players, especially those who have contributed as much or more to the team at lower pay. Finally, because the American and Japanese attitudes are so different, clashes are inevitable.

The American player, for example, often fails to understand, much less appreciate, the wisdom of the Code. The Japanese concepts of "pecking order," "established procedure," "sameness," "fighting spirit," "hard training," and "face" are alien to him, and he seldom makes the effort to adapt that Yonamine did.

The American player has often refused to report to spring training until February 15, the day U.S. camps open (but two weeks after the Japanese officially open theirs). During training, because he was accustomed to rounding into shape in his own way, he would refuse to go along with the time-honored, restrictive, group-oriented methods the team had established. "I've been training this way for years," he would say. "There's no need to run five miles a day just to get in shape. Besides, I have my own system."

The American would frequently balk at the efforts of Japanese coaches to change his stance or the playing style he had become accustomed to. "I've been batting this way for 15 years and I'm not about to change now." This caused additional friction. He would often refuse to carry his own equipment as the Japanese players did. "Major leaguers never carry their own bags." And if asked, along with the other players, to slide head-first in order to demonstrate "fighting spirit," this too he would refuse. Why risk injuring himself.

Furthermore, the American was too easygoing, too open, too casual. He did not show the proper respect for the manager and the owner. "Pals" with the owner? In Japan, owners are not "pals." Some Americans even had the audacity to bring in a personal interpreter/agent at contract time to negotiate with team officials. This was an insult both to the team interpreter, who usually acted as a go-between in these matters, and to the front office who viewed the event as a "family affair."

The American complained too much. There was "too much practice." "The Japanese were too compulsive about time schedules. Clubhouse facilities were poor. There were no showers. The dressing rooms were small and dirty." "The filthiest I've ever seen," grumbled one. "I've seen better in Latin America." This was true, the Japanese would readily admit. Each player had only a foot locker, with a partition. And most of the stadiums were old and decrepit. There were no deluxe lounges. But this was Japan. The Japanese players did not complain.

What really upset the Japanese was the superior attitude of some Americans. They would criticize the way the team used its top pitchers, would make fun of the manager's mistakes in strategy, and shake their heads in amusement at the fanatical training habits of their teammates. "Crazy camp," they would say. "It's insane to train as hard as you do. Save your energy for the season." They would try

Ex-Dodger farmhand John Miller wards off the cold with a cup of green tea at the Chunichi Dragons' training camp as Manager Shigeru Mizuhara (left) looks on sternly

to change everything overnight. "No, no, that's not right," they'd say impatiently, unaware of the embarrassment they were causing the manager and coaches.

Furthermore, it became clear that some of these Americans did not like playing in Japan very much. They looked down on the people. They did not try to learn the language or customs. They laughed when the manager took the team's bats and gloves to the Shinto priest to be blessed. How curious, they thought, going to a "witch doctor." Instead of mixing with the Japanese, they spent all their free time in their expensive American-style homes, or socializing with their American friends at exclusively American clubs. (Except, of course, when they were drinking in local night clubs, spending their high salaries, chasing local girls.)

Gradually, the "Ugly American" image began to emerge as the Japanese realized there were players who simply did not care about the team. They were in Japan for two or three years at most and just wanted the money. That was all.

Of course, the majority were good Americans—good in the sense that they took pride in their ability to play baseball and wanted to do well. They wanted the Japanese to like them. They did not want any trouble. And the personalities of some, like the quiet, determined Clete Boyer and George Altman, even seemed to mesh with the Japanese. But far too often there were clashes. The cultural gap and the added actions of a few unscrupulous players were all it took to give the American a bad name.

One homesick player, for example, took his first two month's pay and then without warning left Japan. Another was asked at the start of the season to go down to the farm team until his batting eye improved. The player, who had already received half his yearly salary, indignantly refused, and was subsequently given his release. A former Dodger coach refused to travel by second-class train with the rest of the team and demanded an immediate raise in pay after two months on the job. He left when the club would not agree.

There was also the player who threatened to punch his manager in the mouth for taking him out of the lineup. As well as the former major-league all-star who cooperated on a magazine article criticizing the way his manager ran the team. Finally there was the former Triple A star whom some consider the "Ugliest American of All." An official of the Central League club that signed him tells his story:

This American was a liar and a cheat. We bought him from a Pacific Coast League team and, when he arrived in Japan, the first thing he told us was that his fiancée was coming to stay with him and he asked the club to pay for her expenses. The club agreed to do this, since he was engaged. Then one day, a few weeks later, he announced that his girl friend had already come the week before, stayed for a few days, and returned to the U.S. He requested that we reimburse him for the ticket—round-trip, first-class from Arizona. The club paid him the money.

I thought this was strange, because I knew he had started living with a Japanese girl. So, out of curiosity, I checked with a friend of mine at Haneda International Airport. No such person by the name he had given was on the list of arriving passengers for that period. Later, on a trip to the U.S. at the end of the season, I stopped off at the girl's supposed home town and checked with the local police. There had never been anyone living there with the name and address the player had given me. It was then I realized the team had been cheated.

Another time, during the middle of his first season, he told the general manager that he wanted to bring his parents to Japan to see him play. The general manager was very impressed with this. He thought the American was a good son to be thinking so much of his parents. So he gave him the money for two round-trip, first-class tickets from the West Coast. I later checked and discovered that his parents never came.

There was more. One time when the team was in Osaka, he was taking batting practice without a helmet. He was told to put one on, but he refused. He got hit in the head by a ball and had to be taken to the hospital. He was all right, as it turned out. There was no concussion, but the doctor advised sending him home.

He had already received his road expenses, about $30 a day, and the club asked him to return it. He said no; he wanted to keep it. The club said he had no right to road expenses since he had not traveled with us. What's more the club had to pay medical expenses for something that was his own fault. The club demanded he return the money. He finally relented and gave it back, but he said he wasn't going to take batting practice anymore, "for his own safety."

At the All-Star break, his batting average was .170 or .180 and he asked the general manager for a bonus. He said: "I made a lot of great plays on the field." The general manager just laughed at him.

He's the worst foreigner we've ever had and I truly dislike him. But please don't use his name, because it will hurt him.

Joe Pepitone stands alone. During his brief stay in Japan, the former New York Yankee all-star first-baseman managed to generate more controversy and arouse the ire of more people than any American player before or since. Pepitone was recruited at the start of the 1973 season by the Yakult Atoms who purchased his contract from the Atlanta Braves. To get him, the Atoms had to pay an estimated $70,000 to the Braves, another $70,000 to Pepitone, and unload their star hitter of many years, aging Dave Roberts.

The Atoms felt that Pepitone would be worth all this. To many, he was the most talented American ever signed. He was still young (32) and he could hit, run, and throw with grace and skill. Furthermore, he was a power hitter who had approached 30 home runs a year in his better seasons with the Yankees. The Atoms were loaded with young talent and were hoping that the addition of Pepitone would bring the team its first Central League pennant.

All Pepitone produced was a giant headache. He had always been regarded as a little "strange"—he had quit baseball more than once in the U.S.—and after his arrival in Japan he lived up to that reputation. His shoulder length hair and Wyatt Earp mustache made him conspicuous enough, but after a squabble about having his own hotel room on road trips, refusing to carry his bag, and once reporting without his baseball shoes, the Atoms began to show some concern.

After appearing in 14 games, batting .163, and hitting one home run, Pepitone arrived at the park one day for a double header and announced that he could not play. He had severe headaches, he complained, and blurred vision. It seems the doorway of his apartment was too low, and every time he went in or out, he hit his head. He was "too ill" even to pinch hit.

Shortly thereafter, Pepitone grumbled that his ankle was bothering him. There was something wrong with his Achilles tendon, and he didn't know when he could return to action. Soon Pepitone stopped going to the ballpark altogether, and startled the Atoms even further by making a sudden trip to the U.S.—returning a month later.

Pepitone's erratic behavior made great copy. "Pepitone Sabotage," the newspapers headlined. One sympathetic writer, who discovered that Pepitone wore a toupee, was moved to speculate that Pepitone's premature baldness—his "weak point" was causing his problems.

There were serious doubts about Pepitone's ankle injury. According to one report, he had gone to three different doctors and none could find anything wrong. Pepitone was also spotted on numerous occasions at *Byblos*, one of Tokyo's liveliest discotheques, dancing away on his injured leg until the wee hours of the morning.

The Atoms were not completely unaware of what was going on, and someone suggested to Pepitone that they might be having him followed in order to check up on their $150,000 investment. Pepitone responded by developing a limp and then, realizing this wasn't enough (since his limp magically disappeared at night), had a knee-high cast put on the leg.

Joe Pepitone, the former Yankee first baseman, is probably the most unpopular gaijin ever to play in Japan

Finally, with a month left to go in the season, Pepitone returned home for good. For the $70,000 he had received, he had played in only 14 games. Clete Boyer (with whom he roomed for a time) was left with a telephone bill of more than $1500 in calls to the States and a grocery bill of over a thousand dollars—both of which the Atoms felt obligated to pay.

After the initial outrage wore off, Pepitone became a standing joke in Japan. An office worker who fouled up a job, for example, would be dubbed a "Pepitone" until he redeemed himself. But more than anything else, perhaps, Pepitone made people sad. He was a player of consummate skill, who at age 32 should have been in his prime. He could have had it all. Instead, he chose to throw it away.

Years before, the manager and front office would usually go along with an American if he produced on the field. The ex-major leaguer, in particular, was surrounded by an aura of superiority. After all, he came from the land of Willy Mays, Mickey Mantle, and Stan Musial. His country was the home of the Yankees, the Giants, and the Dodgers—teams that had demolished the Japanese on post-season tours in the 1950s and early 60s. Baseball the American way had proved itself far superior. And so who was the Japanese manager to set himself above a representative of such a system? The manager knew the American who played for him was far better than he had been during his playing days—and probably knew more about baseball, as well. Thus, if the American didn't want to practice or otherwise abide by the club rules—*shōganai* ("It can't be helped!") If the American wanted to argue with the umpire all the time, so what? Even though it might be embarrassing and uncomfortable, that's the American way. If the American wanted to show up ten minutes before a game (Spencer once hit two home runs and a double in a game without *any* warmups) that was the American's prerogative. Of course, the Japanese players didn't like it but—*shōganai*.

As the level of Japanese baseball began to rise, however (almost in step with the GNP), and the Japanese became more accustomed to dealing with Americans, a new-found self-confidence set in, accompanied by a strong sense of national pride. In time, the Japanese began to revise their thinking and ask the American to do things *their* way.

One of the most dramatic early examples of this shift in attitude involved former Cleveland infielder Ken Aspromonte. In 1965, he became the first man in the history of Japanese baseball to be fined by his manager for "conduct unbecoming a player during a game." The incident occurred when Aspromonte, playing for the Chunichi Dragons, was called out on strikes for the second time in a row. After protesting vehemently to the umpire; he flung away his bat, almost hitting the catcher, and stomped back to the dugout where he kicked a few chairs and overturned the water cooler.

Dragon manager Michio Nishizawa, not pleased with Aspromonte's theatrics, removed him from the game and ordered him not to appear in uniform until further notice. Two days later, with notice still "forthcoming," Aspromonte took the advice of a Dragon coach and visited Nishizawa's house—where he made a formal apology. Nishizawa, pleased that Aspromonte had the "guts" to apologize, reinstated his temperamental American, but slapped him with a 50,000 yen fine (the standard in Japan) for his improper conduct.

Nishizawa's action delighted the Japanese baseball world, which, as the sanctimonius *Nikkan Sports* pointed out, was becoming "fed up with intemperate American imports." *Sports* went on to solemnly proclaim: "This discipline is a warning to some of the foreign players who have been overbearing in their conduct."

Nishizawa's action was just a sign of things to come. The following year, Norm Larker found himself in the doghouse with Toei Flyer Manager Shigeru Mizuhara when he failed to run out an easy infield grounder. Larker was fined and suspended. He protested that his right foot was sore and that he was only trying to protect it. But Mizuhara still ordered Larker back to Tokyo to "reflect on his conduct." Said the resolute Mizuhara: "Larker's conduct hurt the team's spirit when we are trying to overtake the league-leading Nankai Hawks. Though we have some important games in Kyushu against the Nishitetsu Lions, I want to show Larker he is not indispensable. I shall watch his attitude and then decide when he will play again." MIZUHARA CRACKS DOWN ON LARKER ran the happy headlines the following day.

Advised by an intermediary that he should apologize if he wanted to get back into his manager's good graces, Larker soon went to Mizuhara, conveyed his regrets, and vowed to show a better attitude in the future. Mizuhara was so pleased that he quickly reinstated him and, in later years, made Larker the subject of a magazine article titled *My Favorite Foreigner*.

The next American to face Japanese managerial wrath was Mike Krsnich, infielder for the Kintetsu Buffaloes. Krsnich was "expelled" from the Buffaloes' training camp for "insubordination" and was ordered to go train with the farm team. Krsnich's crimes were failure to show up for pre-game practice on time and "generally ignoring orders." Despite being one of the top ten batters in the league, the American was traded soon after, because of his "noncooperation."

The Japanese were now putting out the word to prospective Americans that playing in their country was no longer easy. Japan would no longer be a Mecca for big-league cast-offs. Players would not only be required to "earn" the large salaries they were getting, but they would have to do it the Japanese way.

Clete Boyer helped to enhance the American image abroad

Clete Boyer, upon joining the Taiyo Whales in 1972, demonstrated the kind of attitude the Japanese wanted. In an interview on nationwide television, Boyer said, "I'd like to take this opportunity to tell the Japanese fans that Johnny (teammate, John Sipin) and I are *not* in Japan for the money. I could still get a good job in the States, and so could he. Johnny's good enough to play major-league ball. He should be in the big leagues now. John and I are here because we like Japan; because we want to help out any way we can; and because we want to play against the best."

The shoe was now on the other foot and the Japanese were tying the shoestrings tighter. The new "hard-line" toward foreigners was leading to actions once unthinkable: *outright release* for those who did not toe the mark—regardless of their contributions to the team.

One American, a former Triple A star in the Dodger chain, discovered just how serious this new attitude could be. For three straight years, he was his team's leader in home runs as well as RBIs and despite a batting average in the .240's, he was a dangerous clutch-hitter who had won many a game. Yet the club released him because of his attitude. As a team official explained:

He would come late to pre-game practice too often, and the other players didn't like it. If practice started at 4:00, he'd show up at 4:10. He always had some excuse. One day it would be because the traffic was heavy; another day, because he'd missed the train—he couldn't read the Japanese signs. He never once said he was sorry. He'd criticize Japanese customs as being too military. "Bullshit" was the way he always described them.

He'd criticize the manager behind his back. He would say bad things about him in front of the coaches. But the worst thing was his temper.

He was a dedicated, hard-playing athlete, who wanted to do well; wanted to win. But he just couldn't control his temper. One time he hit a double and the umpire called him out for not touching first base. He got so angry he just walked off the field, into the clubhouse and out of the game. Another time, he was removed for a pinch-hitter in the 12th inning. He had gone 0-4 and was trying to get out of a slump, so he was pretty angry at being replaced. The pinch-hitter drove in the winning run, but the American was too mad to care.

The next day, he told the manager, "I don't like playing for you and I don't care if this team wins or not. You didn't have to take me out."

Later, of course, he calmed down and apologized. But it was too late. We released him at the end of the year. And you know, the season before we had kept another American, an infielder who didn't even bat .200. He was a really good fielder, and we asked him back because he adjusted. He did things the Japanese way. We liked him.

Since the Pepitone fiasco in 1973, however, many Japanese teams have begun to conduct background "character investigations" of potential foreign recruits. And by the mid-1970s, advice to those players who wished to avoid the "Ugly American" tag was somewhat along the following lines. Leave your American ways in America and try to behave a little Japanese. Follow Don Blasingame. He didn't break any batting records, but he played hard. He tried to learn the language and understand our customs. He was a good baseball man and became a coach. Be like Dave Roberts. He learned to speak Japanese fluently. He lived in Japan all year round. He always reported to camp in perfect condition. He was so respected that the team gave him a "day" when they had to release him. Be like Willie Kirkland. Kirkland didn't need an interpreter. He knew when practices began. He knew the bus and train schedules. He was never late and he never complained. In Kirkland's fourth year he batted .219 and hit only 14 home runs. Kirkland was 38 years old. Most other players would have been released, but he was given another contract. The team liked his attitude.

Be like George Altman. "Altman was a former major-league all-star," said one coach, "yet he listened to his coaches." Be like Daryl Spencer. Spencer was outspoken and independent—traits which are not admired in Japan—yet Spencer tried to be a part of the team. He learned to play mahjong and eat Japanese food. ("One of the hardest things I've ever done was to eat the raw egg in *sukiyaki*," said Spencer, "but I did it. I didn't want them to think I couldn't.") The Japanese really appreciate people who try to do things their way.

Finally, be like Clete Boyer. Although Boyer has more major-league "stature" than any other American to play in Japan, he was one of the hardest working players on the field—modest, unassuming, and a dedicated team player. He has a quiet dignity, and a deep sense of personal responsibility to younger players. As his former manager described him: "Boyer-*san* is like a samurai in the way he treats the other players. He takes them out in the evening. He looks after them. He coaches them. He must get very tired."

Boyer comes early to spring training. He signs his contract before leaving at the end of the season, and negotiates his salary upon his return the following year. Boyer once even suggested to a team official that he was overpaid at $80,000 a year. Boyer was appointed the Whales' defensive coach upon his retirement in early 1976, and is now being touted by many as a future manager in Japan. As a strong spokesman for the game recently observed, "If there is any American who can manage a Japanese baseball team, it is Boyer-*san*."

10 the "gaijin's" complaint

(Dialogue between a Japanese manager and his American player, with the help of the team interpreter. The American is just off the injury list.)

MGR: Ask him if he can pinch-hit tonight.

INT: Can you pinch-hit tonight?

AMER: Sure. No problem. I can play the whole game.

INT: He says he would be honored if you would allow him to play the whole game.

MGR: No, tonight he must pinch-hit. That is my feeling.

INT: Manager-*san* says he feels you must pinch-hit tonight.

AMER: OK. I'll pinch-hit. Anytime he wants me to.

INT: He says that he will do anything you want him to.

(*Manager smiles and bows slightly to American.*)

MGR: Tell him that I will only use him in a key situation.

INT: He says he will only use you in a key situation.

AMER: OK. Don't worry. I'll give it all I have.

INT: He says he will do his best for you and the team when called upon.

MGR: (*With serious, thoughtful expression*) Tell him that if he feels he is going to hit into a double play he should strike out instead. That's better for the team.

INT: The manager says that if you have the feeling you are going to hit into a double play, you should try to strike out.

AMER: (*Astounded*) What! Strike out? He must be crazy. I've never struck out intentionally in my life and I'm not about to start now. If he wants me to strike out, then tell him not to put me in the game. I've never heard anything so stupid.

INT: (*Ahem*) He says that he thinks it is very difficult to strike out intentionally. And that perhaps there might be other players on the team who could do it better than he.

MGR: Hmmm. I see. That is something I will have to think about. I understand his thinking. Tell him to be ready if I need him, at any rate.

INT: The manager says he understands your feeling, and says he will reconsider his request. He appreciates your cooperation and asks you to prepare yourself if he needs you tonight.

AMER: (*Calming down*) Sure. Anytime.

It is easy to understand why many Americans want to play in Japan. The sky-high (tax-free) salaries with "benefits," the inordinate kindness Japanese shower on foreign guests, and the excitement of the Orient are all good reasons why a fading American ballplayer might jump at an offer from a Japanese team.

But the realities of Japanese baseball life can be far from pleasant. The American who wants to "make it" in Japan finds he must contend with lingering expectations that he perform the heroic feats befitting an American major leaguer; he must cope with the language barrier and the intricate rituals of everyday life; and he must face the insular mentality that labels him a *gaijin*—the Japanese word for foreigner, which literally means "outside person." Adjusting to baseball, Japanese style, can be an emotionally draining experience and, as more than one American has discovered, a painful lesson in cross-cultural understanding.

Consider the story of Jim LeFebvre, the former all-star second-baseman for the Los Angeles Dodgers. Leg injuries and Dodger manager Walter Alston's youth movement made LeFebvre's future as a Dodger uncertain. So, in 1973, when the Lotte Orions of Japan's Pacific League wanted to sign him, the Dodgers agreed to let him go. LeFebvre was given a three-year contract in the neighborhood of $90,000.

To the Orions, LeFebvre was a real find. They had long known that Triple A stars and fading major-league veterans would not automatically tear up the league, but LeFebvre—he was something entirely different. He was that "genuine big-leaguer" the Japanese had always coveted. He was only 30—the youngest active major leaguer ever recruited. And he was only a few years removed from his status as the premier second-baseman in the National League where he was belting home runs out of the park at a 25 a year clip.

Freshman Lotte Orion manager Masaiichi Kaneda, the high-strung "god of pitching," was ecstatic about his big catch. LeFebvre was his "personal" selection, and Kaneda proudly announced his new American would hit 50 home runs and bat .350 (something only Sadaharu Oh of the Giants could do).

LeFebvre started out fairly well, hitting home runs at a 35 a year clip and batting in the .270's.* But it was not the magic Kaneda had guaranteed, and LeFebvre soon found himself having to defend his play.

REPORTER: Why don't you hit more home runs?

LEFEBVRE: I'm here to play winning baseball.

REPORTER: Your manager said you would win the triple crown.

LEFEBVRE: Contributions to the win and loss column are more important than individual statistics.

REPORTER: But why don't you hit more home runs?

* Le Febvre's introduction to Japanese baseball was characteristic of the problems new arrivals faced. After a session in the batting cage, in which he slammed nearly half the pitches into the stands, he was told that his form was "no good." He would have to stop "uppercutting" the ball.

Clarence Jones of the Kintetsu Buffaloes is welcomed at the plate after his game-winning home run

Kaneda was particularly upset because it appeared he had spoken too soon. Although Kaneda had Korean parents and was unorthodox in many ways,* he was thought by many to be the most "Japanese" of all managers. He was extremely "face-conscious" and LeFebvre's failure to tear down the fences was becoming a public embarrassment—especially in view of the ex-Dodger's enormous price tag. And as the season wore on, the situation only became worse.

In one crucial mid-season game, LeFebvre popped up to end a late-inning Lotte threat; and in another important game a few days later, he made a costly error. The following day, after LeFebvre reported ten minutes late to pre-game practice, Kaneda took the offensive. "He's hitting home runs," he complained to the press, "but he comes late to practice and his overall play is not that of an $90,000 player." In the early innings of a game in late August, LeFebvre muffed another easy grounder. Kaneda immediately yanked him out and, following the game, he declared angrily: "I apologize to my players for the error LeFebvre made. LeFebvre should quit."

Needless to say, LeFebvre was somewhat disconcerted over the controversy brewing around him. He felt he was giving his best † and could not quite understand Kaneda's indignation. "Nobody likes to make a bad play or do poorly in a big game," he said. "I'm a major leaguer. I've got just as much pride as anyone else. I always go out there and give it all I've got. I can understand Kaneda's position. He's upset because I'm not winning the triple crown, but when he said what he did . . . that hurts."

Two days later before pre-game practice, LeFebvre complained of a headache. The team trainer and physician examined him, diagnosed a case of the flu, and advised him to rest. LeFebvre went directly to bed. As far as Kaneda was concerned, that was the last straw. He immediately suspended LeFebvre and accused him of perpetrating the

---

* Upon meeting LeFebvre for the first time in Peter O'Malley's office at Dodger Stadium in Los Angeles, Kaneda reportedly pulled out $10,000 in cash, slapped it on the table and said: "This is a present for Jimmy."

† LeFebvre was in fact a very dedicated and anxious to do well in Japan. One of the Orion coaches, after watching him for a whole season, remarked that he was the "hardest working member on the team," and even went so far as to say that LeFebvre "trained too much."

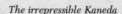

The irrepressible Kaneda

same kind of "sabotage" that Joe Pepitone pulled on the Atoms. He announced to one and all that he was going to look into the possibility of getting another foreign player. When reminded that LeFebvre had a three-year contract, Kaneda snapped: "I don't care. LeFebvre can play on the farm team for the next two years as far as I'm concerned. If he doesn't show any more desire than he has up until now, I'm not going to use him again."

"What was I supposed to do?" wondered LeFebvre, "Go out there and throw up?" No one was listening, however. The press was only interested in Kaneda's strong stand against "LeFebvre Sabotage." It made better copy. And it took Kaneda off a very uncomfortable hook.

By the next day, after the morning papers were out, Kaneda calmed down and lifted the suspension. LeFebvre returned and finished the season with 29 home runs and a .265 batting average. However, his troubles with Kaneda continued into the following season. At one point Kaneda ordered him to "stop hitting home runs." Another time he forced LeFebvre to play when his bad leg began to act up and LeFebvre missed 48 games that year as a result. But he had a strong second half and was a key figure in Lotte's pennant win and first Japan Series victory. That made little difference to Kaneda, who was so embittered with his "defective" star that he reportedly swore he would never deal directly with Dodger owner Walter O'Malley again. He had been taken once and that was enough.

Finally, in May of LeFebvre's third year (LeFebvre was batting .250 with five home runs at the time), Kaneda "requested" his American to voluntarily resign from baseball and become an Orion farm team coach, to make room for another *gaijin* import. LeFebvre reluctantly agreed and stepped aside for Kaneda's next triple crown candidate—a minor leaguer named Bill McNulty who once hit 55 home runs in the Pacific Coast League.*

The LeFebvre affair, although extreme, illustrates the problems the highly touted, highly paid, and highly visible American star faces. As LeFebvre himself cautioned after three years in Japan:

> I give this advice to any player who comes here. Leave your major-league pride in the States. Pretend you're a rookie at a minor-league camp. Try to learn the Japanese way. Don't try to change it. Do that and you might make it. If you don't think you can make this adjustment, stay home.

On a purely practical level, succeeding in Japan involves many difficult adjustments. Training camp is "like being in prison," as one American described it, and the process of getting used to the Japanese strike zone can cost a player as much as ten points on his seasonal batting average. Japanese pitching is also different. Not only do pitchers throw with unfamiliar sidearm and "submarine" motions, but they also "think backwards." Whereas an American pitcher will usually throw a fast ball on a 2-0 or 3-1 count, the Japanese will throw a breaking pitch. Daryl Spencer once explained the logic behind this:

> At home, the 3-1 pitch is the one you really zip. You know the pitcher has

---

* McNulty batted less than .200, and at the end of the season Kaneda—perhaps realizing he had acted a bit too hastily—asked LeFebvre to return as a player in 1976.

to get the ball over the plate and that usually means fastball. But here, when the count is 3-1, you're in trouble, because the pitcher feels he's getting into the groove and can get his breaking ball over the plate. The advice I always gave to newcomers was to figure what kind of pitch you'd expect from an American in a certain situation and then plan on the opposite from the Japanese.

Training methods, the strike zone, and different styles of pitching are not all the American has to worry about. Inevitably the cultural barrier begins to rise before him, and it seems to grow more formidable with each passing day of the season. The American who gets off to a bad start, for example, is in trouble. Unlike most U. S. managers, who give a player time to work things out for himself, the Japanese manager wants immediate results. If his *gaijin* goes 0-10, the odds are that he will wind up on the bench and the batting coach will then take over.*

The conversation ex-S.F. Giant Matty Alou once had with his manager on the Taiheiyo Lions is typical of the difficulties Americans face. Alou, struggling to get his 1976 average over .260, and frequently benched for his inability to do so, spoke one night to his manager.

ALOU: Why do you keep putting me on the bench?
MGR: Alou-san, you've just got to start hitting.
ALOU: How can I do that when I'm on the bench all the time?
MGR: Well, I'm sorry, but you're on the bench because you're not hitting.

The American who has a good start will be left alone, but it isn't long before he is introduced to *chōshi*—a player's "pitch" or "tune" on a given day. Japanese managers will often make out their starting lineups after carefully assessing the *chōshi* of their charges in pre-game practice. The American who has been playing well feels he deserves to start regardless of how he "looks" before the game. But,

---

* Atlanta Braves outfielder Ralph Garr, by contrast, once opened the season with a horrendous 2 for 33. Yet his manager bore with him, leaving him in the lineup, and Garr finished at .367.

in Japan, the look of things is all important. If a player "looks" bad in
pre-game practice, the odds are he'll be on the bench. Daryl Spencer
once gave teammate Gordon Windhorn a firsthand demonstration of
how the "*chōshi* factor" works. As Spencer described it:

Windhorn didn't believe the manager decided his lineup on the basis of
pre-game practice. So to prove a point, I had a "poor" batting practice. The
manager and the batting coach were watching me like hawks. When I
stepped out of the cage, they pulled me aside and told me my *choshi* was no
good and that I should sit out that night, despite the fact I had a couple hits
the day before. The next night, I did well in batting practice and the manager put me back in the starting lineup.

The Japanese manager's keen eye also plays a part when weather
conditions threaten. Because in Japan it is the home team's decision
to start or not start a game, if the starting pitcher's *chōshi* is no good,
the slightest drizzle can be enough to postpone the game. If, on the
other hand, his *chōshi* is good, the manager might wait out a typhoon and then have the groundskeepers out mopping up the field
with towels.

Irrational thinking and intuition, the American soon discovers, are
almost as much a part of the game as percentage baseball theories. A
player may have a .300 batting average against a certain pitcher, but if
the manager has a "feeling" the player won't get a hit in a given time
at bat, he will bench him. Decision making by "inspiration," however
irrational, is the Japanese manager's prerogative. Having the "guts" (a
word the Japanese like very much) to make such a decision is considered the mark of a good leader. This can be frustrating to the western
mind—more than once an American has received the take sign
because his manager had the feeling a "surprise" pitch was about to
be thrown.

Dealing with the Japanese coaching staff can also be frustrating. As
one American moaned: "The biggest difference between the U.S. and
Japan is that in Japan coaches 'coach.' Far too often they don't know
what to do, but they're too proud to admit it."

A pitcher who was having trouble with his control, for example, was simply advised to drink more water and try not to throw the ball over the middle of the plate. Another American pitcher was told that the only cure for a sore arm was to throw more. While to an aging player, whose legs were starting to go, it was suggested he run more in pre-game practice to compensate. Since he was older, it was reasoned, he must work harder than anyone else to stay in shape.

The American who sees things being done wrong and offers to help correct them usually finds his unsolicited major-league advice unwelcome. When a Japanese manager feels he needs advice from Americans, he gets it from the masters across the sea. He either takes his team to the States for spring training, sends his players to the American winter instructional league, or invites renowned coaches like Mr. Joe DiMaggio, Mr. Harvey Haddix, or Mr. Al Campanis. These former players are "teachers." They have the title, position, and the right to dispense American baseball wisdom. In Japan a player is a player. And a coach is a coach. That rule also applies to ex-major leaguers. As Daryl Spencer once described his frustrations on trying to offer advice:

When I first arrived in 1964, our team was doing too many simple things the wrong way. They were doing the pitchout backwards, for example. Instead of throwing it outside, for some strange reason the pitcher would throw

Warren Spahn, guest pitching coach at the Hiroshima Carp's 1975 spring camp, gets the traditional "victory toss" prior to his departure for the U.S.

high inside when the manager thought the base runner was going to steal. That meant the batter was in the catcher's way. Their base running was also poor. Runners were picked off way too much or thrown out trying to steal because they couldn't read the pitchout signs. And time and again in a close game with runners in scoring position, first base open and the pitcher on deck, they'd fail to walk the batter.

At first, they refused to listen to my advice. It really bothered me because they were making so many foolish mistakes and didn't seem to care about changing. If I hadn't been so mad my first year, I'd have probably hit .360. It took them a whole season before they finally got around to doing things the right way. But I learned too—in Japan you have to be diplomatic.

The presence of a free-wheeling American spirit unfamiliar with the intricacies of the pecking order and a status-conscious Japanese manager on the same team is a potentially explosive combination. Almost by definition, the American is a threat to the manager's authority, and the inevitable conflicts that occur make for some curious anecdotes. A former major-league all-star once arrived five days late for his second spring in Japan—because of a delay in visa processing—and discovered he had been fined the outrageous sum of $1000 for each day. Infuriated, he headed for the manager's office carrying the $4000 worth of American baseball equipment he had been asked to buy and demanded an explanation. There, behind closed doors, the following conversation took place.

AMER: (*Indignantly*) This is one hell of a way to start the season. I bring you all this equipment and now you're fining me? A *thousand* dollars a day? You've got to be kidding. I had visa problems that weren't my fault. I got here as fast as I could. Last year, I didn't get here until the middle of the month. So what's the fine for?

MGR: Now, now. Take it easy. Last year was different. You had permission then. Anyway, don't worry about the fine. I told the press that I was going to fine you, but I'm not going to do it.

AMER: That's a relief, but why announce it at all?

MGR: I did it for the other players, to show them I am in command. I'm the manager after all, and I have to show my power.

AMER: Yes, but what about my reputation?

MGR: I'm going to have to ask you to forget about your reputation. You must promise not to tell anyone what I have just told you. At the team

meeting tomorrow, I'm going to announce your fine is being paid.
You don't have to pay. The team will pay and we will use the money
for the players' fund. But you must vow to keep this a secret.

AMER: You must be joking.

The manager wasn't joking, however, and the American reluctantly
consented. The payment of the fine was announced and, as far as anyone knew, the manager had aptly demonstrated his ability to deal
with "overpaid" Americans who thought they had special privileges.

Occasionally the American will refuse to cooperate in the manager's
face-saving charade, and the repercussions can be severe. This happened with Jim Barbieri, an ex-Dodger who played for the Chunichi
Dragons in 1970. Barbieri was in his customary leftfield position one
day, when a shallow fly ball was hit his way. He raced in and attempted a shoestring catch, but the ball rolled past him to the wall.
When the dust settled, Dragon Manager Shigeru Mizuhara emerged
from the dugout and waved Barbieri out of the game—a move that
angered as well as embarrassed the American. In a display of disgust
violating nearly half the provisions of the Code, Barbieri strode slowly
to the dugout, approached Mizuhara, and spat: "You're horseshit!"
Mizuhara understood. "Get out!" he roared. The two men then entered a shoving match that was quickly broken up.

After the game, a coach advised Barbieri to apologize. ("If you do,
he'll like you more.") Barbieri was still fuming "I can't do it," he
replied. "I don't respect the man. No U.S. manager would take a
cheap shot like that." The angry young man remained adamant in his
refusal to apologize and, predictably, was released at the end of the
season.

Embarrassing the manager can be a costly thing to do, even when
it is unintentional and in the best interests of the team. During one
Dragon–Atom encounter at Nagoya, for example, Atom Manager
Osamu Mihara decided to replace his American first baseman Dave
Roberts with a pinch-hitter. Roberts who was the Atoms' leading hit-
ter for six years, with as many as 14 home runs in one season against
Dragon pitching alone, was not exactly eager to oblige. "In fact," he
told Mihara in his fluent Japanese, "I'm certain I can get a hit." The

third-base coach came over and a discomfiting conference was held in front of the dugout.

Roberts persisted and Mihara finally gave in. Roberts then went to bat and promptly sent a line shot over the centerfield wall for a home run. Though good for the team and good for Roberts, this proved an embarrassment to Mihara. But after Roberts crossed home plate, Mihara did a rare thing. He walked over and tipped his cap to him. Still Roberts was released shortly thereafter to make room for, ironically, Joe Pepitone. As Roberts later recalled:

I was happy about the home run, but I knew Mihara felt embarrassed. When the Atoms signed Pepitone, I knew I'd be the one to go. They told me the reason was that having two American stars on the team wouldn't be good. We wouldn't get along. But I think they had other reasons.

Since the appearance of things is all important in Japan, if it even looks as though the *gaijin* is stepping out of line, action must be taken. When Norm Larker was suspended for not running out a ground ball, it didn't matter that he was nursing a lame ankle to stay in the lineup during the pennant drive. What mattered was how it looked to everyone. Larker did not seem to be hustling; and that called for action—suspension by the manager.

Perhaps the most bizarre episode involving a Japanese manager and his American player featured Lotte Manager Kaneda and George Altman. It all began in August 1974. Altman, at 41, was having the best year of his career. He was pacing the league in batting at .351, leading his team in home runs, and was the primary reason the Orions were in the thick of the pennant race. But, although no one knew it at the time, Altman was a sick man. He had lumps in his abdomen and the pain was growing more acute each day. Finally, Altman went to see a doctor. The diagnosis was cancer.

Altman immediately underwent surgery. The Lotte club was shocked. (Kaneda, with questionable taste, pronounced Altman "a dead man with only hours to live.") Although Altman had returned to Chicago, his illness became a rallying point for the Orions. They went on to win their pennant and the Japan Series.

At the team victory celebration in late October, there was a special surprise on hand: George Altman. He had just flown in from the U.S. and, although 20 pounds lighter, was looking as healthy as ever. The operation had been a success. He had a clean bill of health from the doctors. What's more, he was running every day to get in shape for the 1975 season.

Altman's return was a touching event; no American player in Japan was better liked or respected. The Lotte officials welcomed him back. Perhaps he could be the team's designated hitter since the rule would be going into effect in the Pacific League the following season. Kaneda injected a note of caution: "Altman's achievements as a key player on Lotte are noteworthy and we cannot treat him roughly. We have to think seriously about the danger to his life. If he can't play, I am thinking about using him to coach the younger players on the farm team."

But Altman didn't want to coach. He had passed another medical examination in Japan with flying colors and he wanted to play. The trouble began when he sat down with Kaneda to discuss his contract. Lotte wanted to cut his salary by an estimated 15%. Altman refused and asked about a bonus he'd been promised if he hit over .310 for the '74 season (his final figure was .351).* Kaneda was perturbed at this seeming display of ingratitude. After all, Altman had missed 45 games. His fielding was not what it had once been. And what if the illness recurred? In fact, the implication seemed to be, wasn't Lotte's generous offer to employ Altman for another season in itself a bonus?

Contract negotiations ground to a halt and Altman returned to his

---

* Bonuses of this sort, although illegal in the United States, are a common practice in Japan, and for players like Altman, who have to cope with Japanese reasoning, they are a necessary evil. As Altman described his initial frustrations:

After I reached a certain salary level, they just didn't want to pay me anymore. They thought I was making enough. When I was 39, my fourth season in Japan, I had my best year (.320/39/103). They said they didn't want to give me a raise because I was too old and they couldn't be sure how well I'd do the following year. I talked 'til I was blue in the face, but it did absolutely no good. So finally, I had to start asking for bonuses if I hit over a certain figure to get the money that was coming to me.

I don't think bonuses are good in general, because then a player just starts thinking about his own statistics. But I had no choice.

home in Chicago. Shortly thereafter, Kaneda found a Japanese doctor who would tell him what he wanted to hear: Lotte might be endangering Altman's life if they were to let him play. Altman was immediately given his release and advised to retire "for his own good."

Convinced he could still play, Altman returned to Japan in January. Back at his old weight and in perfect condition, he tried out with the Hanshin Tigers. At Hanshin's request, he passed still another check-up and was so impressive in workouts that the Tigers were ready to offer him the first base position, fifth slot in the batting order, and a contract calling for a substantial increase over what he had earned with the Orions.

It looked like a storybook ending for the courageous "ageless wonder"—until Kaneda returned to center stage. "To let Altman play when there is a chance his illness will recur is an act of inhumanity on the part of Hanshin I cannot forgive," he declared indignantly. "What is Hanshin doing?" he asked. "Do they want to win the championship that badly?"

It had been with "tears rolling down my cheeks," Kaneda explained, that he released Altman and urged him to give up baseball. "I was thinking only of George's welfare," he said; "that's why I made him quit. I lost two relatives through cancer and I know what a terrible thing it is. That's why I'm making such a fuss." Kaneda went on to suggest that the doctors who examined Altman were reluctant to tell him the truth, and openly warned Tiger manager Yoshio Yoshida not to use Altman. "If he does," Kaneda vowed, "I'll never speak to him again."

Hanshin officials were stunned by Kaneda's attack. Anxious to avoid an open conflict with the "God of pitching," they naturally decided to delay their decision on Altman. A Tiger executive announced that the team wanted to be absolutely certain there wasn't even "one chance in a million" that Altman would get sick again. For if so, Hanshin would be shamed in the eyes of the nation.

Altman, who was tearing the cover off the ball in batting practice and working harder than any rookie in training, could not believe what was happening. "I'm in perfect health," he protested. "Kaneda's remarks are a disgrace. If I thought my life was in danger, I wouldn't be here now. I wish Kaneda would stop interfering in my life."

Finally, after hours of discussion and consultation, the Tiger president (who no doubt wished the problem would go away) reached a decision. Altman could play for the Tigers providing he made a formal statement on the matter, in effect, telling Kaneda to mind his own business. Altman complied, and signed his contract.

Kaneda responded bitterly:

We at Lotte did Altman a favor by not giving him a contract. It was an act of good will. In that spirit, I'd like to say I hope Altman plays well, if he wants to so much. Rather, I should say I hope he *lives* well.

If Hanshin hopes to defeat the Giants this year, they'll have to improve their defense. Altman's legs are no good and that's a fact they'll have to consider.

Altman put the distasteful incident behind him and proceeded to show that a 42-year-old baseball player who had licked cancer could still swing a mean bat. Despite having to adjust to a different league, he hit a solid .274 with 12 home runs and then retired from Japanese baseball.*

The American who tries to be a part of things on a Japanese team often finds the American style of clubhouse clowning unpopular. Willy Kirkland of the Hanshin Tigers, for example, once teased a fading veteran player who had just been appointed playing-coach and perhaps made an enemy for life. The coach was taking batting practice when Kirkland passed by and yelled playfully in Japanese: "You're a coach now; you don't have to take batting practice." The coach was so enraged by what he took as a slur on his declining use-

---

* Said Altman privately:

I don't think Kaneda wanted me back on the Orions because I suspect he'd already committed himself to another *gaijin* as my replacement. And he didn't want me to play with another team, because if I did well, it would be embarrassing to him.

I saw him once after moving to the Tigers, during a spring exhibition game when a photographer asked me to shake hands with Kaneda for a picture. I was willing, but Kaneda wanted to continue the charade. When I approached him, he turned and opened his mouth in mock surprise—as if he couldn't believe I was still alive.

fulness to the team that he had to be restrained from going after Kirkland. "That was no joke," he said later. "He was making fun of me."

The American who tries to "go Japanese" discovers that it is no simple thing. He starts to learn the language, but finds that mastering Japanese is not easily done in a single baseball season. More often than not he rationalizes: "What's the use. I'll only be here another year or two." If he tries to live like the other players, he finds this involves not just eating fish, rice, or noodles every now and then—but every single day. Such a radical shift in eating habits may well hurt the batting average. As Jim LeFebvre, Altman's teammate, pointed out: "When George got sick in 1974 and left for the States, I lived with the team on the road the rest of the season—Japanese style. I did everything they did. I ate the same food. I tried to be like them. I think I earned their respect, but I also lost ten pounds."

Often the American finds that loneliness and isolation are very real problems. The only one he can talk to is the other *gaijin* on the team. There are Japanese players who know some English, but not enough to really lend a sympathetic ear. Dick Stuart, who came over as a

George Altman raps out a hit for the Hanshin Tigers

bachelor and was for a time the only *gaijin* on the Taiyo Whales, summed up the feelings of many an American player when he said: "The Japanese were extremely nice and courteous to me, but to live alone in a foreign country was an adjustment I just couldn't make."

A married player may find the move to Japan puts a strain on his marriage. This happened to Jim Marshall who played for the Dragons. Marshall put up at a Nagoya hotel while his family lived in Tokyo so his children could attend an American school there. Every off day, Marshall would travel the 200 miles to Tokyo and back to visit his family.

A player's wife will also feel the strain. She may decide to learn something of the culture, but after the usual round of temple and shrine viewing, shopping sprees, flower arranging lessons, tea ceremony classes, and abortive attempts to learn Japanese, she begins to complain. She grows weary of the pigeonhole the Japanese set aside for their women; she tires of the crowds, the noises, the pollution, and the prices; of people pointing at her as she walks down the street ("Look! There's a *gaijin!*") and she longs to return home. She also begins to have doubts that her husband is pining away in his hotel room on those long road trips once she discovers how many Japanese girls are willing to make themselves available. More than one American player has returned to Japan for his second year—alone.

Perhaps the most difficult thing for the American to cope with is the chilling realization that Japan does not really want him to succeed. If he can help his team win a pennant, fine. But trouble comes when he does *too* well. If he is the top ball player on the team, it bothers some of his teammates who feel uncomfortable being led by a foreigner. Other top players on the team may be upset at being outdone by a *gaijin*. It even agitates league officials who do not want the record books cluttered with *katakana*—a form of writing reserved for foreign names and words. One league commissioner had this to say after a season in which Americans performed particularly well:

It's a funny situation when a foreigner is the ace pitcher of the team or the home-run leader. Foreigners, at best, should be by-players to bolster Japanese teams, but not front-line starters.

The commissioner went on to point out that teams led by foreigners had suffered a decline in attendance.

Americans threatening to win a particular batting crown often complain of a subtle conspiracy to prevent them from succeeding: scorers who call a bullet off an infielder's knee an error instead of a hit, umpires who signal a neck-high fast ball a strike, and opposing pitchers who "work around" the *gaijin* yet "come in" to his Japanese opposition.

Rumblings of this nature were made in 1969 when Dave Roberts was threatening to win the Central League triple crown, and in 1971 when George Altman was in a PL batting race. Roberts, who was leading the league in the three big departments in early August, suffered a shoulder separation when the opposing Yomiuri Giant pitcher ran into him on a play at first base. The accident effectively eliminated Roberts from the race, and Giant stars Oh and Nagashima went on to divide league batting honors.

Altman, finished with .320 and lost the batting title to teammate Shinichi Eto of the Orions who hit .337. Altman describes his failure.

Late August that year I was leading Eto .340 to .326 and I guess the opposition figured they ought to start doing something about it. So in one game, against the Hawks, for example, their manager moved his second baseman and his first baseman farther apart when Eto came to bat. Eto, who likes to hit to the right side of the field anyway, hit nothing but ground balls all night—right where the second baseman normally plays—into the outfield. He went 4 for 4. It was right then that I figured my chances of winning the batting title were almost non-existent.*

---

* Altman had similar troubles—but for slightly different reasons—in 1969, his second year. As Altman described those woes: "I'd had a pretty good first year in Japan, so in spring training the following season, a reporter approached me and asked if he could write a story about my quest for the triple crown in the coming campaign. I told him: "No, don't write that. My only goals are to do better than I did last year." Well he went ahead and wrote the story the way he wanted: "Altman aiming for triple crown" or something like that, which took care of me that season. The Japanese don't like braggers, especially foreign ones. I got absolutely nothing to hit from the pitchers and nothing but called strikes from the umpires. By mid-year, I was batting about .240. I remember before one game, an umpire came up to me, smiled, and just to rub it in, said: "Hi, George. You going to win the triple crown this year?" That's the year I really learned to be leery of the Japanese press.

The most blatant conspiracy involved Daryl Spencer of the Hankyu Braves. In Spencer's second season, 1965, he was making a serious bid for the Pacific League home-run title. By early August, he was leading the league with 32—six ahead of Nankai Hawk catcher Katsuya Nomura, the perennial league champion. Spencer was moving at a pace that would put him over 50 for the year and was dangerously close to becoming Japan's first full-fledged American home-run king. Spencer and Nomura were also in a neck-and-neck race for batting and RBI honors but it was the prestigious home-run title that held people's attention. Americans had won batting titles before, yet no *gaijin* had ever won a home-run crown.*

Spencer had no idea of the furor that was about to erupt, but a conversation he had with a team coach did suggest how seriously the Japanese viewed the situation:

COACH: Spencer-*san*, you must concentrate on the batting title and forget about the home-run championship.

SPENCER: Why?

COACH: Because Nomura always hits many home runs in September and it is doubtful you can wrest the home-run title from him. But his batting average always drops toward the end of the season.

SPENCER: Don't worry. I can win the home-run title.

COACH: No, we want you to win the batting title. You see, no one has ever won a triple crown. We feel that Nomura is good, but is not worthy of the triple crown if the great batters before him couldn't do it.

SPENCER: Hell, don't worry about that. Nomura's not going to win the triple crown. Maybe I'll do it.

COACH: No, Nomura must win the home-run title and you must win the batting title.

If Spencer was temporarily confused by this, things became clearer the following weekend, when the Braves traveled to Tokyo for a three-game series with the Lotte Orions. In the first game on Saturday, Spencer was walked twice. The following day, in the opener of a double-header, he was walked four times. Orion ace Masayaki

* Unless one counts the league-leading six Bucky Harris hit in the spring season of 1937 under the old one-league setup.

Daryl Spencer draws another intentional walk in his race against Katsuya Nomura of the Nankai Hawks, for the 1965 home-run crown

Koyama threw him 16 straight balls, passing him intentionally every time he came to the plate, regardless of the game situation. In the second game, Spencer was walked twice more; once with the bases loaded on *four* straight pitches. Koyama candidly explained his unusual tactics after the game: "Why should we let a foreigner take the title? If we (the pitchers) are to give the title to anybody, why not give it to Nomura?"

Other pitchers in the league, while not as candid as Koyama, seemed to agree with him. Walking Spencer became a fad. In frustration, Spencer would swing deliberately at outside pitches, tempting pitchers to try for a strikeout instead. Other times he would languish at the plate with his bat reversed or cradled harmlessly behind his back. And still the pitchers walked him.

"I just lost all competitiveness," Spencer said. "I thought Koyama was a truly great pitcher until I heard him say what he did. There were only two teams in the league—the Flyers and the Lions—that were fair to me. The others all took their cue from the Orions. The Hawk pitchers (Nomura's teammates) were the worst, of course."

The Braves manager gallantly offered to have his pitchers retaliate by walking Nomura, but Spencer refused. Instead, he graciously broke his leg in a motorcycle accident with two weeks left to go in the season. And happily, Nomura captured the home-run title, 42–38, winning the triple crown in the process.

It wasn't until 1974 that an American finally won the coveted home-run championship. Clarence Jones of the Kintetsu Buffaloes somehow managed to hit 36 out of the park, more than anyone else in the league. The Japanese pretended not to notice. Instead they talked about Jones' .226 batting average and 112 strikeouts, or better yet, Sadaharu Oh's 49 home runs, .332 batting average, and second straight triple crown in the other league.

From those who have played baseball in Japan come the following comments on the difficulties of life there.

I'm just mentally tired from playing the Japanese style. I don't like to complain because Japan has been good to me, but it's a strain to adjust. They don't stress winning enough. Americans won't tolerate mistakes like they do here, and they repeat them over and over. In a game, you never see a Japanese show any initiative. He just does what the coaches tell him. It's hard to play here if you're oriented to winning. Japanese get behind in a game and all the fight seems to go out of them.

In the U.S., a man is respected for what he does. If a guy comes through on the field, nothing else matters. In Japan, it's much more than that. You have to put up with all the small stuff—the bullshit. That means being on time to the minute. If you're late, they expect you to apologize. It means not arguing with the umpire. They want you to smile after you strike out. A Japanese gets angry and kicks the shit out of the umpire. If an American so much as argues with the call, he's branded a bad sport.

One time the president of the team ordered me to attend all the conferences on the mound. Man, I just refused to go. I'd feel like an ass out there knowing that everyone in the stands knows I can't speak Japanese.

You get tired here. In the States you have more free time. But here, you're constantly on a schedule. There are less games, but they're always calling practices and meetings. Everything's so regimented. First the running coach gets you before the game, then the batting and fielding coaches. Everyone does everything together. Sometimes that gets on your nerves. Sometimes you feel real good, real tuned up and you don't want to do a lot of running or take a lot of cuts in the batting cage. But you don't have any choice.

It's rough being a *gaijin* here. Everything you do is magnified. They expect you to hit a home run every trip to the plate. If you screw up they think you're loafing. Open your mouth at the wrong time and there's a big story in the papers next day. They're always messing. They just won't let you alone to play. They make you sacrifice bunt in the first inning. You can be hitting the ball real good, but go 0-3 in a game and they'll pull you out for a pinch hitter. That really destroys your confidence and your rhythm. Sometimes, the pressure really gets to me, and I wonder if it's all worth it, despite the money they pay. So many times, I've gone back to my room, shut the door and just screamed.

Yet on the positive side, playing in Japan can be very rewarding in far more than just monetary terms. Rare indeed is the American who doesn't derive some value from his experience there.

I've made friendships here that I'll treasure all my life. And I've learned there's a different way to look at life. This is their country and their game. In many ways, playing in Japan has made a man out of me.

There are no kinder, warmer, more honorable people than the Japanese. They've really made me feel welcome. I mean they really *care* how I feel. It actually bothers them if they think I'm not happy with my apartment or if they feel I'm getting homesick. They go out of their way to accommodate me. People in the States are too self-centered. They expect everyone to do things the American way. They don't seem to have the time or patience to understand foreigners that the Japanese do.

In the U.S. everyone is looking out for himself, but here the players care more for the team and the team more for the player. When a player quits playing, he stays with the organization. The team finds a place for him. These guys really know how to get along. It's incredible. They're together almost all the time from January to November. They live together, eat together, play baseball together. I've never seen one fight, one argument. It's a real pleasure. In the States, there's always somebody who mouths off and tries to start trouble.

It's nice to play in a place where the pitcher isn't trying to stick the ball in your ear half the time and if a guy slides into you, he says he's sorry.

I could never make the kind of money in the States that I'm making here. And I really enjoy living in Japan. It's so much safer than the U.S. Guns are illegal in this country. When I go out at night I never have to worry about being mugged. Half the time I don't even lock the door when I'm gone, because I know nobody wants to rip me off.

The American is not the only "outsider" in Japanese baseball, he's just the most visible. Koreans also fall into the same category. But while the American is merely resented, the Korean is often looked down upon.*

The Korean—usually born and raised in the country—often plays the game because he finds it difficult to get anywhere else in Japan's social hierarchy. In fact, there are so many Korean players that, as one knowledgeable writer observed, "If you removed them all there wouldn't be any more Japanese baseball." A few are openly proud of their heritage, but many more take advantage of their resemblance to Japanese, assume a Japanese name, and try to pass as natives. As a result "Korean spotting" has become a minor pastime for the fan.

Koreans, though a credit to the game, have not been warmly accepted into the fold. If the excellent Korean outfielder Isao Harimoto loafs on a fly ball, one might just hear, "Well, he's Korean after all. What do you expect?" Even the great Kaneda, popular as he is, can't completely escape his origins. "Did you know Kaneda is a Korean?" a recent American arrival to Japan was informed. "Kaneda is lucky his team won a pennant. Everyone knows a Korean can't lead a Japanese."

Then there are such mixed-blood players as the Hiroshima Carp's star third-baseman Sachio Kinugasa who is half-Japanese and half-black. A product of the post-war occupation, he was born and raised in Japan. One day, American Jim Hicks, a former Chicago Cub player recruited by the Carp, was swinging away in the batting cage in training camp when a coach advised him to cut down on his swing. "You must not hit the ball so aggressively," the coach warned. "You must do it the Japanese way. Just meet the ball."

Hicks turned and pointed to Kinugasa and said: "What about him?

* Partially because the Japanese once occupied the Korean peninsula (Japan doesn't sympathize with losers—failure only makes one inferior in Japan) and partially because the Koreans tend to be outspoken and aggressive—almost in direct contrast to the Japanese.

Look at the way he swings. He really goes out and attacks the ball. He doesn't just meet it, he really hits it."

"Yes," said the coach patiently, "but he is not a Japanese."

The American who wishes to stay on in Japan as a coach or manager, and make a meaningful contribution to the game, faces considerable barriers. A segment of the baseball establishment holds that no foreigner belongs in the upper echelons of Japanese baseball. There is the danger he will pollute the game with too many unhealthy western ideas. But even more, the American faces a frustrating insularity that believes that no outsider can really understand Japan. "Understanding Japan involves an ability to feel what is going on, and this takes a lifetime to nurture."

In 1970, when the Nankai Hawks made Don Blasingame the first Caucasian head coach in Japanese baseball, there were cries that because Blasingame did not speak Japanese, he wouldn't be able to function. But since Blasingame's knowledge of the game and his no-nonsense manner were all that Hawk manager Katsuya Nomura wanted, Japan's first "white head coach" worked out quite well. While Blasingame was learning Japanese, he taught the Hawks over 40 defensive plays, ran the team when Nomura was catching, and received a share of the credit for the Hawks' 1973 Pacific League Championship.

The Blasingame experiment was so successful, in fact, that the Hankyu Braves decided to call 42-year-old Daryl Spencer back in 1971 to be a part-time player and coach. Spencer delivered some key pinch-hits (even playing a spry first-base on occasion) and his baseball acumen helped the Braves to two straight Pacific League flags. But, unfortunately, Spencer was American. He was too impulsive, too free with his opinions, and his superior knowledge of the game made the Brave coaches look bad. Furthermore, he was too impatient to put up with the marathon meetings the coaching staff went through everyday; he preferred an occasional game of mahjong with the players to break the grind—something a coach isn't supposed to do. Spencer was not retained a third year.

As Spencer, now living in Wichita, recently recalled:

Head Coach Don Blasingame of the Nankai Hawks demonstrates proper bunting form during a spring camp lecture session

I love Japan in many ways. I think I have a lot to offer and that I could help some teams there. I watched the Braves grow from a last-place club into a champion. But, I spoke my mind one too many times, and I think I'm blackballed.

Added one veteran baseball observer in Spencer's defense:

It's too bad about Spencer. Japan should be less sensitive and more appreciative to him for what he has done for the game. He was perhaps the most exciting *gaijin* player to ever play here and his knowledge of baseball is what made the Braves what they are today. I can't think of any other *gaijin*, with the possible exception of Yonamine, who has done as much for Japanese baseball; and I can't think of any other *gaijin* who knows more about the game here. It's really a pity that no team is using him.

In 1972, the Chunichi Dragons made the Hawaiian born Japanese-American Wally Yonamine their manager.* It was a bold move and

* Yonamine was the third foreigner to become a manager in Japan. Bozo Wakabayashi, a Nisei, managed the Hanshin Tigers during the mid-1940s and Kaiser Tanaka, another Nisei was the Hanshin manager in 1957 and 1958.

the appointment was not without its opposition. During his first years, critics sniped at Yonamine. They cried that his language ability wasn't good enough, even though he was fluent in the language. "He can speak all right," said one reporter, "but he can't read. How can he know what we're writing about him?" "His training is too easy," complained another "and he uses the wrong players." "He's too concerned about money," said a third; "he tells his players to improve so that they can make more money. How crude." "Yonamine's opinions as a manager are not valued in inside baseball circles," sniffed an ethno-centrist in summation.

The Dragon front office turned a deaf ear to Yonamine's critics. They knew what they were getting and they respected his ability. Yonamine responded by bringing the Dragons a pennant in 1974—and in a most dramatic, fitting manner. He broke the mighty Giants' nine-year stranglehold on the Central League flag and in the process defeated his old teammate and batting rival, Kawakami, the same man who had once seen to Yonamine's premature departure from the team.

Many viewed the Dragons' ascension to power as a major turning point in Japanese baseball, the dawning of a new era in managing techniques. One liberal spokesman wrote: "Yonamine is perhaps the best manager Japan has had in 30 years. The Dragons' organization has the most progressive training methods in the country. He doesn't overwork his players in training—especially the pitchers." Yonamine's departure from the "live for today" world of the Japanese manager was perhaps his most significant accomplishment. His judicious use of his pitching staff, for example, may well keep the Dragons a Central League power for years to come—and win him the everlasting devotion of his top hurlers who won't have to worry about prematurely changing vocations. With an eye to the future, Yonamine has continually shown concern about the depth of his team. In a typical Dragons contest, for example, as many as 15 or 16 players may see action. Yonamine was so effective a leader that local businesses sought out his advice on management techniques.

Encouraged by the Dragons' success, the Hiroshima Carp appointed former Cleveland Indian coach Joe Lutz as their 1975 field manager—making Lutz the first "white pilot" in the history of Japanese baseball. This radical move by Carp management was an attempt to revive sagging local interest in the team, which had slumped to a new low after numerous lackluster second-division finishes. It was all the more daring because Lutz spoke not a word of Japanese. Although the stocky American had spent the 1974 season with the Carp as a coach and was familiar with the team, he had to run the club and communicate with his employers through an interpreter.

Lutz made some much needed changes in Carp baseball. He immediately slapped a ban on starting pitchers throwing in relief and tried to shift the emphasis of the game to the individual (no mean feat in Japan) by allowing his players more freedom at the plate and on the base paths. "I tried to get them to be more aggressive," said Lutz. "Instead of dictating what a player should do with a runner on base in the early innings, I told them to advance the runner any way they wanted." Lutz also announced a reduction in workouts following the all-star games—an effort to combat the Japanese tendency to run out of gas in the last half of the season.*

The Carp got off to an impressive start—their new hustle amazed Carpophiles—but it soon became apparent that all was not well with the house of Carp and its blue-eyed master. Rumors circulated that the players didn't like being managed by a *gaijin*—especially one who couldn't speak their language. And for a Japanese to be fined by a *gaijin* for not running out grounders at full speed was something the players couldn't abide.

The Carp front office was troubled by other things, however. Lutz's remarks about the quality of Japanese umpiring were disquieting enough, but his frequent harassment of the officials was becoming a deep source of embarrassment. Lutz defended his actions.

---

* One of Lutz's more revolutionary innovations was a seminar he conducted at Hiroshima University for wives of Carp players. These classes, in which he was assisted by several of the faculty, dealt with everything from diet and protein to sex before a game (it's OK) and were an effort to get the normally stay-at-home wives more involved. "I was astonished to discover," Lutz said, "that the wife of a 17 year Carp player and the wife of another who had been with the team for 12 years had *never* met!"

I argued with the umpires for two reasons. I wanted the players to know I would back them up and I hoped my actions would get us a break later on in the game. I explained this policy to team management time and again—I even took the trouble to explain what I was doing to a crew of umpires. But no one understood.

This was purely American reasoning, however. The umpires felt belittled by Lutz's actions, and it was doubtful Carp players felt supported—since they had no idea what their manager was saying when he stormed on the field.

For his part, Lutz was growing increasingly disillusioned. He was upset over his inability to communicate and at what he felt were impingements on his authority.

I didn't feel I had complete control of the team. The front office would make decisions and I was always the last to hear about them. Players would violate curfew and I would learn about it from outside sources like the press. Once the league commissioner sent me a letter regarding a fine on one of our players. I first heard about it from a reporter and then found the front office had been discussing the matter for three days without consulting me.

I just got the feeling after a while that I didn't know what was really going on. There was a total lack of communications.

The situation came to a head less than a month into the regular season when Lutz protested an umpire call and after some bumping and shoving was ordered out of the game. He refused to go, arguing for ten minutes until the Carp general manager, in a highly unorthodox move, came down on the field and asked him to leave. Lutz did and after the game he submitted his resignation "in the best interests of the team." *

Lutz's resignation touched off a flood of eulogies around the league, all praising the value of "Lutz baseball." "We Japanese," said one rival manager, "have much to learn from his brand of baseball." It

---

* For Lutz that was the final insult. As he later revealed: "I think I would have quit anyway. Perhaps things might have been different if I'd had my own interpreter instead of one who worked for the front office. They were extremely kind to me, but as things stood there was just too big a wall between me and everyone else."

also prompted a wave of regrets that the experiment hadn't worked out. The league commissioner sighed: "Lutz just doesn't know enough about Japanese baseball," and added, "Foreign managers are simply not suitable for Japan."

Lutz's departure at Hiroshima Airport was a scene to behold. More than 400 fans, driven perhaps by pangs of guilt, showed up to wish him a safe journey. They showered him with dolls, candy, leis, cigarettes, and all offered "sign-cards" begging him for one last autograph. "We may never see him again," said one well-wisher with a slight touch of panic. A young woman presented her two-year-old son. "Please sign his back," she begged, "so that he will grow up to be strong and brave like you, *Lutz-san!*"

But as Lutz flew off into the sunset, the Japanese baseball world returned to near-normal. The new Carp manager vowed to follow "Lutz baseball"—a fitting tribute to the former American master—and an inspired Carp baseball team went on to win the 1975 Central League pennant, its first ever. And the "Legend of Lutz" became a prominent topic in the Japanese winter stove leagues.*

---

* Perhaps because of the Carp's heady climb to the pennant, Taiheiyo Lion Club owner Nagayoshi Nakamura went in search of an American manager of his own. In early 1976, he signed the famed Leo Durocher to a phenomenal contract estimated at $220,000 a year—with an option to manage "as long as he wanted." Durocher, however, put off his arrival because of other commitments; and in mid-March, when the 69-year-old former umpire-baiter asked for a six-week delay to recover from a bad cold, the Lion owner canceled Durocher's contract.

Some in the press believed that Durocher never intended to come in the first place. Was the whole thing just a ploy to increase Lion season-ticket sales? Others held that Nakamura set it all up simply to get rid of his manager, with whom he was reportedly at odds, but whose first-year record did not warrant a precipitous firing. One paper complained that Durocher was taking Japan too lightly and went on to mention Frank Howard, Joe Lutz, and Joe Pepitone—other *gaijin* who had brought Japan woe—with the headline: "Fans betrayed in another shabby drama."

11 the Giants

Iku-*san* is the cheerful manager of a thriving *sake* house in Tokyo's *shitamachi* (old district). Iku-*san*'s clientele represents a cross section of Tokyoites: construction workers, day laborers, shopkeepers, white-collar workers, carpenters, and fish vendors. They all come to Iku-*san*'s place at the end of the day to let off steam, have a few drinks, and to watch the baseball game. Like other *sake* houses and coffee shops, Iku-*san*'s place has a big color TV for all to see. And every night of the season, it is tuned to Channel Four—Nippon Yomiuri Television—for the Giants' game. The volume is always turned up loud enough to be heard over the din of laughter and clinking glasses.

If you ask Iku-*san*'s customers to name their favorite team, the answer is predictable. "I've been a Giants fan since I was a child," says the man who sells chickens down the street. "Yes, the Giants," adds his friend, the proprietor of the *Fuji* snack shop next door. "When the Giants lose, I get so angry I take it out on my wife. And I don't read the newspaper the next day. But when the Giants win, I'm up at 5 o'clock the next morning waiting for the paper to be delivered so I can read about the game."

If you ask Iku-*san*'s customers why they like the Giants so much you get a variety of answers. "The Giants have always had the best players," says one. "They had Kawakami, then Nagashima and Oh. They are the greatest baseball players who ever lived."

"Giant players are loyal," contributes another. "Kawakami would never manage any team except the Giants. Neither would Nagashima. Kawakami was the team's best batter; now he's a team executive. Nagashima is following the same path."

"The Giants always look good in their uniforms. They're handsome," adds a jovial old lady in a kimono. "Giant players have good manners and they conduct themselves properly on the field," chimes in her friend. "They have grace and style and their technique is good." And a slightly inebriated off-duty taxi driver yells from the end of the counter, "I'm a Japanese! That's why I like the Giants."

But when Iku-*san*, the bartender, says: "The real reason everyone likes the Giants is because they are the best," everyone nods his head in agreement. "The Giants are winners. That's their tradition," he explains. "We Japanese like winners."

"And what's more," he adds with a mischievous grin, "the Giants won nine straight Japan Championships without any foreign players." To the question, "What about Oh, the Giants' first-baseman. His father is Chinese, isn't he?" Iku-*san* nods and replies, "But Oh has a Japanese heart. He was born and raised in Japan. He went to school here. He has a Japanese mother and a Japanese wife. He looks like a Japanese. He talks like a Japanese. He *is* a Japanese."

Suspend your powers of disbelief momentarily and imagine the following: The New York Yankees have won the American League Pennant and the World Series 11 times since 1961, including one streak of *nine* years in a row. (Once they finished last.) NBC has telecast every Yankee game nationwide, each evening during prime time for 15 years, and continually leads all other networks in ratings for that time slot. During this same span the Yankees have drawn near capacity crowds for every single game they have played: at home, on the road, and even during the exhibition season. One out of two baseball fans in the United States is a devout Yankee enthusiast.

Envision all this, and you have a fairly good idea of how successful and popular the Yomiuri Giants are in Japan. They are, in short, a national institution. Since professional play began in 1936, they have totally dominated Japanese baseball in a way that really has no parallel in America.

Winners of nine pennants under the old one-league system, the Tokyo Giants, as they are also known, continued their dominance when the second league was inaugurated in 1950. Lead by Manager Shigeru Mizuhara, and spearheaded by Hawaiian Wally Yonamine and Tetsuharu Kawakami, the "god of batting," the Giants swept to eight more Central League pennants in that decade. Kawakami took over as manager in 1961, and with Oh and Nagashima providing the fireworks, the Giants added 11 more pennants—including an unprecedented nine Japan Championships in a row (1965–1973).

Yet, unlike the New York Yankee teams of the 1950s and early 1960s, who caused a mass exodus of fans from their Stadium in the Bronx when they ticked off American League pennants with such mechanical ease, the Giants have always been incredibly popular. The team drew an average 2,200,000 fans a year until 1970 when the seating capacity of the Giant home stadium, Korakuen, was expanded to its present 50,000. The annual average then rose to well over two and a half million. That's approximately 40,000 fans for each of the 65 home games the Giants play. In the U.S., with the standard 81 home-game schedule, that would be equivalent to three and a quarter million—a figure that *no* American team has even approached.

The Giants have drawn 20,000 fans to a spring training workout, and once played a pre-season game in a snowstorm before an overflow crowd that stayed to the end. Almost every game the team plays is televised nationally, sometimes on two channels at once, and viewer

The 1973 Giants display yet another pennant to their fans at Korakuen Stadium

ratings in the "Japanese Nielsen" for Giant games run from 20 to 30 percent. The major sport dailies normally devote front-page coverage and close to half their baseball content to the team's activities. Even *Tokyo Chunichi Sports*, an affiliate of the news group that owns the Chunichi Dragons, and *Sankei Sports*, once affiliated with the Atoms, have continually given the Giants a disproportionate share of the print. Annual surveys consistently show that nearly half those who follow baseball in Japan are *Kyojin* (Giant) fans.

For years, *Kyojin no Hoshi* (Star of the Giants), an animated cartoon series describing the trials of a Japanese youth who undergoes punishing training by his father to make him worthy of becoming a Giant, was one of the most popular programs on the air. In fact, there's scarcely a youngster who doesn't own a Yomiuri Giant cap.

In 1974, the Giants failed to win the Central League pennant for the first time in ten years, losing by one-tenth of a percentage point to the Chunichi Dragons.* Several veterans retired and the team embarked on a major rebuilding program. And although the 1975 Giants occupied last place all season long, their popularity and attendance remained sky-high. In an incredible display of loyalty, over 2,800,000 fans turned out to watch the team—an all time record for a single season.

When the New York Yankees had a monopoly on the American League pennant, "Yankee-hating" became a national pastime. So the love the Japanese have for a team that grinds out championships with monotonous regularity must indeed seem puzzling to Americans unfamiliar with Japan.

The Giants' "lovability" can of course be partly traced to the fact that the team is owned by the Yomiuri conglomerate of the Shoriki family—a vast media complex well-equipped to propagate the Giant legend. It includes the *Yomiuri Shinbun*, one of the largest selling daily newspapers in the world,† the *Hōchi Shinbun*, a leading sports daily, and Nippon Television, the third largest TV network in Japan.

---

* Ties are counted in Japan.

† The *Yomirui* has a circulation of 7,000,000, seven times that of the New York *Daily News*, in a country with a population less than half that of the U.S.

No other club is as fortunate. When the Yomiuri media machine moves into action it virtually buries every other team in baseball. Yomiuri newspapers ensure extra space for photos and stories about the Giants. And the network, besides telecasting their games, inundates its program schedule with shows featuring Giant players. Consequently, the nation often knows more about the Giants' latest rookie than it does about the established stars on other teams.

The Giants popularity is not entirely the result of a massive PR campaign, however. From the beginning, the Yomirui organizations has attracted the best players. First there was Eji Sawamura, the pitcher who threw that magnificent game against Ruth and Gehrig and the other American All-Stars in 1934. Then there were Takehiko Bessho, and the White Russian Victor Starfin, both 300 game winners. From 1938 to 1958, Giant first-baseman Kawakami was considered the greatest hitter in baseball. And then along came Nagashima and Oh, who raised the stature of the Giants to unbelievable heights. To cap this, even the great pitcher Kaneda joined the team in his later years. These players created a long line of Japan Champions and a baseball aristocracy.

The Giants have always been at the forefront. They were the first

Fans swarm the Giants' team bus

professional team; and they were the first to use an American after the war. They were also the first to drop Americans, when Kawakami established his "pure-blooded" Japanese Giants. The success Kawakami achieved, dominating other clubs that relied on American players, forever endeared the House of Yomiuri to a nation struggling to regain its self-esteem after the war.

Then too, the Giants have a deep sense of tradition. When Kawakami retired, he paid a ritualistic visit to the grave of Giant founder Matsutaro Shoriki (who had died in 1969) before moving up to the Giant front office. And when Nagashima, who had been "like a son" to Kawakami, took over the job as manager, he was inducted in a ceremony at Korakuen Stadium equivalent to a coronation.

The overwhelming popularity of the Giants has done serious damage to other teams at the gate. In 1973, for example, the Central League had its tightest race in history; six games separated the first and last place teams in the final standings. Yet the average attendance for non-Giant games in the Central League was so low (10,000) that only the Giants made a profit. The following year, interest was heightened because the Giants finally lost. Yet even so, only three teams besides the Giants managed to make money.

The situation in the Pacific League that same year was far grimmer. Every team finished in the red.* In the early 1960s, one of the stronger Pacific League teams, the Toei Flyers (later to become the Nippon Ham Fighters), was drawing over two million a year. But with the Giants' surge to dominance, attendance dwindled to less than half that of the Central League. Even pennant winners played before empty parks.

The Pacific League has always been in trouble; and the owners, frustrated in numerous attempts to establish inter-league play and to reap some benefits from the Giants' drawing power, have tried everything to stimulate flagging fan enthusiasm. One team, the Hankyu Braves, decided to adopt a caricature of Popeye, wearing a gladiator's helmet and smoking his pipe, as a team insignia, but then dropped

---

* All stadiums in Japan are independently owned, so clubs are deprived of additional revenue from concessions.

the idea when King Features asked $5000 for its use.

On a more practical level, the league began scheduling games on Friday, traditionally an off-day in Japanese baseball, and arranged to have all games televised from beginning to end (instead of the customary one hour and 26 minutes). In 1973, the league instituted a split-season, with a five-game playoff at the end of the year between the two winners for the pennant. And in 1975, it adopted the designated hitter rule.* The result of all these efforts: No appreciable rise in attendance, low TV ratings, additional seasons in the red for each team.

As long as the Pacific League was unable to produce a "Giants" of its own, fans continued to stay away. One team, the Lotte Orions, was forced to move to Sendai because it could not afford to pay the rent on its park in Tokyo. The Nishitetsu Railways Corporation and the Toei Motion Picture Corporation finally gave up. In 1973, Nishitetsu sold the Lions to the Taiheiyo Land Development Corporation and Toei sold out to Nittaku Homes, who in turn sold the team to Nippon Ham a year later. The financial burden was simply too much to bear.

The prestige of the almighty Giants undermined rival teams in other ways. Many young prospects signed on with them, not for higher salaries, but for the status that came with wearing a Giant uniform. One star high-school player, turned down an $80,000 offer from Toei to sign with the Giants for $30,000 less. A draft system, instigated in the late 1960s, helped restore equity; but occasionally a player would still refuse to sign with the club that drafted him hoping somehow to land on the Giants. Such was the appeal of being with Yomiuri. It was like being a Tokyo University graduate or an employee of the Bank of Japan. In Japan, it was the tops.

Baseball people outside the Giants' camp are not happy with what some regard as the underhanded manner the Yomirui organization has used its power. In league meetings, for example, the owner of the

---

* League owners stopped short of more radical changes, such as one suggesting that the pitcher be required to tell the batter what the next pitch would be; or a second idea by the same person that the number of allowable strikes be lowered to two.

championship team traditionally wields an inordinate amount of influence; and there are suspicions that Matsutaro Shoriki, former owner of the Giants, used his to gain unfair advantage. As one writer complained:

Umpires' salaries are determined by owners' conferences, which, in effect, meant that Shoriki had control over them. In the period between 1963 and 1973, it seemed very strange, but in nearly every instance of a dispute involving the Giants and the umpires, the decision eventually went in favor of Yomiuri.

The pressure on the umpires was very subtle. That's the Japanese way. There are no open threats. All a Giant official has to say to an umpire is: "I saw the game the other night. . . ." The umpire understands the message. And if he knows what is good for his future as an umpire, he will not make life difficult for the Giants.

And then of course there is the power of the Yomiuri media. Central League players habitually complain, for example, that "To fight against the Giants means to fight mass communication." One baseball writer elaborates:

If a particular batter is hitting well against the Giants, the *Hōchi Shinbun* will conduct psychological warfare against him. It will dig up some gossip or a scandal and make it a big story in the paper. Since no other team except Chunichi is affiliated with a newspaper, this kind of thing is not written about the Giants, even though the top Giant players have been known to keep mistresses. Chunichi and the Giants seem to have an unwritten agreement not to attack each other.

"Giant power," in all its forms, is a great source of irritation to non-Giants. So when a Central League team marches into the hallowed grounds of Korakuen for a three-game series, it musters up all its fighting spirit and is prepared with its best pitcher rested and ready to answer the call in all three games if necessary. Teams that fall short of the pennant will still look back upon the season with pride if they won the majority of their games against the Giants.

The failure of the mighty Giant machine to win its 10th straight pennant in 1974 was a traumatic experience for Giant lovers in more ways than one. The painfully obvious need for fresh talent had thrown the Giant front office into a panic and they did the unthinkable: they hired a *gaijin*. This radical move stunned Japan's pure-blood cult who could not believe the royal house of Yomiuri would ever again "integrate," but it dramatically emphasized just how low the Giant star had fallen.

The "chosen one" was Dave Johnson—a former Atlanta slugging star—who, although coveted by many teams in the States, had somehow managed to gain his release from the Braves. Along with the privilege of becoming the first non-Oriental American ever to wear a Yomiuri Giant uniform, the 32-year-old second-baseman was given a substantial two-year contract plus a record $120,000.

All that was expected of the four-time all-star who hit 43 home runs for Atlanta in 1974 (a major-league record for second-baseman) was that he play third and fill the gaping hole in the lineup created by Nagashima's retirement. Unfortunately, he found the various adjustments hard to make. A late start, separation from his family, the language barrier, and the absence of another American on the team, all

Ex-Atlanta Braves' slugging star Dave Johnson rounds the bases

Nagashima and members of his team listen to Shinto priest's prayer for good fortune in the 1975 season

seemed to affect Johnson considerably. While a broken bone in his shoulder which kept him out of action for more than a month, the loss of 25 pounds, and Nagashima's penchant for benching him if he went hitless for a few games didn't help his morale much either. Johnson struggled through a dismal first season. He batted .197, hit 13 home runs, and the Giants finished in last place for the first time ever.

Johnson was naturally the scapegoat for the Giants' nosedive. The press rode him mercilessly and one paper even took to writing his name as J-*son* (*son* means "loss" in Japanese). Yet nothing could hide the overall disintegration of the once-proud *Kyojin*. The dramatic change in their status sent a wave of anxiety rippling through the country. One paper, *The Japan Stock Journal*, even wondered if the collapse of Japan's favorite baseball team bore a dark connection to the country's woeful business slump.

The spectrum of Giant fandom is a wide one, but among the most fervent are the middle and upper-echelon brass in big business. Underlings are extra prudent at work after the Giants lose a game because the boss or section chief will be in a bad mood.

Does the decline and fall of the Giants have anything to do with, say, the present state of the economy? It was in 1974 that the economy experienced zero growth, the year the Giants lost the pennant. Sports page talk about the Giants now is wait until next year, of shrewd trades, or promising rookies coming up. Nagashima will stay. If the economy recovers, can the Giants be far behind? Something has to be done to put the boss in a better frame of mind.

Perhaps the most traumatized of all was rookie manager Nagashima. Japan's national idol spent the season hiding in a corner of the dugout where the TV cameras couldn't find him. On the last day of the season, he herded his charges before the loyal fans at Korakuen Stadium to lead them in a formal apology for their poor performance. Nagashima then presumably headed for the nearest Shinto shrine—to pray either for a climb in the GNP or a marked rise in Johnson's batting average the following season. *

---

* Nagashima's prayers were answered. In 1976, Johnson raised his batting average a hundred points; and so did several other Giants. The acquisition of the great Korean batter and a second American, pitcher Clyde Wright, sparked an overall rejuvenation of the team. Although the Giants were far from being pure-blooded anymore, they were back in their rightful place at the top. And to their faithful millions, that was all that mattered. At the same time, the GNP began to rise again.

12 A REAL WORLD SERIES

The ace hurler of the Tokyo Giants, Tsuneo Horiuchi, cooly eyes the big American batter at the plate before glancing in at his catcher for the sign. It is the top of the 9th; two out. The Giants are leading the winners of the American playoffs 7–0 in the fourth game of the first annual international world series.

The Giants have won the first three games, taking the opener and Game Two at Korakuen Stadium in Tokyo, before flying to the United States and winning Game Three at the American team's park. Giant batting stars Oh and Nagashima have each blasted three home runs in the four games, and the pinpoint pitching of the Giant staff has held the Americans to just one run in three games.

It is three o'clock in the morning back in Japan, but the entire nation is awake, glued to their television sets to watch the satellite relay of the game. With the count two strikes and a ball, the Giants are just one strike away from their first world championship. Horiuchi goes calmly into this windup and fires. Curve ball at the knees over the outside corner. Strike three!

The crowd of 70,000 Americans sit in stunned silence. They cannot believe what they have just seen. While in Japan, 100,000,000 people break into a sustained cheer that shakes the tiny island nation. The Yomiuri Giants have just swept the Americans four straight and are the baseball champions of the world!

From the time he founded the *Dai Nippon* Club in 1935 until his death in 1969, owner Matsutaro Shoriki often spoke publicly of his special dream: a *real* world series between his Giants and the winners of the American series. A four-game sweep over the Americans is probably what he had in mind, since the history of Japanese-

American competition over the years has been such a nightmare.

Shoriki made his initial foray into international baseball in 1931, when as a promotional device for his newspaper he sponsored a tour of American major-league all-stars.* This pickup team which called itself the Major League Stars, featuring such greats as Lou Gehrig, Charley Gehringer, Lefty Grove, Al Simmons, and Lefty O'Doul, romped to a 17-0 record. The games, played against amateur competition, were so one-sided that the results often resembled football scores. Shoriki invited the Americans back in 1934. This time with Babe Ruth and Jimmy Foxx along, they again breezed to a 17-0-1 mark.

The second trip, however, was significant for Japan in two ways. First, 19-year-old Eji Sawamura pitched that great game in which he struck out Gehringer, Ruth, Foxx, and Gehrig in succession, a feat which gave the country its first authentic baseball hero. And second, the American pros were so popular that Shoriki (with some friendly persuasion from O'Doul who had acted as a co-leader of the tour) decided to form a professional baseball team of his own—the Giants. Two years later, Japan had its first pro league. Deteriorating relations between the two countries then prohibited any further trips.

During World War II, *"Rusu* (Ruth) is a bum" became the greatest insult Japanese soldiers could hurl at their American enemies. By 1949, however, Shoriki was at it again. With the blessing of General Douglas MacArthur, Shoriki invited his old friend Lefty O'Doul to make a return visit—this time as manager of the Pacific Coast League's San Francisco Seals. For the first time, Shoriki was able to send up professional competition against the visiting Americans, but it made little difference. The Seals won all six games with ease.

The Seals' venture was helpful in breaking the ice between the two

---

* American professional teams to visit Japan before that time included the Reach All-Americans, a group of major- and minor-leaguers sponsored by the A. J. Reach & Co. sporting goods manufacturers, who played a 19 game tour in 1908, a combined N.Y. Giant–Chicago White Sox team led by John McGraw and Charles Comiskey that made a stopover in Japan on a worldwide tour, and the Hunter All-Americans, a squad of big leaguers led by Herb Hunter, a former National League utility infielder, who made a visit in 1920. It was Hunter who was instrumental in getting Ty Cobb to spend the 1929 season in Japan as a coach, and who later organized the 1931 tour.

countries. MacArthur was effusive in his praise of O'Doul: "You have done more than all the diplomats have in breaking down the aloofness existing between the people of Japan and the occupation personnel." O'Doul joined a small, select group of foreigners when he was given an audience with the Japanese Emperor. His Imperial Majesty remarked upon meeting the Seals' manager, "I am glad to meet the greatest baseball man in the world."

O'Doul was back in 1951, leading a group of major-league all-stars that included Joe DiMaggio and diminutive left-handed pitching star Bobby Shantz. Lefty's charges swept to a 13-1-2 record. DiMaggio hit his last home run as a player in Japan and Shantz became the first major-league pitcher ever to lose to the Japanese, when he suffered a 3-1 setback to a Pacific League all-star team.

From then on, post-season visits by American teams became a regular affair. By agreement, they were sponsored alternately by the *Yomiuri* and *Mainichi* newspapers with the understanding that the U.S. Commissioner of Baseball would select a worthy representative to play in Japan. The purpose of these tours was to let the fans see major-league baseball, give the Japanese players an opportunity to learn something, and to promote good-will and mutual understanding between the two countries. The ultimate plan of course, particularly of Shoriki and his Giants, was to develop Japanese baseball to the point where it would be on a par with the American game.

The Japanese improved gradually, although as records of the "competition" over the next decade indicate, they did not pose much of a threat to American baseball dominance. In 1953, for example, Ed Lopat and a team of all-stars, posted an 11-1 record, while in the fall of that same year, the N.Y. Giants finished an exhibition tour at 12-1-1. In 1955, the American League Champion New York Yankees with Mickey Mantle, Yogi Berra, and Whitey Ford waltzed to 15 wins and a tie in 16 games, and the following year, the National League Champions, the Brooklyn Dodgers with Duke Snider, Roy Campanella, and Don Newcombe, racked up a lethargic 14-4-1 record. In 1958, the St. Louis Cardinals with Stan Musial were 14-2-2; in 1960, the San Francisco Giants with Willy Mays, Orlando Cepeda, and Willy McCovey were 11-4-3; and in 1962, the A. L. runner-up Detroit

Brooklyn Dodgers at the Hiroshima Peace Shrine in 1956

Tigers with Al Kaline, Norm Cash, and Jim Bunning compiled a 12-4-2 mark.

It was obvious to any American observer that Mickey Mantle, Stan Musial, Al Kaline, and company were not exactly at peak form for the games. Most of the players were somewhat rusty and, unwilling to risk injury in meaningless games, scarcely played with reckless abandon.

The post-season trip to Japan was considered a vacation for the players and their wives. They saw Mt. Fuji, the shrines at Nikko, and the temples and gardens in Kyoto. They purchased Japanese watches, cameras, silk screens, woodblock prints, and explored the little shops in the twisting, narrow sidestreets of the Ginza and Asakusa. They ate *sukiyaki* and *tempura,* sampled *sake* and *Kirin* beer. For most, it was their first trip to the exotic Orient and it proved an exciting adventure.

When the idea of a formal international "world series" to replace the good-will exhibition tours was first broached in 1962, it was rejected outright by U.S. Commissioner of Baseball, Ford Frick. It was too soon, Frick said. The Detroit Tigers 12-4-2 record on their 1962 tour demonstrated that. Frick suggested instead, that the Japanese champions have a "junior world series" with the American Triple A winners. The Japanese commissioner refused. Japan wanted to play the big-leaguers or no one.

One reporter, wise to the ways of the East, then suggested that the Japan champions play a regular post-season tournament with the last-place team in the majors. If the Japanese lost to the likes of the newly founded Mets, he reasoned, at least they would be losing to a major-league team. A series defeat by a Triple A team would be a loss of face and prestige too hard to bear. But if the Japanese team did manage to defeat the big-league cellar dwellers, the next year they would play the next-to-last-place team, gradually moving up, through the 24 American clubs, according to their performance. In this way, the Japanese would eventually earn the right to play the U.S. champion. The idea was poorly received, however, once it was calculated that it would take Japan at the very least 24 years to make it to the top of the ladder.

The United States had underestimated the seriousness of the Japanese—Shoriki, in particular. Shoriki was in the process of assembling the most devastating team Japan had ever produced. In addition to the "O-N Cannon," they boasted a slew of .300 batters—sharp, line-drive hitters who could spray the ball to all fields, a sturdy pitching staff that from 1966 would be led by the brilliant Tsuneo Horiuchi, plus a solid defense which included the best double-play combination and possibly the speediest outfield in either league. They were young and tough and well-schooled in fundamentals. They played as a team, and they seldom beat themselves with mistakes. These "pure-bloods" of manager Tetsuharu Kawakami were poised to dominate Japanese baseball for the next decade and Shoriki was eager to match them against America's best. He would not settle for anything less.

To illustrate, in early 1965 Commissioner Frick selected the Pittsburgh Pirates to make the post-season tour that fall. Shoriki, whose newspaper underwrote the costs of the trip, rejected the National League team. Shoriki's "official" excuse was that the Pirates were unknown in Japan and would not draw good crowds. But everyone knew his real motive. He wanted the American champion to play his "superteam."

Frick argued that Pittsburgh would be a "worthy representative." They were a strong pennant contender, led by such stars as Roberto Clemente, Bob Friend, Bill Mazeroski, and Bill Virdon. Frick reiterated his contention that a real world series was premature. He admitted that the Japanese were improving, but said they had a long way to go before they could play consistently on the level of a team like the Pirates.*

Shoriki was adamant in his refusal to accept the Steel City team. Frick said that the Pirates would go to Japan or no one would. The impasse could not be broken and there were no "good-will" games that fall.

In November 1965, the 80-year-old Shoriki made another attempt to get an American champion to visit Japan. He sent his son, Toru, to the United States in an effort to persuade Frick to let the newly crowned L. A. Dodgers come in the fall of 1966. Toru conveyed to Commissioner Frick his father's deep conviction that Japanese baseball, and, in particular, his Giants, "had improved to such an extent that they would be able to make a good showing against the U. S. champs."

Frick was still reluctant. "How can the Japanese compete when American players no longer usable in the majors were playing regularly in Japan?" he wondered. The younger Shoriki informed Frick that the Yomiuri Giants had won the 1965 Japan championship handily with a team of *all* Japanese players. Toru urged the proposal be accepted, if only because it was his aging father's dream to have a real world series.

Frick, who was on the verge of retiring, agreed to take up the Japanese proposal at the 1965 winter meeting of team owners. However, the idea was greeted with little enthusiasm. When Frick announced

---

* The major weakness was that the teams had no depth. A player of major-league class would be playing alongside a Class B level player. Japanese teams did not have the bench strength American big-league teams had—that is, the pinch-hitters, defensive specialists, relief pitchers.

his retirement and a new commissioner, William Eckert, was selected, Shoriki decided to try once more.

This time his son Toru delivered a personal invitation directly to Dodger officials. When they consulted the new commissioner, he agreed that the Japanese should have some say in the choice of whom they would invite, and gave his approval. The Dodgers then agreed to go, but they made it clear they would not be coming as National League Champions, but, in the words of one Dodger official, "as ambassadors of good will in baseball uniforms." *

Though satisfied, Shoriki was not happy when the Dodgers lost the 1966 World Series in four straight games to Baltimore. Nor when the two Dodger greats Sandy Koufax and Don Drysdale decided not to come. Shoriki suspected his Giants were being taken lightly.

In their 18 games in Japan, the Dodgers struggled to an embarrassing 9–8–1 slate, and were beaten by the Giants in *four* of the seven games the two teams played together. Giant fans were exuberant at their club's achievement. They allowed that the absence of the two great Dodger pitchers might have made some difference, but noted that the Dodger's number three pitcher Claude Osteen had been bombed out five times in a row, and that Sadaharu Oh had ripped Dodger pitchers to the tune of five home runs and a .344 batting average.

Kyojin supporters basked in the glow of laudatory comments made by their visitors. Dodger Manager Walter Alston, for example, had nothing but praise for the Giant's slick infield defense, their teamwork, and the sharp, level swings of their batters. He said that Oh and Nagashima would be stars on *any* U.S. team, and judged that with three or four dependable starting pitchers the Giants would be a major-league team. Dodger catcher John Roseboro added his opinion

---

* The Giants warmed up for their fall meeting with Los Angeles by taking on the Mexico City Tigers that spring. The Tigers, a Double A level team played a 13 game tour and lost every single match—including five lopsided tilts to the Giants. So vast was the difference between Yomiuri and the Mexican squad, that one commentator described the Tigers as the worst he had ever seen, and claimed their manager was "unfit to be handling a professional baseball team." Giant players ungraciously added their conditioning had "gone bad" just by playing the Mexicans. Clearly the Giants were ready for headier stuff.

that young Giant hurler Tsuneo Horiuchi was worth a quarter of a million dollars. And Walter Dillbeck, who headed a group that founded the ill-fated Global League, said flatly: "The Japanese are ready for the majors."

The Dodgers' woeful record ("a disgrace" was the way one American official put it) complicated the situation for the American side. "How can you not include us in the world series when we have just won 4 of 7 from your National League Champions?" wondered Giant fans.

This was a difficult question to answer diplomatically. It was obvious that four Giant wins against a Dodger team minus Koufax and Drysdale were meaningless. Without them, the Dodgers were just an ordinary team. Nevertheless, the Commissioner's office was in an awkward situation. Finally the reply came that Japanese participation in any world series was a virtual certainty in the future, but the timing was not yet right. For the present, the U.S. would like to continue sending high quality teams—teams, of course, that met with Japanese approval.

The following spring, Yomiuri was invited to train with the Dodgers at Vero Beach in Florida. And once again, those seeing Manager Kawakami's Giants for the first time were duly impressed. Said Wes Parker: "Nagashima is as good as Ron Santo. Their infielders seem very sure about what they're doing. They react well. They look like they've been practicing the same things eight hours a day for years." Don Drysdale, who visited Japan with the Brooklyn Dodgers in 1956, appraised the Japanese now as "bigger and faster," and ex-Dodger great and batting coach Duke Snider added: "Oh is the best hitter in camp."

Alston enlarged upon his initial evaluation: "They're my kind of hitters. They don't have much power, but they make contact with the ball. They're very hard to strike out. Their pitchers all look about the same. They don't throw exceptionally hard, but they all have good curves and control. They seldom beat themselves with walks. And I like the way Kawakami handles his club. His strategy is sound."

Dodger General Manager Fresco Thompson who had also made the 1956 trip with Brooklyn said: "The Japanese have improved more in the last ten years than American players. They work harder than we do and they're better at fundamentals." He added that the Dodgers would have won two more pennants in the early sixties with Nagashima at third.

The Giants returned to Japan in a state of euphoria. Kawakami, particularly buoyed by all this praise, said boldly: "The Americans have nothing more to teach us." And Tetsuya Shimamura, a writer for *Sankei Sports* echoed the view of a growing number of believers when he wrote: "The Giants may now be slightly inferior to major-league clubs in the throwing arms of their outfielders and batting power, but in the performance of their infielders and baserunning, the Giants are equal or even superior to major-league clubs. The time to play a real world series has come." The Yomiuri front office was so confident that it toyed with the idea of entering the Giants in the U.S. major leagues, and leaving their farm team to play in Japan.

The Giant bubble developed a leak, however, in 1968 when the St. Louis Cardinals went to Japan. The Cardinals, owners of two straight National League pennants, were coming off a seven game loss to Mickey Lolich and the Detroit Tigers in the American series. (Once again much to Shoriki's chagrin.)

The Redbirds, led by the incomparable Bob Gibson, the slaphitting, basestealing duo of Lou Brock and Curt Flood, and powerful first-baseman Orlando Cepeda, put a stop to the *Kyojin* Express and romped to a 13–5 record. The Giants, who had scheduled ten games with the Cards, managed but two wins.*

As the U.S. breathed a sigh of relief, Giant fans assured themselves it was only a temporary setback. After all, Nagashima had been sidelined the whole series with an injury, and four of their losses were by two runs or less. On the brighter side, Oh batted .356 and belted six home runs. More importantly, the Cardinals praised the Giants as

---

* Suffering from a two-week layoff after the 1968 world series, the Cardinals started off badly. Cardinal star Bob Gibson was shelled from the mound in the first game, and the Redbirds dropped two of the first three. This prompted such growls from Giant Manager Kawakami as: "We want the Americans to practice and be in shape when they arrive here to play us." Cardinal Manager Red Schoendienst assured the Japanese his Cards were "serious" about the games and then proved it as St. Louis went on to win ten of the next eleven.

much as the Dodgers had. Red Schoendienst, for example, had this to say:

I don't have any particular advice for the Japanese. The only thing they lack now is power. They have every fundamental—pitching, right-field hitting, sliding. Their running and fielding are superb. The players know the strike zone. They don't hit bad balls. They're real hard to strike out.

The only thing I can think of is the way the pitchers are used here. I have seen pitchers throwing in the bullpen every day. Pitchers wear out fast that way. They need at least three days rest after a game. Otherwise we haven't much advice to give them.

Matsutaro Shoriki died in 1969, leaving his dream of a real world series unfulfilled. But his son Toru picked up the torch. And in March 1971, a visit by the San Francisco Giants started rumblings of baseball parity once again. The Giants were invited by the Pacific League Orions to spend part of spring training in Japan, and to play nine games—one with Yomiuri. San Francisco, considered a solid National League pennant contender, had Willy Mays, Willie McCovey, rookie-of-the-year Bobby Bonds, and two of baseball's best pitchers in Juan Marichal and Gaylord Perry. But they took home America's first losing record: three wins and six losses.

Fans of the Japanese Giants (who won their lone game with the American Giants 6–5, on two home runs by Oh) were now convinced

Bob Gibson pitches to Oh during the St. Louis Cardinals' tour of Japan in 1968

the gap had been closed between the two countries. If a weak sister Pacific League club like Lotte could win three of five against a National League "powerhouse" like San Francisco, Yomiuri should certainly be able to hold its own against any American team. The pressure was back on.

The Japanese did not want to hear any excuses about "lack of training" or "not being serious," as some San Francisco apologists hinted. The next American team to come had better be in shape and ready to put out 100%.

In early 1971, when newly appointed U.S. Baseball Commissioner Bowie Kuhn picked the 1970 World Champion Baltimore Orioles to play the Japanese in October of that year, the stage was set. Yomiuri, it appeared, was finally going to get the chance it had been waiting for.

The Orioles were in the process of creating an American League dynasty. They had won two pennants in a row and were favored to take the flag again in the upcoming A. L. Season. They had devastated the Cincinnati Reds in the American series the year before, winning in five games.

The Orioles were loaded with talent: Brooks Robinson, alltime great Frank Robinson, 1970 MVP Boog Powell, and all-star second baseman Don Buford. They had four 20 game winners: former Cy Young award winner Mike Cuellar, speedballer Jim Palmer, Pat Dobson, and the mainstay of the pitching staff, Dave McNally. Baltimore was touted by many observers as the greatest team ever put together.

An unprecedented 11 of the 18 games would be against the Yomiuri Giants. And since, both the Orioles and the Giants were fully expected to win hands down in their respective countries, it would be the closest Japan had yet come to Shoriki's dream. A good showing by the Giants, and the United States would have to consider renaming its annual fall classic.

The Giants spent part of their spring training that year in Dodgertown, at the invitation of Walter O'Malley and the Los Angeles team. During their stay, they played six exhibition games, winning three and losing three. By chance, one of those games was with the Baltimore Orioles. The Giants lost, 6–4, but the experience seemed to erase any remaining doubts they might have had about their ability to compete against the much larger Birds. As Kawakami said afterward: "Their physical superiority seemed indeed overwhelming before the game, but later I found they were not as powerful as I thought." The bespectacled Giants' pilot then added that if his pitchers "pitched low and worked the corners," he believed they could beat the Orioles in their upcoming series.

Those who felt the Giants would emerge victorious in their postseason date with destiny based this view not only on Yomiuri's past performances in games with the Americans, but also on a number of other factors extending from the assumption that the Japanese way of doing things would prove superior to the American way.

The Giants trained harder. Giant batters, unlike Oriole batters, toiled long and hard in the batting cage. They were skilled in the art of hitting to all fields and fouling off bad pitches. They knew how to advance the runner. They played as a team.

Oriole pitchers were faster than those Giant batters usually faced; but the Giants would choke up on the bat, concentrate, wait for the pitch they wanted, and punch it into the open hole. And, of course, Oh and Nagashima, great international sluggers that they were, would hit their share of home runs.

Giant pitchers, although not especially fast, had good breaking stuff and pinpoint control. Unlike Oriole pitchers, they threw every day in the bullpen. Oriole batters were big and powerful. No one in Japan could hit a ball as far as Boog Powell or Frank Robinson. But that would be no problem. Giant hurlers would keep their breaking pitches low and work the corners. The ball would be hit on the ground and Giant infielders would gobble it up.

Yes, the time had come for Japan to show the rest of the world what real dedication could accomplish. All those years of hard work were about to pay off. The mighty Giants would be taking a string of seven straight Japan titles into their series with Baltimore. The *Kyojin* dynasty was at its peak. The most powerful team in the history of Japanese baseball was finally prepared to do what was once thought impossible—beat the Americans at their own game.

As the 1971 baseball season progressed, tension and excitement over the forthcoming Oriole–Giant clash began to mount in Japan. Both the Tokyo team and Baltimore were comfortably ahead in their respective leagues, and the Japanese baseball world was looking past the play-offs and world series to the match-up between these two titans.

Reporters sent to America to scout Baltimore echoed Kawakami's view that the Giants could beat the Orioles. They confidently assured their readers that the Yomiuri team was at least equal, and, in some areas, even better than Baltimore. They pestered Orioles' manager Earl Weaver about his views on the upcoming battle who, apparently unaware of the importance of the match to the Japanese, brushed off the exasperating reporters with his usual bluntness. He had enough to worry about just winning his division race.

Now as the days dwindled down, the eleven scheduled Giant–Oriole contests began to take on even deeper significance. To the man on the street, the powerful Yomiuri club was part of the new status Japan enjoyed in the world with its booming economy and skyrocketing GNP.

The Japanese were tired of playing second fiddle to the Americans. Where once they had looked upon America as a benevolent older brother, they now wanted equality. The younger brother had grown up. Furthermore, President Nixon's surprise trip to China had been a slap in the face, and his Administration's stiffening attitude toward Japan in trade affairs cast serious doubts as to just how concerned the older brother really was about the younger. These events triggered a wave of anti-American feeling throughout the country. And, as a result, a Giant victory over the American team would be just that much sweeter.

Every cab driver and bartender in Tokyo, when not railing against the Nixon *shokku's* (shock), had something to say about the upcoming series. "Hey, *gaijin-san*, what do you think of the Oriole–Giant games? The Giants are ready this time. Just wait until Oh and Nagashima get a hold of those American pitchers. Hah! Hah! You'll see. You Americans have been champions too long."

This mania crested as the Giants wrapped up their seventh straight Central League title and the Orioles waltzed to their third consecu-

Above: Korakuen's scoreboard shows the final result: Aaron 10, Oh 9

Left: Oh shakes hands with Hank Aaron after their home-run contest in Tokyo in November 1974

tive Eastern Division crown with a three-game sweep over the Oakland Athletics. When the Orioles took the first two games of the world series against the N.L. pennant winners, the Pittsburgh Pirates, Japanese heads nodded knowingly. Yes, this was the best American team by far. The match-up against their Giants would be a good one.

The Pirates, unaware of their role in this prescribed drama, won the next three games to take a 3–2 series lead. What was wrong, the Japanese wondered. Were the Orioles overconfident? No, just looking ahead to their more important series with the Giants, they reassured themselves. No need to worry. They'll snap out of it. They want to come to Japan as champions. Baltimore reassured the uneasy multitudes in Japan when they won the sixth game to even the series at three games apiece. But then came the bombshell. Baltimore *lost* the seventh and deciding game to Steve Blass and the Pirates 2–1. The Orioles were *not* world champions. A Yomiuri official announced that he was "stunned" at the Oriole downfall, and moaned that "the failure of the Orioles to win the world series has undoubtedly discounted the meaning of the games they will play against the Giants."

The Japanese were terribly disappointed. Even if the Giants now won a majority of their games against Baltimore, it would be a shallow victory. There would be no incentive for the Orioles, with no real world championship on the line, and they probably wouldn't play as hard. Some even asked if perhaps the Pirates could not be sent instead. No, they were informed; this was impossible. Maybe next time.

But Japan did not want to "wait until next time," and minds began working in devious ways. Supporters of the Giant cause thought of a way their heroes could still become the world champions. They calculated in this manner: The Pirates record against the Orioles was four wins in seven games—a percentage of .571. Thus, if the Giants won seven of their eleven games with the Birds—a percentage of .636, they could lay rightful claim to the world title.

Baltimore's defeat in the series took on a new light with this reasoning. Somehow the Giants' task seemed a little easier; victory over Baltimore more probable. The Orioles would let down for sure. In fact, by the next day, the whole matter appeared settled. Or at least it was for one announcer who, in describing the final pitch of the Japan Series, called it the "pitch that will determine the champions of Japan . . . er . . . no. The champions of the world!"

The clamor in Japan over the Giants' rating as a world baseball power was not completely lost on Baltimore. The team had heard of the impact in Japan of their loss to Pittsburgh. "We didn't want to spoil them," remarked Frank Robinson sardonically. But unlike their predecessors, they would be coming to Japan at full strength and—unwilling to further disappoint their hosts—determined to play their usual brand of all-out baseball.

The series began with all the hoopla usually associated with such events in Japan. A huge welcoming party met the Orioles at Haneda airport, and this was followed shortly thereafter by a special reception for them in Tokyo. The opening game—the first of those eleven "crucial" Oriole–Giant encounters—was played beneath a clear blue autumn sky. Kimono-clad beauties presented bouquets to the Orioles. The U.S. ambassador read a special message from President Nixon and the Japanese foreign minister made a speech. Japan's Self-

Defense Force Band played the "Star-Spangled Banner," Bowie Kuhn threw out the first ball, and Shoriki's dream of a real world series was at last underway.

Oriole speedballer Jim Palmer started on the mound for Baltimore. With no control and no curve, Palmer worked six innings and gave up four runs. But Frank and Brooks Robinson each homered, Nagashima made a crucial error, and the Orioles swept to an 8–4 win, outhitting the Giants 12–10. There was the usual post-game praise. The Japanese marveled at the size and power of 6′ 4½″ 250 pound Boog Powell ("He's as big as a *sumo* wrestler"), the fielding genius of Brooks Robinson, and the awesome speed of Palmer ("Too fast," Oh said, shaking his head in disbelief). Giant fans admitted the Orioles were good, but took comfort in their team's 10 hits and four runs. It was still early. Wait until tomorrow. Giant ace Horiuchi would be pitching and the Giants wouldn't be so nervous.

The second game was played before another capacity crowd and another nationwide TV audience. Horiuchi vowed to hold the Orioles scoreless for five innings. He didn't. He gave up six runs before his departure in the sixth inning. There was a look of surprise and dismay on his face when Frank Robinson and Don Buford hit his best pitches out of the park. Screwball artist Mike Cuellar pitched for Baltimore and held the Giants to five hits. He shocked everyone when he picked off the first two Giant baserunners. ("Where does he get that move?" the fans buzzed. "I've never seen that before.") There was frustration on the faces of the Giant batters as Cuellar served up a wide variety of breaking pitches, floating change-ups, curves, and knucklers. The Giants made five errors, and the Orioles won the game 8–2.

The Giants were beginning to worry. The Oriole pitchers were too fast. It made their change-ups more confusing. Oriole home-run power was awesome. Even little (5′9″) Don Buford hit 400 foot shots. ("Where does he get the power?" the Japanese wondered.)

The Baltimore onslaught continued in the third game. Pat Dobson, displaying good stuff, tossed a three-hitter at the Giants. Buford showed more home-run power and the Orioles won 10–1. In Game Four, however, the Giants gained a tie, 3–3, and KO'd Palmer in the

4th inning. Horiuchi hurled nine innings, but lost a shutout and a win when the O's rallied for three runs, including a two-out home run by catcher Andy Etchebarren in the 9th. It was a bitter pill for Horiuchi and the Giants to swallow, but at least they seemed to be regaining their composure.

The Giants took a break as the Orioles met the Japan All-Stars in the fifth game of the tour. Cuellar's breaking pitches and change-ups continued to baffle the Japanese. He pitched a four-hitter and the Orioles won 4–1. The following day, the Orioles downed a combined

Mike Cuellar of the Baltimore Orioles demonstrates his screwball to Nagashima during the club's 1971 trip to Japan

Giant/Nankai Hawk squad 2–0. Sore-armed Dave McNally, the Oriole ace, made his first and only appearance and threw seven shutout innings. His variety of pitches amazed the Japanese and won McNally a great deal of attention in the sports dailies.

In Game Seven, the series between the Orioles and Giants resumed, with the Japanese vowing to come back. Horiuchi threw nine strong innings, and surrendered only two runs. *But Pat Dobson pitched a no-hitter.*

The Giants were beginning to get the picture. They had been vastly overrated. Giant batters were not only unfamiliar with the Oriole pitchers' speed, but were also not accustomed to such a variety of curves and change-ups. Oh and Nagashima had only one home run between them. Nor were Giant pitchers used to Baltimore's awesome power. Although they threw low and hit the corners according to Kawakami's plan, Frank Robinson, Boog Powell, and others simply golfed their offerings into the stands. No Japanese pitcher had the pick-off moves of Cuellar and no Japanese outfielder could throw as hard as Marv Rettenmund, Frank Robinson, or Paul Blair. That the Orioles were superior in all aspects of the game was becoming quite apparent. The question was now no longer whether the Giants would win seven of eleven, but whether they could win at all.

Game Eight, Baltimore vs. the All-Stars, was the clincher. Sunday afternoon's capacity at Korakuen and a nationwide TV audience were placing their hopes on an All-Star win to salvage some sorely needed prestige. It was the All-Stars' second and last crack at Baltimore. And if Japan's best couldn't beat them, no one could. Palmer started for the Orioles and promptly loaded the bases with no one out. There was expectation in the air. A big inning might lead to a rousing win. Perhaps it wasn't all over. But Palmer quickly dashed such hopes by striking out the side and going on to pitch a near perfect shutout. Baltimore won 8–0. Buford, Elrod Henricks, and Frank Robinson all homered while Boog Powell chipped in the most powerful shot of the series, a wicked shot that caromed off the centerfield wall some 400 feet away. Said Kawakami dejectedly after the game: "There is no Japanese who could ever hit a line drive like that."

Disappointed and confused children turned to their fathers as they filed out of the stadium that day. "Papa, why can't we beat the Americans?" "Papa, why don't Oh and Nagashima hit any home runs?" "Papa, when will the Giants win?"

The verdict was in as far as the media was concerned. "The biggest Japanese players look like pygmies compared with the Orioles." "When an Oriole bat hits the ball, the sound gives a ring not heard in local baseball." "Too strong."

The "Oriole *shokku*," said one writer, "has sent a chill down the spine of Japanese baseball. It has made Japan realize that a 'real world series' is still far away in the future." "It's like the old story of the frog in the well *," added another, "we who believed we had been getting strong, did not realize just how vast the difference is."

In the remaining games, the Giants tried desperately to regain some face. They tied the Orioles in the ninth game, but lost the tenth. Kawakami moaned: "We must win at least one game." And, in the eleventh contest, his Giants almost did it. Going into the 7th inning of that encounter, Horiuchi (the only hurler who did consistently well against the Orioles) had a 5–0 lead. Kawakami anxiously watched his star set down the Orioles inning after inning, getting nearer and nearer to the coveted first victory. Could it be?

"All right gang, let's get some runs," yelled Weaver as the Orioles came to bat in the top of the seventh. "We're five down. Knock a hole through that kid's head." Paul Blair led off the inning with a double to the left. Don Buford followed him and smacked a single to right. One run came in. Up stepped big Boog Powell. "Cm'on Boog," urged his teammates, "Hit a home run and they'll give you a free color TV." Mighty Boog nodded and hit the first pitch "like a ping-pong ball" deep into the right centerfield bleachers. In came two more runs and out went Horiuchi.

The Orioles were not finished. A single put still another runner on first to set the stage for weak-hitting shortstop Mark Belanger. Belanger had not hit a home run all season. Such was his lack of power that he drew an ovation from his teammates when he managed to clear the fence in batting practice. "Hey, Mark," yelled Weaver,

* Japanese proverb: A frog in the well doesn't know the ocean.

"you're the only one who hasn't won a home-run prize. Hit one out and make your wife happy." Belanger sent a high fastball into the left centerfield stands to tie the score at 5–5.

The Giants came back with two runs in the bottom of the inning to take a 7–5 lead, but in the top of the 8th, the Orioles were at it again. Weaver, noticing Giant infield was back in deference to the power of his team, turned to the inning's leadoff batter, Paul Blair. "OK, Paul, show 'em what a bunt down the third base line looks like." Blair agreeably dropped down a perfect bunt and made it to first ahead of the throw. The next batter, reserve infielder Tom Shopay, was not to be outdone as he too laid a perfect bunt down the first base line and beat the throw. That put runners on first and second, none out, with Boog Powell up once again. "Cm'on Boog," yelled a teammate, "Get yourself another TV." Powell shrugged and swung away. Pow! Another home run to deep right center. Three runs came in and the Orioles went ahead 8–7.

Those in the press who sat close enough to hear were aghast. "They're treating us like children," a reporter said in amazement. "They can score at will. There's no telling how strong the Orioles are when they feel like playing."

The game ended in a 10 inning 9–9 tie, but the ease with which the Orioles had deprived the Giants of almost certain victory left those in the press box openly wondering if the Giants could *ever* beat the Orioles.

A: If the Orioles played in the Central League, how many games do you think they'd win?

B: All of them?

A: They would have to let up sometime. Palmer and Cuellar have their off days. Perhaps on a lucky one, Horiuchi and two or three other pitchers could defeat them. I estimate they'd probably lose 10 or 20 games in the 130 game schedule.

B: I suppose so. How many games do you think Dobson could win?

A: Every one he started? 35 or 40? Well, maybe he'd lose one.

B: The Orioles hardly used their best pitcher, McNally. Just think how good he'd be if he were pitching his turn.

A: Powell and Frank Robinson would probably hit 60 home runs or more.

B: Buford could hit 40. He is small, but he's very strong.*
A: He must be the best lead-off batter in the world.
B: And the most powerful too.
A: The Orioles are definitely the strongest team in America.
B: True, true. How could the Pirates be better?

The remaining games were played with little enthusiasm. Dobson shut out the Giants two more times, and the Orioles finally managed to lose—twice in fact. Once to a combined Giants/Hankyu Braves team, 8–2, when a weary Palmer was knocked out of the box, and again to a combined Giant/Chunichi Dragons squad 9–1. In that game Weaver started relief pitcher Grant Jackson and brought in a utility infielder named Jerry Devanon to hurl the last three innings—a move that some Japanese found insulting.

· The last game was at Korakuen Stadium against the Giants; the general tone was in marked contrast to the series' opener. The stadium was only half-full and there was no TV coverage. Oriole relievers Tom Dukes and Dick Hall, dividing mound duties, delivered the final humiliation—a 5–0 shutout.

That last win gave Baltimore an 8–0–3 mark in their eleven games against the Yomiuri Giants. Those eight wins included four shutouts and one no-hitter. Vaunted sluggers Oh and Nagashima were stopped cold. Nagashima finished with a .258 batting average and two home runs. Oh was held to .111 and three home runs.

The Orioles left Japan with words of thanks and gratitude for their Japanese hosts, praise for their opponents on the field, suitcases full of souvenirs, and an overall record of 12–2–4.

The Giants picked up what was left of their pride and fighting spirit, and headed for the autumn exhibition league.

The phrase "real world series" was laid to rest—at least for the time.

A variety of explanations were put forth for the Giants' miserable showing. One aging doctor in a bizarre magazine article attributed their downfall to a basic flaw in the Japanese character:

* The average height of a Japanese ballplayer is 5'11" 170 pounds. The average American ballplayer is about 6'1" 190 pounds.

A difference of personalities existed between the Orioles and the Japanese. The Oriole players were not afraid of the ball. Even in a pinch they were not afraid. No matter what the situation, they endured it and did not try to escape.

But the Japanese players, including the Giants, quickly displayed a "rejection-reaction." The pitchers lost their control, the players were making errors one after another, and the batters, in the face of the 20-game winning quartet, were easily disposed of. This was completely the appearance of the "rejection-reaction."

Before the war, this reaction could not be seen in the Japanese. If you examined the movements of babies you would understand. If you put a stethoscope on a baby's chest, he would cry but he would not reject it. While a child these days won't cry, he will push the stethoscope away with both hands—"rejecting" the examination.

The Japanese character has changed and the war was the turning point.

Others suggested President Nixon's personal call to Oriole manager Weaver just before the series. As one commentator reasoned, the U.S. was frightened by Japan's economic power and embarrassed by the dollar devaluation. Something had to be done to restore America's image as world leader, and a decisive win by the Orioles would certainly help. That was why the Orioles played with more zeal than any previous team to visit Japan. (If only Prime Minister Eisaku Sato had called Kawakami.)

Then came the "size and strength" arguments. Baltimore was better, so the reasoning went, because they were bigger. That was all there was to it. Size was the only difference. The Japanese were just unlucky to be so small.

Weaver scoffed at this. "Power is something you gain with training," he said. "Look at Buford. He's only 5'9" and 160 pounds. Look at the power he's got. Last year he hit 19 home runs. That was fourth on the team."

"If the Japanese think they lost because of a difference in power," Buford added, "they should do something about it. I lifted weights to build my wrists. I practiced shadow swinging with a heavy bat. That's how I got my power."

Weaver then reiterated the old axiom that pitching and defense make for a winning team, areas in which the Giants were weakest.

Weaver criticized the lack of stamina displayed by their hurlers, while Oriole pitcher Dobson zeroed in on other aspects. "Maybe the Japanese don't have the speed of Americans," he said, "but speed is not that important. The key thing in pitching is throwing at different speeds from the same motion. No matter how fast you are or how good a curve you have, if you throw at the same speed all the time, you've had it. The Japanese have good breaking stuff and good control, but they just don't throw a good change-up. And that's got nothing to do with size." Dobson also characterized Japanese pitchers as "too predictable." With a count of 0–2, he pointed out, the Japanese would invariably throw three straight balls.* It didn't take the Oriole batters long to figure out that all they had to do was lay back and wait for the strike that was sure to come.

Equally important was the total breakdown of the Giant defense—normally solid, surehanded, and a hallmark of the team's success over the years. Errors, missed double plays, and off-target throws accounted for more than one Oriole win and led to suspicions the Giants were choking. Whether this was a manifestation of the "rejection-reaction" is doubtful, but the Giants were visibly nervous. The Japanese have often been described as the "worst clutch performers

---

* These are known as "amusement pitches" in Japan because many Japanese managers will fine a pitcher who gives up a hit or a run when he is ahead on the count. As a result, the average number of pitches thrown by a Japanese pitcher in a game is 140, compared with 120 in the States.

Don Buford slides home

in the world." For them failure is a most traumatic experience. And, in this case, the pressure of playing for "national honor" seemed to take its toll.

There were other factors. The superior throwing arms of Oriole outfielders as well as some patented Brooks Robinson saves, and the fast-paced play of the Baltimore team (some games were over in less than two hours) upset the rhythm of the Giants. But, simply stated, the Orioles were a better team. They played to the peak of their potential; the Giants did not.

Then how could the Japanese have been so certain of victory in the first place? How could they been so totally wrong?

Perhaps the answer lies in the Japanese people's almost desperate need to be recognized and respected as a nation. Because how the world views Japan is more important to the Japanese than most Americans will ever understand. It is why the nation feels such a tremendous sense of collective pride when the Japanese volleyball team wins an Olympic gold medal. It is why the nation sinks to the depths of shame when three Japanese radicals shoot up an airport full of people at Tel Aviv. It is why the nation worries that the world will think it has suffered a regression after a Yukio Mishima commits *hara-kiri*. And it is why the Japanese badger every Western tourist regard-

Tom Seaver goes against Oh during the New York Mets' 1974 visit. Oh hit a single

Mets' Manager Yogi Berra and first baseman Ed Kranepool pose with a prize they received after a victory during New York's 1974 tour

ing his feelings about Mt. Fuji, Kyoto, *sake*, and everything else under the Rising Sun.

The Japanese simply ignored the facts before the Giants–Orioles series. They took all the compliments from teams on previous goodwill tours and built them into something more than they were intended to be. And they failed to recall that previous touring teams had not played up to their potential. This because they *wanted* to win so badly; to achieve recognition from the American baseball community. They were simply tired of being looked down upon.

The Japanese knew they were approaching major-league status and that the Giants were as good as some major-league teams. Whatever was lacking could be compensated for by "Japanese spirit." If they wanted to win badly enough, they would. Unfortunately, this reasoning proved wrong. The Japanese had set their sights too high. And the subsequent fall was painful indeed.

When the shock over the Orioles' performance eventually subsided, it was replaced by a mood of resignation. "We Japanese practice and practice," sighed one reporter, "and still we're badly beaten by the Americans. Sometimes I think we should just forget about competing with the U.S. and play baseball for the simple enjoyment of it."

But time heals all things and soon, in characteristic fashion, the Japanese stole quietly back to the practice fields to assimilate what they had learned from the foreigners. Batters began to lift weights. Pitchers began to practice their pick-off moves. And Harvey Haddix was invited over to teach the all-important change-up. The Japanese were back at the task of making Japan a baseball power.

In 1974, three long years after the Oriole debacle, the Yomiuri Shimbun resumed the post-season tours of American teams by inviting the "Miracle Mets" of New York.* The Mets arrived somewhat spent and without many of the stars that propelled them to their 1969 and 1973 pennants. Although Japanese fans were eager to see the great Tom Seaver and his "riser ball," it was retiring idol Nagashima, appearing in his last games as a player, that accounted for the tour's high interest.

The Mets were not in the Orioles' class. It took them six games to get their first victory and they then struggled to an overall 9–7–2 record. In eleven games against Nagashima and his "Young Giants"— a team destined for last place the following season—the Mets scored a woeful 3–6–2.

There were scattered complaints about the Mets' brand of play. One writer even suggested that the "Miracle Mets" be renamed the "Disgusting Mets" and called for a halt of the post-season tours. An apology to the fans from Mets' Manager Yogi Berra prompted speculation in the Japanese press that Berra would lose his job upon the team's return to the States. There was no more talk of a "real world series," however. The Japanese just discounted the games as meaningless.

The Mets, for their part, found they had vastly underrated the Japanese and were forced to play far-above-average baseball to win. Berra ranked the Giants better than his Mets at fundamentals, although he too criticized Japanese pitching.

There were other outward and visible signs of a new regard for Japanese baseball. During the Mets' tour, for example, CBS staged a home-run contest between Hank Aaron and Sadaharu Oh. The close

* The Japanese declined an invitation to join a minor-league world series tournament held in Hawaii in 1972.

Upon his retirement as manager of the Yomiuri Giants, Tetsuji Kawakami pays his respects to team founder Matsutaro Shoriki

match, which Aaron won, was televised in America. Some months later, in early 1975, the ball and glove of Japanese pitching great Masaiichi Kaneda were "inducted" into the Cooperstown Hall of Fame—a first for Japan. At the same time, a U.S. promoter revealed plans to inaugurate a "best-in-baseball" competition between the top pitchers and batters of Japan and America. Catfish Hunter, Nolan Ryan, and others would take on the likes of Oh and the powerful Tiger catcher Koichi Tabuchi, while Johnny Bench, Reggie Jackson, and others would face the leading Japanese pitchers.

Although there is no serious talk of baseball parity for Japan at the present time, it will not be long before the "Young Giants" or some other Japanese team is ready to issue another challenge to the United States. Soon, in fact, there *will* indeed be a "real world series." And when that happens, the day must follow when the flag of the Rising Sun is flowing in the wind over another important flag: that of the World Champions of Baseball.